D0403626

The New Canadian Tax & Investment Guide

Henry B. Zimmer, C.A.

The New Canadian Tax & Investment Guide

For Executives, Professionals & Business

Hurtig Publishers

Hurtig Publishers Ltd.
10560-105 Street
Edmonton, Alberta

First Printing — October, 1980
Second Printing — December, 1980

Canadian Cataloguing in Publication Data

Zimmer, Henry B., 1944–
 The new Canadian tax & investment guide
 for executives, professionals & business

ISBN 0-88830-190-1

 1. Tax planning — Canada — Popular works.
2. Income tax — Canada — Popular works.
3. Investments — Canada. I. Title.
KE5682.Z82Z54   343.7104   C80-091036-2

Printed and bound in Canada
by T.H. Best Printing Company Ltd.

Contents

ONE   **Our Silent Partner**   1

TWO   **Minimize Your Salary & Maximize Your Benefits**   9

Company Cars   9
Loans to Employees and Shareholders   13
  "Imputed" Interest on Loans   Low Interest Loans
Holiday Trips, Including Travel Expenses
  for an Employee's Spouse   19
Discounts on Merchandise Ordinarily Sold by an Employer   22
Recreational Facilities and Club Membership Dues   22
Stock Option and Stock Purchase Plans   23
Other Benefits   26
Getting the Competitive Edge   26
  Convention Expenses   Job-Hunting Expenses
  Contract Negotiation Fees for Athletes
Tax Avoidance vs. Tax Evasion   29
Employment Benefits Summary   30

THREE   **Postponing Your Income**   35

Planning for Retirement, Loss of Office, and Job Transfers
  Outside Canada   35
Non-Statutory Deferred Compensation Programs   35
  Choosing between the RRSP *and* IAAC
  The Employer's Tax Position
  Beware of Constructive Receipt   How Much and When
  Protecting the Employee
Planning for Non-Residency   44
  Income-Averaging Annuity Payments to Non-Residents
  Definition of a Non-Resident

Death Benefit Programs   50
Payments for "Loss of Office"   52
Income-Averaging Annuities Contracts   52
    Summary of Qualified Incomes

FOUR   **RRSPs, Pension Plans & Other Statutory
Deferred-Compensation Programs**   55

Registered Retirement Savings Plans   55
    Should I Have an RRSP?   *Spousal Plans*
    Deductibility of Interest   RRSP *Interest vs. Mortgage Interest*
    No RRSP *Annuity Before Age Sixty*
    Bequeathing Your RRSP *to a Spouse*
    Bequests of RRSPs *to Other Beneficiaries*
    Becoming a Non-Resident   Temporary Residents of Canada
    What Kind of Plan Should I Have?
    Insurance Companies vs. Banks and Trust Companies
    "Cashing In" an RRSP *for a Life Annuity*
    Two New Options: Fixed-term Annuities and RRIFs
Registered Pension Plans   71
    An Employee's Allowable Contributions
    Past Service Contributions
    Increasing Contributions for Past Service
    Your Own Pension Plan
Deferred Profit-Sharing Plans (DPSPs)   77
Registered Home Ownership Savings Plans   78
    Analysis of RHOSPs   *The* RHOSP *as a Gifting Program*

FIVE   **A Tax Shelter Update**   83

Tax Shelters in the Real Estate Industry   83
    The "Good Old Days"   1972 Tax Changes
    Multiple Unit Residential Buildings
    Soft Cost Write-Offs for Real-Estate Developers
    The Tax Position of Real-Estate Developers
    Investors' Soft Cost Write-Offs
    The Future of Real-Estate Tax Shelters
    Evaluating Real-Estate Shelters   Type of Investment

A Real-Estate Case Study   The Risk Factor
Film Investments   105
Evaluating Movie Investments
Finding a Common Denominator
Oil and Gas Exploration Shelters   109
Complex Accounting   Evaluation of Oil and Gas Projects
Summary   112

SIX   **Maximize Your Investment Yields**
Without Incorporating   113

Planning around Earned Income   113
The Investment Income Deduction   113
Pay Off Your Home Mortgage   114
After Burning the Mortgage...   115
Transactions with Family Members   116
Husbands and Wives   Overcoming the Rules
Transfers of Capital Property between Spouses
Beating the System
Transactions with Persons Other Than Spouses   112
Loans to Older Children   Family Planning
Transfers of Capital Property to Children and Others
Tax Planning to Defer Capital Gains   126
The Use of a Tax Reserve   Estate Freezing
Additional Use of Tax Reserves
An Opportunity for Adventurous Planning
General Tax Planning for Capital Gains   131
Tax Planning for Personal Residences   132
A Word of Caution for Habitual Renovators
Changing the Use of a Principal Residence

SEVEN   **Maximizing Your Investment Yields**
Through Incorporation   137

Overview of the Corporate Tax Structure
    for Investment Income   137
The Taxation of Canadian Dividends Received
    by an Individual   138

The Investment Income Deduction   142
The Use of Investment Companies   142
Opportunities for Income Splitting through a Corporation   144
Sheltering Capital Gains   147
Sheltering Public Company Dividends   148
Control of the Investment Corporation   149
The Formation of Discretionary Trusts   150
Capitalization of the Investment Company   152
Interest vs. Dividend Income   153

EIGHT   **Incorporating Your Earnings—
The Ultimate Solution?**   159

Advantages of Personal Service Companies   159
Professional Corporations   161
Management Companies for Professionals   162
Choosing between Professional Corporations and
    Management Companies   164
Federal Legislation Governing the Use of Service Companies   164
The Future of Service Companies   166
    *Athletes   Entertainers   Incorporated Executives
    Commissioned Salesmen and Other Consultants*
Organizing the Personal Service Company   171

NINE   **Tax Planning for the Private Canadian Business
Where the Small Business Rate Applies**   173

The Canadian-Controlled Private Corporation   174
Definition of Active Business Income   175
The Meaning of the Small Business Tax Rate   176
Opportunities for Tax Planning   177
Remuneration of Spouses   179
Remuneration Guidelines for One's Children   181
Directors' Fees   183
Remuneration Guidelines for the Owner-Manager Where
the Company Qualifies for the Small Business Deduction   183
    Meaning of Tax Deferral   Salaries vs. Dividends

The Dividend Tax Credit   Effect of 1978 Tax Changes
Additional Implications of the New Rules
Tax Planning for a Proper Salary-Dividend Mix   Summary
Tax Planning for the Family   196
Separate Classes of Shares

TEN   **Maximizing Profits from All
Private Canadian Businesses**   199

Taxation Guidelines for Business Income That Does Not
    Qualify for the Small Business Tax Rate   199
    Other Factors
Income From Manufacturing and Processing   205
    Calculating Manufacturing and Processing Profits
    Tax Planning for the Manufacturing and Processing Incentive
Tax Planning for Owner-Managed Manufacturing and
    Processing Operations—Salaries vs. Dividends   207
The Inventory Deduction   211
    Planning to Maximize the Inventory Deduction

ELEVEN   **The Art of Buying a Business and the Use of
Holding Companies**   215

Introduction   215
The Taxation of Inter-Corporate Canadian Dividends Out
    of Business Income   216
Tax Planning Opportunities   218
The Relationship Between Dividends and Capital Gains   222
Corporate Reorganizations   223
Bringing Buyers and Sellers Together   226
Sheltering a Vendor's Tax   226
The Ideal Corporate Structure   227
Expanding the Business Empire   229
The Era of the Holding Company   230
    Small Business Development Bonds
    Lease-Option Acquisitions

TWELVE   **A Common-sense Approach to Estate Planning**   233

Capital Gains Planning for Non-Residency   234
Deemed Dispositions on Death   235
The Use of Spousal Trusts   237
Income Tax Requirements for Spousal Trusts
Capital Encroachment Powers   "Over-Protecting" a Spouse
Appointment of Executors   243
Special Rules — The Family Farm   245
Tax-Free Transfer of Small Business Holdings   245
Estate Planning and Life Insurance   248
The Time for Planning is Now   251

EPILOGUE   **Taking the "Ax" out of Tax**   253

GLOSSARY   255

CHAPTER ONE

Our Silent Partner

This is not a book to assist you in preparing your tax return. Nor will it save you money when you file in March or April next year. By then, it is too late. Tax planning is a twelve-month-a-year exercise, every time you are up for a pay increase or manage to put away a thousand dollars for investments, or think about starting (or buying) a business.

If you have bought this book, you probably already realize that you are paying too much tax. Any Canadian whose taxable income reaches $25,000 will begin to pay between 45% and 50% out of each additional dollar of earnings to a silent partner — Revenue Canada. Although these high brackets are reached at what is today a relatively modest income level, the rate structure is geared so that taxpayers with incomes over $100,000 pay, on the average, taxes which are not above 65%.

When someone earns in excess of $100,000, things tend to fall into place by themselves. The individual can afford the best professional advice and he will probably utilize tax shelters since after all, the most he can lose is thirty-five cents on the dollar. Corporations as a vehicle for sheltering income are also readily available. However, for the vast majority of people who earn less than a six-figure income many of these opportunities are not as accessible. Any legitimate advantage in dealing with the silent partner should therefore be pursued. To some extent, getting an edge is difficult, since the government is the one who makes up the rules of the game. However, if one learns the rules, playing the game can even be fun as well as profitable.

Of course, the Income Tax Act is complicated — especially since the 1972 Tax Reform added capital gains and many other concepts that were unheard of earlier. For many accountants and lawyers, the study of taxation has become a full-time job and much time has been spent by these two professions in self-education. However, while accountants educate accountants and lawyers educate lawyers, little attempt has been made to educate the public. Granted, there are some excellent articles on tax matters which appear from time to time in publications such as the *Financial Post* and several books have been written on the subject of tax return *preparation* and basic tax planning. This book, however, explains effective tax *reduction* for business persons and executives. Many examples are used to highlight tax-planning opportunities and simple numerical calculations are employed to reveal the basic logical pattern that is the key to understanding the deeper mysteries.

In the past, most professionals have not really tried to explain away the "mysteries". In fact, why should they? A good friend of mine, a partner in a national accounting firm, refers to the Tax Act as the "Accountants' and Lawyers' Relief Act". Among accountants (and I assume among lawyers as well) average incomes have quadrupled since 1972. The public has been intimidated by professional jargon and most practitioners have done very little to dispel the myth that income taxation is beyond the average taxpayer's comprehension. In a recent article in *Financial Post Magazine*, Andrew Allentuck says of tax experts:

> In the battle to preserve one's income from Revenue Canada's long arm, the tax accountants of the nation are everyone's ally. No longer dull, reclusive types who once retreated to nibble cheese dips if and when they were invited to office parties, they're now Cadillac and Mercedes-borne, Rosedale and Mount Royal-residing oracles of fortune. As the soothsayers of Rome interpreted the meanings of entrails, the tax accountants preside over the mysteries of the Income Tax Act. In the eerie shadow world of fictitious corporations, capital loss carry-backs, and Class 32 Multiple Unit Residential Buildings, they tell those supplicants who come with $85 to $150 an hour how to vanquish the dreaded tax man.

Actually, taxation concepts are not especially difficult to understand. Over the past two years, I have presented some 120 seminars to perhaps 2500 business owners and executives across Canada. These people have shown that the average taxpayer not only wants to understand how the system works but, with just a little effort, he can also make the system work for *him*. One only needs a translation of the tax rules into plain English.

As you read through this book, you will find that learning the rules is easy. Comprehension does not require an accounting or legal background. You need only assimilate some facts, and use some common sense and a bit of imagination. While the Canadian tax system is, in general, well thought out and logical in its structure, there are a tremendous number of grey areas, loopholes, and most of all, opportunities for legitimate tax planning. If you are capable of earning over $25,000, you should be able to appreciate the business logic underlying the tax rules. Also, if you can harness a little imagination to legitimately bend these rules, there is no reason why these lessons cannot be translated into the skills required to increase earning power as well.

Since the price for legal and accounting services is high, many business owners and executives have expressed to me a desire to educate themselves to intelligently discuss tax matters with their advisors — especially where the professionals have difficulty coming down to a layman's level. As one of my clients said to me recently, "I've got to learn what this is all about. After all, it's *my* money."

This book is a collection of the topics with which I have dealt in tax seminars all over Canada. I have found speaking to the public extremely gratifying. Recently, an Edmonton businessman said that he had learned more in one day from me than he had from his accountants in eleven years, and a Vancouver doctor told me, during the first coffee break in the morning, that he had already absorbed enough to cover the cost of my seminar and the loss of a day's earnings. Invariably, I have been asked by participants whether any book is available covering the material that I teach. So here it is.

There is a chapter on fringe-benefit plans — such as company cars, employee loans, and business-pleasure trips where the value of these benefits is often much more than a (fully taxable) raise in pay. I will deal with planning for retirement and the conversion of high-bracket salary income into a post-retirement allowance. You will be brought up to date on the tax deferral advantages of personal service companies, especially for doctors, dentists, commissioned salespeople, and executives capable of earning consulting revenues from several different sources.

Chapter Five explains the use of tax shelters in real estate, movie films, and oil and gas projects. The material emphasizes the importance of first finding a good *investment* before concentrating on its shelter aspects. Many people do not realize that there is a large difference between a "tax shelter" and a "tax loss". A shelter is *not* effective if it involves a loss of dollars or a reduction in the value of one's investment — even where the loss is tax deductible.

Another chapter explores ideas for maximizing investment yields by splitting income with family members, both by way of direct transactions and through the use of investment corporations. It deals with some of the misconceptions pertaining to investment yields which result from erroneously trying to apply U.S. guidelines to Canada. For example, U.S. rules do not differentiate between the earning of interest and dividend income. However, for anyone in a tax bracket of 40% or higher, a Canadian dividend is worth at least one and a half times as much as an equivalent yield of Canadian interest on an *after-tax* basis. Thus, if a stock pays a 6% dividend, this is equivalent to pre-tax interest of 9%.

I will show you that for many individuals, the difference between buying a blue-chip Canadian stock and investing in a term deposit (or Canada Savings Bond) translates to only a 2% net annual cash difference in favour of the interest-bearing security. However, when one takes capital-appreciation potentials and inflation into account, the balance often swings in favour of share investments.

We will also examine the major tax-planning concepts for owner-managers of private companies. There are some readily understandable guidelines that can be evolved with respect to salary and dividend policies so as to optimize after-tax retentions in any active business situation.

For anyone planning to buy a business, I will explain how there is a "right way" and "wrong way". Without proper planning, anyone who buys the shares of a Canadian private company could be *overpaying* unnecessary income taxes of as much as $70,000 for every $100,000 of purchase cost! With proper planning, this needless tax can be legitimately avoided. Other material introduces estate-planning concepts, such as the points that a will should contain, and suggests some guidelines for a common-sense approach towards allocating assets to family members.

Before we go any further, however, a word of caution is in order. My intention is not to replace accountants and lawyers. First of all, this would be self-defeating since I am not yet ready to retire, and second, even if you digest the entire contents of my book, this will not make you a "tax expert". My purpose is to show you what is available, so that when you do sit down with your *own* advisors, at least you have a common starting point. After having read this book, you should be able to discuss specific matters with the professionals who are there to assist you in implementing the proposals which I suggest. In many cases, your own advisors will be able to make important modifications suitable to your own specific circumstances.

In addition, an important point should be put into proper perspective. While the cost of an hour's time with a tax accountant or tax lawyer can be as much as $150, it is very rare that the evolution of a tax-planning outline should take more than three or four hours in total. The actual *implementation* of the tax-planning ideas can then often be accomplished with the assistance of one's non-specialist advisors, whose rates are usually considerably cheaper. In addition, barring major changes in the tax laws, a tax plan, once initiated, should be effective for many future years.

I have been consulting on tax matters almost exclusively to small businesses and executives for the past five years. In only two or three cases has my charge exceeded five hundred dollars. This is not because I undercut the competition. It is because I leave the implementation of my proposals to my clients' regular advisors.

What if you don't think you have a tax problem? You will still find that a tax check-up is important. In the same way as you go to your physician for a physical check-up at least once a year, a periodic tax check-up can save you money by detecting problems that you may not even know exist. While $150 an hour sounds expensive, a fee of $500 spread over several years is not costly if you will save considerably more.

Another word of caution. The contents of this book are based on the tax law in force as of June 30, 1980. Each year, the federal government brings down at least one budget which makes modifications to the rules. Often, many of the changes are not of interest to the average taxpayer. In addition, the general framework of the Tax Act remains the same from year to year. However, keeping up with the tax rules is an ongoing process. This book is your starting point. Beyond checking out specific tax-planning concepts with your own advisors, I strongly recommend that you keep up to date by reading digests of budget proposals which appear in publications such as the *Financial Post* or the *Financial Times*. Your own accountants should be able to explain the relevant changes to you a few days after each budget.

It is important to understand how to properly evaluate tax changes. Before becoming excited about a legislative amendment, or an opportunity for planning, always compare the tax theory to the actual dollars of tax cost or saving as the case may be. For example, the December 11, 1979, Budget was defeated because of a Conservative Government proposal to raise the price of gasoline by eighteen cents a gallon. When I first read that proposal on budget night, I stopped for a moment to calculate what *my* cost was going to be. I estimated that I use approximately twenty gallons of gasoline each week, or about one thousand gallons a year. Thus, my gross increased cost would have been $180, which, of course, translates to something considerably less on an after-tax basis. (This is because my car is used partially for business purposes and part of my gasoline becomes a tax write-off.) To keep my example simple, assume that the average taxpayer would have paid an extra $150 a year. That would have been the "cost" of that particular ill-fated budget — less than a 1% hike in personal tax rates.

The same budget, however, proposed for the first time to

allow a taxpayer carrying on an unincorporated business to pay a salary to his or her spouse and to deduct that salary for income tax purposes. In many instances, the savings for Canadian families would have been several thousands of dollars. This is because each taxpayer must file a separate return and the ability to split income between a husband and wife is one of the key concepts for effective tax planning. Which of the above tax changes got all the media publicity? When the government fell, the good died with the bad. (Fortunately, the Liberals reintroduced many of the Conservative Amendments in April 1980, and it is now permissible to pay a salary to a spouse who is an active participant in a family business.)

In addition to saving taxes, I hope that you will learn tax awareness from this book. You must learn to think in terms of after-tax dollars and to discount additional income that you receive by the tax burden of earning it. Conversely, costs and expenses should be discounted by the appropriate tax bracket where these outlays are deductible.

To take a common example, most of us who earn employment income from one source or another receive cost-of-living increases. If the cost of living goes up by 8% in one year, then an 8% raise is often received exclusive of merit increases. However, for most of us, a raise in pay translates on an after-tax basis to only about fifty cents on the dollar. Thus, our 8% cost-of-living increase becomes only 4% in our pockets. It is true that to the extent that certain of our costs are fixed, we may be unaffected by increases in the cost of living. How many of us envy our neighbours who have owned their homes for the last ten or fifteen years and are thus "immune" from rising house prices? Nevertheless, 8% still equals 4% — maybe not in mathematics but in "real-life" arithmetic.

As you increase your understanding of taxation, you will also become aware that while the laws change from time to time and certain loopholes are in fact blocked, other valid opportunities for tax planning will always present themselves. Parliament giveth, Parliament taketh...

CHAPTER TWO

Minimize Your Salary & Maximize Your Benefits

Whether you own your own business or work for someone else you probably derive at least a portion of your income from salary. In general, you should only draw as much salary as you need to meet your particular living requirements after income taxes. Once you earn sufficient salary to pay living expenses, the next step is to look for fringe benefits. Very often, these benefits can be worth more than salary, since your employer can provide goods and services which you want without the full impact of taxes otherwise payable on an equivalent amount of salary.

This chapter will deal with some of the more common and readily available fringe-benefit programs you can obtain by virtue of employment. Naturally, if you are self-employed, you are more likely to be able to take these advantages than if you have to ask someone else. However, as you will see, it is often advantageous for the employer as well to provide some of these benefits because the cost may be less than salary or, at worst, the expense is about the same. At the end of this chapter there is a summary of many of the available fringe-benefit programs that also discusses which of these benefits are taxable and who must pay the tax.

Company Cars

The best benefit one can derive from employment is a company car — an automobile owned or rented by the employer, who covers all operating expenses as well. For this benefit to apply, however, it is important that the employee have at least some business requirement for the vehicle to justify the costs to the company of providing it.

For years, even before the Tax Reform of 1972, Revenue Canada insisted that employees report a taxable benefit from having a company car. The benefit has always been calculated by the following formula:

$$\text{Operating expenses} \quad X \quad \frac{\text{Personal mileage}}{\text{Total mileage}}$$

If you examine the above formula, the logic is easily apparent. By taking operating expenses and multiplying by a percentage factor for personal use, the actual benefit is easily extracted. For example:

$$\$3000 \ X \ \frac{4,000 \text{ miles}}{12,000 \text{ miles}} = \ \$1000 \text{ benefit}$$

In an Interpretation Bulletin, Revenue Canada has indicated that operating expenses do *not* include depreciation of the vehicle (if the car is owned by the company) as long as the car is used *primarily* for business purposes. The presumption is that if the car is used mainly for business, the company would own the vehicle in any event and would suffer essentially the same depreciation whether or not that automobile was also subject to personal use.

While the above formula "makes sense", further analysis shows that it is not really practical for two reasons. First, no company that has more than two or three vehicles bothers to segregate costs on a car-by-car basis. The bookkeeping would be horrendous, especially since in many cases, employees also share common gasoline credit cards. Secondly, the formula breaks down because of audit difficulties. Revenue Canada always does its audits of businesses "after the fact". In 1980, for example, Revenue officials would be auditing taxation years from 1976 to 1978. How then is an assessor to verify personal mileage and total mileage on an automobile that might have been scrapped or traded-in several years previously?

Before 1972, Revenue officials would often ignore the formula and arbitrarily assign personal benefits from the use of company cars. This naturally led to a lot of ill will and many disputes. That year, in an attempt to codify the rules more carefully, Parliament approved the use of a simpler formula to deal with this problem. The benefit to be taken into income by an employee was prescribed to be the *greater* of the actual benefit (the portion of operating costs of the car related to personal use) or a "minimum standby charge". The minimum standby charge is computed as follows:

- If the car is owned by the company: 1% per month X the original cost of the car X the number of months of availability.
- If the car is leased: 1/3 X the monthly car rental (exclusive of insurance and maintenance) X the number of months of availability.

The above formulas are quite straightforward and can easily be verified even in subsequent years. They take into account *availability* of the car for personal use, not actual use.

Although a strict interpretation of the law requires the *greater* of the actual or the minimum benefit to be reported, it appears that Revenue officials are content to collect perhaps a smaller amount of tax from everybody who has a company car by just applying the minimum formula. This substantially reduces the amount of audit work otherwise necessary to recover a few additional dollars.

It is my experience that Revenue officials will only try to get more than the tax on the minimum benefit in certain specific situations. These would include the family-owned company where, for example, someone is driving an automobile not in keeping with his or her activities within the company. Thus, if my consulting corporation provided a Mercedes 450 SLC to the office manager, who is my wife, the Revenue officials might be justified in trying to tax more than just the minimum.

If you take some simple numbers and apply them to the minimum standby charge formula, it becomes apparent what the real value of a company car is — in spite of the tax cost. For example, assume that a $15,000 car is owned by a company and is available throughout the year to a particular employee. The benefit would be $1800 ($15,000 X 1% X 12 months). If the individual is in the 50% tax bracket and has $1800 added to his *income*, the only *cost* to the employee is $900 of tax. For an out-of-pocket cost of $900, the employee has a $15,000 car available throughout the year for which the company has paid *all the expenses*. What better benefit could one ask for? Certainly, the average executive would be willing to forgo an increase in pay which would be fully taxed at his highest marginal rates in favour of a $15,000 car which would only cost him $900 a year.

Similar advantages exist if the car is leased. If that same $15,000 automobile is leased at $450 a month, the taxable benefit is also $1800 (⅓ X $450 X 12 months), and the same $900 tax is payable (if the individual is in the 50% bracket).

The benefit is enhanced significantly if the individual also owns his own company. A Canadian small business will often pay a tax rate of approximately only 25% on its profits. Thus, as shown in the next table, a company can afford to pay for a $15,000 car using only $20,000 of "earning power". The individual owner, on the other hand, would have to appropriate at least $30,000 of gross salary (if he is already in a 50% bracket) to net the same $15,000. Thus, there is a tremendous saving in earning power if one owns a business and the corporation purchases a car.

PRE-TAX DOLLARS REQUIRED TO PURCHASE $15,000 CAR

Ownership	Gross Earnings	Taxes Payable	Net Cash Flow for Car
Corporation	$20,000	$ 5,000 (25%)	$15,000
Individual	$30,000	$15,000 (50%)	$15,000

For larger companies, it would generally be more expedient to lease automobiles for key executives. The employees would presumably sign agreements stating that in the event of resignation or dismissal, they would assume the balance of the leases. (If an employee is not financially stable, the company would presumably withhold this benefit.) Since turnover is greatest among new staff, company cars could be reserved for employees who have attained certain income levels and a certain length of service.

It is unfortunate that for taxpayers resident in Quebec, the provincial tax rules pertaining to company cars are not nearly as generous. The benefits which must be calculated for tax purposes are significantly higher. Nevertheless, to have an automobile furnished by an employer is still advantageous in that province.

Loans to Employees and Shareholders

If a business makes a loan to an employee, there are no requirements contained in the Tax Act governing the repayment of that loan within any specific time frame — as long as the employee is not a shareholder of the corporation. Thus, a loan from an employer to an employee can be made for an indefinite period and can remain outstanding as long as both parties agree. If the loan is ever forgiven, the forgiveness of debt would, at that time, create income from employment. This rule is to prevent tax-exempt and other non-profit organizations from making advances to their employees (instead of paying salaries) and then, later on, forgiving these loans. A non-profit organization would not need a tax deduction and, in the absence of the above rule, an employee could escape taxation.

Where an employee is also a shareholder, there are, however, some very strict repayment rules that ordinarily apply where a loan is made. The reason for these rules is that the government does not want shareholders borrowing money initially taxed at comparatively low corporate rates without the imposition of personal taxes. In the absence of any special rules, a corporation with profits of $10,000 would have as much as $7500 of funds available for shareholders' loans after paying Revenue Canada as little as 25% of its profits.

The general rule on shareholder loans is that if a loan is outstanding on two successive year-end balance-sheets of the company, it is *retroactively* included in the shareholder's income. Thus, the maximum length of time that a loan can remain unpaid is two years less one day. (The "two years less one day" would only apply if the loan is taken out on the first day of a company's fiscal year.)

One cannot subvert the system by simply repaying a loan just

13

before the deadline and then borrowing back the funds. Other provisions within the Tax Act provide that a "series of loans and repayments" is equivalent to not having repaid the loan at all. In addition, one cannot use family members for purposes of taking these loans for extended periods of time. A loan to a member of a shareholder's family is basically the equivalent of a loan to the shareholder himself.

There are four specific exceptions to the above rules, which provide the individual with an opportunity to borrow money for an extended period of time. These exceptions are:

1. A loan made in the ordinary course of business by a company whose ordinary business consists of making loans.
2. A loan made to a shareholder who is also an employee to acquire shares of the company out of treasury under a stock option or stock purchase plan.
3. A loan to acquire an automobile to be used by a shareholder-employee in the performance of his duties.
4. A loan to a shareholder-employee to acquire or construct a dwelling house for himself and his family to live in.

In all cases, the Income Tax Act requires a reasonable repayment schedule to be decided upon at the time the loan is made and to be subsequently adhered to.

The first exception is of limited significance. It is in the Act in order to prevent what would otherwise be an unfair tax treatment where an individual borrows money from a chartered bank in which he has a few shares. Thus, if I deal with the Royal Bank of Canada and borrow $40,000 for business purposes, it would be somewhat ridiculous for me to have to take that amount into income if, by coincidence, I have one hundred shares of Royal Bank in my investment portfolio.

The second exception, however, is very important when it comes to "buying into" a business — whether that business is privately owned or whether the stock option or purchase plan involves a public company. It appears that the government wants to encourage employees to become shareholders of (or extend their shareholdings in) employer corporations. Thus, where a corporation makes a loan for this purpose, a reasonable period may be used in order to effect repayment. It must be stressed, however, that the exception applies only to shares issued out of treasury and not to shares acquired by an individual from another shareholder.

The third exception is minor because the greatest benefit that one can derive from employment is probably a *company* car. Thus, a loan to an individual to buy his *own* car is of limited use.

However, in the case of a privately owned company, one of the best tax deals emanates from the fourth exception, which is a housing loan. The first advantage of such a loan arises because corporate tax rates tend to be significantly less than personal rates. Where the employer is a privately owned company, often seventy-five cents out of each dollar of profits is leftover on an after-tax basis. These funds can then be used as an advance to the owner for purposes of buying or building a home. This is much cheaper than using only fifty cents (or less) out of each dollar of after-tax *personal* earnings.

HOUSE PURCHASE ALTERNATIVES

Personal After-Tax Funds

Salary to shareholder-employee	$100,000
Less: Personal taxes of 50% (minimum)	50,000
After-tax funds available to purchase a home	$ 50,000

Corporate After-Tax Funds

Earnings taxed in corporation	$100,000
Corporate taxes (25%)	25,000
After-tax funds available to shareholder as a loan for his home	$ 75,000

The second advantage is that the employee-shareholder gets the use of corporate dollars *today* which he must only repay over a period of time, presumably with "cheaper" dollars because of inflation. A reasonable repayment program for the principal itself might be ten or fifteen years.

If you own a controlling interest in an incorporated business, you would be well advised to speak to your advisors with regard to such a loan *before* you purchase or build any residence. The residence need not be a city home. A country house (or second home) will also qualify as long as it will be owned primarily for personal use and could not be construed as a rental property.

Note that the very generous provision in the Tax Act permitting such a loan applies only in situations where a house is being built or bought. It does not apply to the refinancing of an existing home. However, if your intention is to make a major extension to an existing residence, it may be possible to get an advance ruling from Revenue Canada allowing a company loan for that purpose under the same favourable tax conditions.

"Imputed" Interest on Loans

Before 1979, I would have classified a non-interest-bearing or low interest loan as the best of the employment benefits and I would have relegated company cars to number two. This is because there was no requirement that interest be charged on loans to either employees or to shareholders — or that interest be calculated as a taxable benefit. All this changed on January 1, 1979. The new rules are as follows:

- If interest is not charged by an employer, it must be "imputed" as a taxable benefit at the average bank prime rate of the preceding year and added on to the T–4 slip. For 1980, the rate is 11%.
- In order to avoid bookkeeping for small loans, there is an annual $500 exemption from imputed interest. Thus, if an employee gets a loan of $4500 throughout 1980, there will be no benefit for income tax purposes ($4500 X 11% = $495).

There are, however, two exceptions to the rules that otherwise require an interest calculation to be treated as a taxable benefit. The first is where a loan is used for the purpose of acquiring shares in the employer's company under a stock option or stock purchase plan. (These important benefits are covered later in this chapter.) Again, the government encourages employees to buy into their employers' companies and a loan for that purpose can be made under very favourable conditions. It can be repaid over whatever length of time is reasonable and *without* interest considerations.

The second exception and, in some cases, the more significant is a "relocation loan". The rules allow a corporation to make an interest-free relocation loan of up to $50,000 (per family unit of husband and wife) if an employee has been moved from one place in Canada to another pursuant to a change of job location. The proceeds of the loan must be used to acquire a residence that is at least 40 kilometres closer to the new work location than the employee's old residence would have been. The purpose of such a provision is to encourage employee mobility. The housing relocation loan is available as a benefit not only to employees who are being transferred from one place to another, but also to individuals who are being "head hunted" by companies operating in other cities. This loan can be used to induce an individual to accept a new job that also involves a move.

The best advantage, however, is obtained where a privately owned business decides to expand its horizons. For example, take the case of a business operated out of Calgary by two partners. A decision is made to open a branch in Edmonton approximately 300 kilometres away. One of the owners agrees to move from Calgary to Edmonton to run the new division. Although housing prices in the two cities are, at the present time, comparable, the corporation could still make a loan of up to $50,000 to the individual moving from Calgary to Edmonton. Since this person is a shareholder, a reasonable repayment period (i.e., ten to fifteen years) is required for the principal. However, *because it is a relocation loan, no interest need be charged or imputed.*

Even where a loan is made to an employee under conditions where interest must be calculated, it is important to note that there is still an opportunity for the individual to derive a significant benefit. This is because the *only cost to the employee is the tax on the amount added to his income.* Take the example of an individual in the 50% bracket who has been promoted but has not been asked to relocate. As a fringe benefit, the company offers him a loan of, say, $50,000 towards the acquisition of a new home. Here are the tax consequences of that loan:

Loan made	$50,000
Imputed interest factor (1980)	11%
Taxable benefit	$ 5,500
Less: Basic exemption	500
Net taxable benefit	$ 5,000
Out-of-pocket cost to employee in 50% bracket	$ 2,500
Earnings required to pay taxes of $2,500	$ 5,000

If that same employee were to get a raise in salary, and would then borrow $50,000 for his new home from a lending institution, the following would result:

Loan obtained from lending institution	$50,000
Interest rate (minimum)	13½%
Interest cost (non-deductible)	$ 6,500
Earnings required to pay interest of $6,500	$13,000

In this case, the required earning power needed by the employee to finance his house is almost three times as high as under the employer loan alternative. Clearly the employee should be willing to forgo some increase in salary in order to benefit from the use of company funds.

If a loan is made, the employer would be incurring an "opportunity cost" of otherwise having $50,000 in investments. The company would, however, save a corresponding outlay in the form of additional salary. Often, using the services of the company's accountant, who knows both the relevant corporate tax rate and the employee's personal tax bracket, an arrangement can be worked out which will be advantageous to both parties. Although the 1979 rules for imputing interest make employee loans somewhat less attractive than before, a significant advantage is still obtainable.

Low Interest Loans

In some cases, the employer's policy is to charge a low rate of interest on loans to employees. There does not, however, appear to be much logic in this practice where the loan, in turn, is to be used for personal purposes. Under such an arrangement, the employer must recognize interest income which is fully taxable, while the employee's tax relief is limited to the $500 annual exemption.

It would be better to reduce the employee's salary by the amount of the interest otherwise charged to offset any loss to the employer. As explained previously, coping with a taxable benefit is much cheaper than an actual outlay of cash.

Holiday Trips, Including Travel Expenses for an Employee's Spouse

Revenue officials take the position that the value of a holiday trip, prize or incentive award must be included in an employee's income as a fringe benefit — even if the person paying the costs is a customer or supplier of the employer. Travel benefits include the expenses of an employee's spouse as well. However, within this rather general framework there are a number of exceptions. The most important would be the case where a holiday trip can be combined with a valid business purpose. Where a business purpose exists, the taxable benefit can be reduced or even be eliminated in some cases.

A friend of mine who is a chartered accountant was asked by a client of his to prepare a report on the tax implications of Canadians investing in U.S. real estate. My friend informed his client that although a significant amount of research could be done from Canada, it would still be advantageous for him to meet with a tax accountant or lawyer based in the United States to discuss some of the finer points. The client readily agreed. It so happened that my friend was invited to a family wedding in Los Angeles which was scheduled to take place within the following month. It doesn't take much imagination to guess where my friend made arrangements to meet with a qualified U.S. tax practitioner.

Another case involves a privately owned real-estate brokerage house which has offices in major cities in both Canada and the United States. This firm services many clients from both Europe and the Orient who are investing in North American real estate. For several years, this particular company has had a policy of providing a rather interesting fringe benefit to employees. Each year where a commissioned salesperson reaches his or her quota, the salesperson is rewarded with a free trip. In year one, the employees based in western Canada go east while the eastern employees go west. In year two, the Canadian employees go south to the U.S. while the U.S. employees come north to Canada. In year three, the trip is to Europe, in year four to the Orient and in year five to Hawaii.

In each case, the employee is required to file a detailed report on his return to his own office. The report must compare real estate prices in the places that he has been to those at home and the employee must, as well, list contacts that he or she has made in the other city or cities. These reports are kept on file by the company. Not long ago, Revenue officials did an audit at the company's head office. They proposed to allow the first four trips as being for business only, without any taxable benefit implications, while they decided that the fifth-year's trip to Hawaii should be treated as a fully taxable benefit.

The company objected on behalf of its employees, stating that many investors are buying real estate in Hawaii and that there is as much business justification for that trip as there is to anywhere else. At one point, the company's controller asked my advice. I suggested that the company back off and allow its employees to be taxed on the value of the Hawaiian trip. My reasoning was simply that even if they could convince Revenue to allow, say, 30% as being for business purposes, the authorities could just as easily change their minds and contend that 40% or 50% of the other four trips was for pleasure purposes. Sometimes, a compromise with Revenue officials will save more in the long run — especially when one takes into account the professional fees incurred in handling a dispute. I don't know if the controller took my advice, but in any event, the message is clear. Wherever possible, combine business and pleasure. As a general rule, I suggest that you avoid business meetings in both Florida and Hawaii since Revenue Canada appears to take a very negative attitude to expenditures incurred in these two locations.

If you take your spouse on a business trip, Revenue's general outlook is that those costs are a taxable benefit. The exception is where the spouse accompanies the employee at the specific request of the employer and for purposes of enhancing the employer's business efforts. In this case you should obtain written instructions from your employer requiring you to bring your spouse along on a trip. The letter should indicate that it is anticipated that there will be meetings in the evenings involving customers, clients or suppliers and their spouses and that your spouse is expected to contribute to these meetings by promoting the employer's activities. This letter could be extremely useful during a subsequent Revenue audit — but it will only work where there is an arm's length relationship between you and the employer. This means you cannot be related by blood, marriage or adoption. If an employee also happens to own the business, there is no great advantage in getting the individual in his capacity as president of the company to sit down and write himself a letter requiring that he take his own spouse away on business.

When it comes to the cost of bringing spouses along to conventions, Revenue's attitude appears to be somewhat mixed. (Your own expenses are discussed later in this chapter.) In many cases, the authorities will add on taxable benefits where participants take their spouses along, although, in recent years, many organizations seem to have been making efforts to eliminate or reduce the tax exposure. Most convention agendas now make bona-fide attempts to include the spouses of participants in business-related sessions. At one convention where I was a speaker, there was a specific program for wives on how to help their husbands cope with stress. At another convention, a colleague of mine from the University of Calgary spoke to the members' spouses on how to interpret financial statements of small businesses.

Discounts on Merchandise Ordinarily Sold by an Employer

If an individual obtains a discount on merchandise ordinarily sold by his employer, Revenue Canada does not require the value of that discount to be included in income. Presumably, keeping track of such discounts would involve an effort more costly than the tax dollars lost to the government coffers.

Revenue's generosity does not, however, extend itself to the construction industry. Where an executive is able to acquire a home built by his employer, and the cost is less than its fair market value, many of the District Taxation Offices will try to impose a taxable benefit. The amount of the benefit is, of course, subject to negotiation. If you work in the construction industry and are able to benefit from the purchase of a company-built home, avoid any disputes by purchasing at a price which would give your employer at least a small profit margin.

While on the subject of construction companies, I strongly suggest that you stay away from the practice of letting a company pay for improvements to your own residence while charging off the cost of these expenditures against job construction projects. Anybody who does something of this nature is committing fraud, which is punishable by severe penalties.

Recreational Facilities and Club Membership Dues

In an attempt to cut back on expense-account living, Parliament passed a law as part of its 1972 Tax Reform prohibiting the deduction as a business expense of membership fees in any club providing dining, recreational and sporting facilities. Thus, if a company pays these membership fees, they are non-deductible even if the facilities are used for proper business entertainment and promotion. Although the membership fees are automatically disallowed, house accounts (such as green fees or actual costs of meals and beverages) are deductible if it can be shown that these specific accounts arose in the course of business entertainment.

When the above rules were brought in, Revenue Canada was

faced with an administrative dilemma. If the department were to adopt the policy of taxing these memberships as a benefit to individual employees, then a double-tax situation would arise. (This results any time an expense is disallowed to a company while the outlay is also taxed as a benefit to an individual.) In order to circumvent double taxation, Revenue issued an Interpretation Bulletin exempting employees from having to include these benefits in income. Officially, the exemption only applies where an employee uses the facilities *primarily* to further the employer's business objectives. Administratively, however, it appears that the department has taken a rather lax approach in enforcement. Therefore, club memberships paid for by a company can be an excellent benefit for senior executives. This is especially true where the individual is in a substantially higher tax bracket than the employer corporation.

NB

The benefit is even greater where the individual happens to be a major shareholder of the company as well. Again, as is the case with company cars, less earning power is needed to pay for a club membership on an after-tax basis where the corporation bears the cost. This is illustrated in the table below.

PRE-TAX EARNINGS NEEDED TO PAY CLUB MEMBERSHIP DUES OF $750

Personal Earnings

Salary to individual	$1,500
Less: Incremental taxes at assumed 50% marginal bracket	750
After-tax funds for membership dues	$ 750

Corporate Earnings

Profit retained by corporation	$1,000
Less: Taxes thereon at 25%	250
After-tax funds for membership dues	$ 750

Stock Option and Stock Purchase Plans

Where an individual is employed by a *public* corporation and the individual obtains the right to acquire shares of his employer company out of treasury, the tax rules impose an employment benefit. The amount to be added to income is the difference between the price to be paid for the shares and their fair market value at the date the employee exercises his option. (The fair market value of the shares on the date the option was granted is not relevant for tax purposes.) This can be illustrated by a simple example:

Fair market value of each share at the time the option is exercised	$20.00
Less: Option price to be paid	14.00
Benefit from employment (per share)	$ 6.00

Where the option is for public corporation shares, the fact that a taxable benefit arises is not too onerous. These shares generally tend to be marketable and it is usually possible for some of the shares to be sold in order to pay taxes on the benefit. In addition, since these shares are saleable, an employee can borrow money to pay his taxes using the shares as collateral. Finally, a stock option benefit is one of the special income receipts which qualifies for "income-averaging annuity" treatment. This permits the tax consequences of the option to be spread over several years. (Income-averaging annuities are discussed in the next chapter.)

Stock option plans are thus quite attractive for employees of public companies who are able to acquire shares at less than the going trading price. Although the individual must contend with a taxable benefit at the time the option is exercised, any future growth beyond that point is treated as a capital gain — only one-half of which is taxable. A capital gain will only arise at the time the shares are sold.

Because the above rules used to apply to options granted to employees of *private* companies as well, stock option plans in these companies were not favoured during the early 1970s. This was for several reasons:

1. Shares of private companies are not marketable. Thus, an employee cannot sell some of his shares to pay his taxes.
2. Shares of private companies are not readily pledged as

collateral for bank financing. Accordingly, an individual faced with a tax liability would be hard-pressed to borrow against his shares for the purpose of making payment.

3. It would be difficult to sell some of the shares and use the proceeds to invest in an income-averaging annuity designed to spread the tax bite over a number of years.

In mid-1977, however, Parliament decided, for the first time, to differentiate between option plans granted by public corporations and option plans of Canadian-controlled private companies. An employee of a private company is now permitted to buy treasury shares at literally *any price* from one dollar up to fair market value. As long as the employee continues to hold these shares in his own name for at least two years after the date of acquisition, no taxable benefit need be calculated. The only tax consequences that will arise occur at the time of sale. The difference between the actual purchase price and the selling price becomes a capital gain, only one-half of which is taxable.

Thus, it is theoretically possible for key employees of Canadian-controlled private corporations to acquire substantial interests in an employer-company for as little as one dollar. The only requirement that must be adhered to (in addition to the two-year minimum holding period) is that the employees must deal at arm's length with the controlling shareholder or shareholders. Because of the very generous tax treatment afforded to employees of Canadian private companies, a share-interest in the business is definitely one of the key benefits to be negotiated wherever possible.

From the standpoint of the controlling shareholder, admission of key employees as "partners" can be a very viable alternative to an outright sale. Consider, for example, the case where a man has built up a business and now wishes to retire. Unfortunately, no one within his family wishes to assume the responsibilities of administration. The owner could, in such circumstances, issue sufficient shares to one or more key employees so that they wind up with, say, 25% of the equity. These key employees would remain as custodians and would receive salaries for their continued efforts. In addition, if the business does well, 25% of the profits from all future growth will accrue to their benefit, while the remaining profits would remain within the family of the retired owner.

Other Benefits

The section which concludes this chapter summarizes other fringe benefits from employment which executives and business owners should consider. The tax implications to both employees and employers are outlined.

Getting the Competitive Edge

There are many opportunities to capitalize on the differences between the tax rules pertaining to employment income and those pertaining to business income. For example, certain expenses are deductible when incurred by a company but are not deductible to employed individuals. Although it is difficult to generalize, a number of concrete examples should serve to make this point.

Convention Expenses

Under the tax rules, convention expenses are not a proper deduction in arriving at employment income. Thus, for example, where an individual attends a trade or professional convention and bears the costs himself, unless the individual is self-employed, these costs would not be deductible.

Consider an individual who wishes to attend a particular trade or professional conference. He asks his employer to subsidize the costs, but the employer refuses on the grounds that it is contrary to company policy. The employer, however, informs the employee that he may go if he is willing to take the time off as part of his annual vacation. If the employee is tax conscious, he should then suggest that the employer pay the cost of the convention and reduce his salary accordingly.

From an employer's standpoint, it makes no difference whether an amount is paid as a salary or as a convention expense. The full payment in either case can be written off for tax purposes. However, where an employer pays convention costs and reduces an employee's salary, the employee gets a smaller amount reported on his T–4 slip. Having less income to report in the first place is equivalent to having a higher income offset by a tax deductible expense.

This is a prime example of getting the competitive edge — finding a situation where an expense is deductible to an employer which would not otherwise be deductible to an individual employee.

Job-Hunting Expenses

Although moving expenses are tax deductible, there are no provisions in the Income Tax Act relating to "job hunting" expenses. Another example of getting the competitive edge can be illustrated by a situation involving a friend of mine. In 1977, this individual decided to move west to Calgary from Montreal. He flew out and started looking for employment. After about a week, he found a job with an employer who agreed as part of the remuneration package to retroactively reimburse my friend's moving expenses after one full year's employment. This seemed to be a fair deal, but my friend decided to push a little further. He asked for the reimbursement of his job-hunting expenses as well. The employer refused on the grounds that the company had not really sent for him in the first place and that he did not come out to Calgary exclusively for that particular interview. My friend understood the logic behind the company's decision not to reimburse these costs and was prepared to back down.

I suggested to him, however, that he could very easily obtain the next best thing to a reimbursement, which would be to have the job-hunting expenses treated as tax deductible. I asked him to go back and approach the employer with a suggestion: reimburse the job-hunting expenses and start salary payments one or two weeks later. The employer readily agreed because (from a company standpoint) salary paid and travel costs incurred to hire an employee are both equally tax deductible. From the individual's position, however, starting on the payroll a week or two later produces less gross income for tax purposes.

Contract-Negotiation Fees for Athletes

A third example of capitalizing on the difference between the tax rules for employment and business income pertains to contract-negotiation fees for athletes. During the early 1970s, I acted as a consultant on tax matters to a couple of attorneys who had built a thriving business representing Canadian athletes in their contract negotiations with hockey clubs. Those were the days when the National Hockey League and the old World Hockey Association were competing with each other for players and offering large salaries and signing-bonuses to talented hockey stars. The problem which we encountered was that although the athletes were paying fees to have their contracts negotiated, the tax rules did not permit these fees to be deducted.

When the problems of one athlete apply to fifty or sixty others, the dollars involved become extremely significant. Accordingly, I arranged a meeting with senior Revenue officials in Ottawa to discuss this matter. The authorities were sympathetic, but they felt that they were bound by the law which contains no provision for the deductibility of these expenses. They asked me, however, if I had a suggestion which could alleviate this problem.

I simply proposed that they permit hockey clubs to pay the players' agents *directly* and reduce the amount of the salary or signing-bonus of each athlete accordingly. I explained that from the club's standpoint, a payment to the athlete or a payment to his agent is still a valid business expense. Under either alternative, the agent would take the amount received into income. However, where a hockey player's salary is reduced by an amount equal to the direct payment from the club to his agent, this is the same as a tax deductible expense. This is because the player's *gross* income would be less than would otherwise be the case. The Revenue authorities agreed to this arrangement.

Tax Avoidance vs. Tax Evasion

All of the previous examples fall under the definition of effective tax *avoidance*. There is nothing fraudulent about arranging one's affairs to produce the smallest tax bite possible in any given circumstances. There is, however, a fine line of distinction between tax avoidance and tax evasion. Evasion is something that one should stay away from since this is an offense punishable under both common and criminal law. To illustrate the difference, here is a short story outlining one of my favourite examples of evasion.

There is a privately owned appliance store that operates in a major Canadian city. Over a period of twenty or twenty-five years the owner of that store got to know his regular customers quite well, and he eventually came up with a very interesting idea for promoting sales. When a customer who owned his own business came in to buy, say, a television set for personal use, the store owner would approach him with the suggestion that he could invoice the television to the customer's business as an air-conditioning unit. The customer's business could then pay for the set and could also obtain a tax write-off through future depreciation. From the appliance dealer's standpoint it wouldn't make any difference to his cash flow, but from the customer's position, getting a company to pay (on a tax deductible basis) for a personal expenditure would be an excellent benefit.

Somehow or other, Revenue officials caught on to what was happening. They did an audit of the appliance dealer's operations and compared sales invoices to related shipping documentation. Naturally, the discrepancy became apparent. The invoices described air conditioners sold to companies while the shipping documentation was for television sets delivered to personal residences. Both the appliance dealer and all the customers who had participated in this particular venture lived to regret this little scheme.

Tax fraud is, of course, subject to severe penalties. Granted, it is often difficult for a layman to differentiate between permissible avoidance and punishable evasion. Usually, if you are in doubt, listen to your stomach. The more queasy you feel about a particular manoeuvre, the more likely it is that you are crossing over into forbidden territory. When in doubt, consult your own advisors. That is one of the reasons you have them. In the meantime, use your imagination. I am sure that most business owners and executives can find ways to *legitimately* get that competitive edge.

Employment Benefits Summary

1. Description of benefit: Furnish executives with company cars.

TAX IMPLICATIONS TO EMPLOYER:
Operating expenses are tax deductible. This would include costs of leasing if cars are rented. If cars are owned, capital cost allowance is permissible at 30% per annum.

TAX IMPLICATIONS TO EMPLOYEE:
If the car is used primarily for business purposes, a minimum standby charge will be added to the taxable income of the employee. To calculate this charge, see page 11.

2. Description of benefit: Holiday trips and conventions.

TAX IMPLICATIONS TO EMPLOYER:

The expenses incurred in furnishing holiday trips and/or convention costs will be deductible in arriving at business income.

TAX IMPLICATIONS TO EMPLOYEE:
The value of trips, if for holiday purposes, is to be included in income as a taxable benefit. Where there is a business purpose, however, such as a trade convention, then a portion of the "benefit" may be excluded from the employee's income. If the spouse accompanies the employee, this will usually result in a taxable benefit.

3. Description of benefit: Tuition fees for courses.

TAX IMPLICATIONS TO EMPLOYER:
Treated as an expense in arriving at business income.

TAX IMPLICATIONS TO EMPLOYEE:
The tuition fee payment must be included in the employee's income. However, the employee *also* gets a deduction for tuition fees paid on his personal tax return. Thus, the taxable benefit and the fee deduction cancel each other. This is more advantageous than if the employee were to pay the expenses himself. On personally paid tuition fees, one is still "out of pocket" the difference between the cost and one's tax bracket.

4. Description of benefit: Non-interest-bearing or low interest loans.

TAX IMPLICATIONS TO EMPLOYER:
There are no adverse tax implications to the employer for failing to charge interest at going rates. Even if the employer has to borrow money to lend these funds to an executive, there will probably be no disallowed interest expense as long as the employee is at arm's length and is not a shareholder.

TAX IMPLICATIONS TO EMPLOYEE:
From the employee's standpoint, interest will be imputed as a taxable benefit on employer loans at the average bank prime rate of the preceding year. For 1980, the rate is 11%. Any interest actually paid by the employee reduces the amount of the benefit for tax purposes.

The first $500 of imputed interest each year is exempt from inclusion in income. There are further exemptions where the loan is a "relocation loan" of up to $50,000 towards the acquisition of a home, or where the loan is for the purpose of acquiring shares in the employer company or of a related corporation.

5. Description of benefit: Group life insurance.

TAX IMPLICATIONS TO EMPLOYER:
Premiums paid for group life insurance for employees are a tax deductible expense.

TAX IMPLICATIONS TO EMPLOYEE:
To the extent that the premiums paid by the employer are for coverage in excess of $25,000 each year, the premiums will be

31

included in the employee's income as a taxable benefit. However, a group rate is generally much cheaper than personally owned insurance and the only "out of pocket" cost to the employee is his tax on the amount of the benefit.

6. Description of benefit: Payment of provincial hospitalization and medical-care insurance fees.

TAX IMPLICATIONS TO EMPLOYER:
This expenditure is tax deductible.

TAX IMPLICATIONS TO EMPLOYEE:
The value of the payments must be included in income as a benefit from employment. However, the incremental tax in the employee's marginal bracket is the only "expense" to him. This will be less costly than paying for the entire health care program personally.

7. Description of benefit: Disability insurance program.

TAX IMPLICATIONS TO EMPLOYER:
Premiums paid under an employees' disability insurance program are a tax deductible expense.

TAX IMPLICATIONS TO EMPLOYEE:
Where the company pays for disability insurance, there is no taxable benefit at that time. However, any benefits received under the program are taxable. If, however, the employer simply initiates the program and premiums are paid by employees, the premiums are non-deductible, but benefits, if and when received, are tax-free. Often the employer pays the cost of short-term disability insurance while employees pay for long-term coverage. This ensures the receipt of tax-free income in the event of a long-term illness.

8. Description of benefit: Discounts on merchandise sold by the employer.

TAX IMPLICATIONS TO EMPLOYER:
The employer, by selling merchandise at a discount, generates less

revenue than would otherwise be the case. This is effectively the equivalent of a tax deductible expenditure.

TAX IMPLICATIONS TO EMPLOYEE:
Revenue Canada, in an Interpretation Bulletin, does not consider a discount on merchandise ordinarily sold by an employer to be a taxable benefit to the employee.

9. *Description of benefit: Employer provides cafeteria or dining room where meals are furnished at a discount.* (The feasibility of this program depends on availability of personnel, space, and know-how.)

TAX IMPLICATIONS TO EMPLOYER:
The costs of subsidizing such a program will be tax deductible.

TAX IMPLICATIONS TO EMPLOYEE:
The discount on meals is not a taxable benefit.

10. *Description of benefit: Payment of club membership fees in clubs providing dining, recreational and sporting facilities.*

TAX IMPLICATIONS TO EMPLOYER:
The costs of membership fees in such organizations are *not* deductible.

TAX IMPLICATIONS TO EMPLOYEE:
Revenue Canada takes the position that as long as the individual is a member of a dining, recreational or sporting club in order to promote the business activities of the employer, there is no taxable benefit. The advantage of having the employer make these expenditures is that the employer corporation is often in a lower tax bracket than the employee. Since the fees for clubs providing such services are not deductible, it is best to utilize the "cheapest" after-tax dollars.

11. *Description of benefit: A corporate-sponsored private health care plan including dental care.*

TAX IMPLICATIONS TO EMPLOYER:
Costs paid by the employer are tax deductible.

33

TAX IMPLICATIONS TO EMPLOYEE:

The premiums paid by the employer are not a taxable benefit. If the employee must pay into such a plan, his payments are not deductible. Employee payments do qualify as allowable medical expenses for purposes of the deduction available in arriving at personal *taxable* income.

12. Description of benefit: Stock option plans where the employees are permitted to buy shares out of treasury.

TAX IMPLICATIONS TO EMPLOYER:

There is no tax deductibility with respect to a stock option or purchase plan. Amounts received from employees are simply treated as receipts of capital.

TAX IMPLICATIONS TO EMPLOYEE:

Where the employer is a private corporation, rules have recently been implemented whereby the corporation may issue shares out of treasury to arm's length key employees at *any* price (up to fair market value). There is no taxable benefit upon receipt of the shares, as long as the employee continues to own these shares for a minimum of two years. If the required holding period is met, the shares simply have a cost base equal to what was paid and any proceeds over and above this amount give rise to a capital gain on disposition.

If such a plan is implemented, it is always important to have a buy-sell agreement for the mutual protection of the majority shareholder(s) and the key employees.

CHAPTER THREE

Postponing Your Income

Planning for Retirement, Loss of Office, and Job Transfers Outside Canada

If you are a business owner or executive age fifty-five or older, you should be giving some thought to planning for retirement. In this chapter, I will show you that a knowledge of the tax rules can certainly be helpful. Even if you are under the age of fifty-five, this material deals with significant loopholes and advantages that could apply if you ever become a non-resident as a result of a job transfer outside Canada, or unemployed after several years of service to a company.

The basic theme of this chapter is the conversion of income from salary into a "retirement allowance". We have already seen that a raise in pay is simply taxed in your top marginal bracket. With respect to retirement allowances, there are other options — and even a relatively young person may become eligible to receive such payments.

Non-Statutory Deferred Compensation Programs

There are two kinds of deferred compensation. The first is referred to as "statutory" deferred compensation. This means that specific rules governing these concepts are set out within the Income Tax Act. Statutory deferred-compensation programs include retirement savings plans, company pension plans and deferred profit-sharing plans. These will be dealt with in Chapter Four. The second type of deferred compensation is "non-statutory". Non-statutory means that the plan is not covered specifically within the framework of the Income Tax Act. Actually, non-statutory deferred compensation is based on a voluntary agreement between an employee and his employer.

Let us begin with an example involving an employer which is a large corporation (perhaps a public company), and which has been in existence for many years. (Later on, I will show you that retirement allowances can be extremely useful as a tax-planning vehicle for owner-managed businesses as well.) A typical scenario involving a large company is as follows:

The chairman of the board calls a senior vice president into his office. The vice president is earning a salary of $70,000 a year — almost sufficient to put him into the top marginal tax bracket. The vice president is fifty-five years old and is ten years away from retirement. The chairman of the board suggests that the last thing that the vice president really needs is additional salary. After a raise, about sixty cents on the dollar would only disappear as additional taxes.

The chairman then advances a proposal which would allow the executive to defer all or part of the *additional* compensation that he otherwise would receive by way of annual raises over the next ten years. If the vice president accepts this offer, his salary will become relatively frozen at its current level. (Of course, if the executive does require additional funds from time to time, these arrangements can be altered.)

The additional salary that the vice president would otherwise receive on an ongoing basis from year to year is then "put away", and at the time of retirement, *a lump sum is paid out as a retirement allowance*. The lump sum would reflect the forgone salary plus (presumably) an interest factor which would have previously been negotiated between the parties.

What is the advantage of such an arrangement? There are actually three opportunities to save taxes where retirement allowances are received instead of ordinary salary. First, by simply retiring *early* in a given taxation year, the vice president can take a substantial portion of the retirement allowance into his income and gain a significant tax advantage.

It is important for you to understand the difference between *marginal tax brackets* and *effective taxes*. On the first $100,000 of a retirement allowance, for example, the tax bite would only be about $40,000 where this is the executive's *only income* in the year of retirement. If the executive can organize his affairs to keep his other income in that year small, the advantage becomes readily apparent. The effective tax rate becomes 40% rather than the 60% marginal rate that would have applied all along had this retirement allowance been received on a year-by-year basis as (additional) salary. There is an absolute tax saving of 20%.

In addition, a retirement allowance qualifies, in whole or in part, for a transfer into a registered retirement savings plan (RRSP). The amount that can be treated in this manner is *unlimited*. It bears no relationship to the ordinary maximum annual limit for RRSP investments, which is only $5500 (see Chapter Four). Thus, if the vice president in my hypothetical example retires at age sixty-five and has other income and other assets, he may choose to "roll over" his retirement allowance in whole or in part into an RRSP. The advantage is that funds do not have to be withdrawn from an RRSP until the beneficiary reaches age seventy-one. In the meantime, the investment income earned by these funds accrues and compounds on a tax-deferred basis. Using current rates of interest, any amount put into an RRSP at age sixty-five would probably be worth at least double by the time the executive reaches the age of seventy-one.

As a third alternative, a retirement allowance is one of nineteen different kinds of "special" incomes which qualify for a transfer into an income-averaging annuity contract (IAAC). The income-averaging annuity rules were introduced in 1972 as a method of levelling the peaks and valleys created by the receipt of non-recurring incomes in certain years. A complete list of the nineteen different items which qualify for income-averaging annuity treatment appears at the end of this chapter. You would probably benefit from reviewing this list with your own accountant.

If you have received one or more of these nineteen different categories of income (of which a retirement allowance is one) you are permitted to take the cash and purchase an offsetting tax-deductible annuity. The annuity must start to pay a return within ten months after the purchase is made. Thus, you will receive annual payments of principal and interest over the term of the annuity. *All* amounts received under the income-averaging annuity are then included in income in the year or years received. The advantage of the annuity is that instead of being taxed on a large lump sum in one year, the tax burden is spread over many years. This is illustrated by the following schedule, which continues the example of the vice president.

	Year of Retirement	Additional Taxable Income of Subsequent Year	
		1	2–5
Retirement allowance	$100,000		
Purchase of IAAC	80,000	$20,000	$20,000
Net special income	$ 20,000		

In this case, a portion of the retirement allowance is rolled over into a five-year annuity to yield $20,000 a year (combined principal and interest). Instead of being taxed on $100,000 in one year, the tax is therefore spread over a six-year period — the year the retiring allowance is received and the subsequent five years.

An income-averaging annuity can be purchased for *either* a specific term (generally up to fifteen years) or for life. If a life annuity is chosen, there can be a maximum guaranteed period of up to fifteen years. This means that if the taxpayer dies before fifteen years have elapsed, payments will continue to his heirs until that guaranteed period has been reached.

There are two special rules worth noting. The first is that the maximum amount that can be invested into an income-averaging annuity in any given year is the special income item(s) minus the equivalent of one year's annuity receipts. (See the above schedule.) The second special rule is that annuity receipts must begin within ten months following the purchase. The intention is to spread the special income over the year it is received and each subsequent year. Income-averaging annuities may be purchased in the year that the special income is received and up to sixty days thereafter. If the taxpayer so desires, he may therefore delay the acquisition of his income-averaging annuity until March 1 of the subsequent year in order to have payments commence January 1 of the year following. In this manner, it is possible to obtain a one-year delay in the recognition of annuity income. In the above example, the vice president could recognize $20,000 of income in the year of retirement and not recognize any additional income until the *second* subsequent year.

How, then, does the income-averaging annuity relate to the concept of retirement allowances? Basically, conversion of salary into such an allowance simply facilitates a second conversion of the allowance into an annuity pension commencing with the year of retirement. At that time, most people will be in lower tax brackets than in their working years and will also require the cash flow which was not otherwise needed in the period immediately before retirement. Although the previous example reflects a five-year payout, most people will opt for a life annuity program.

Choosing Between the RRSP and the IAAC

Therefore, which alternative should a retiring individual choose? If the individual has substantial other incomes and other assets at the time of retirement, he would "roll over" his retiring allowance into an RRSP. This would enable him to completely defer the recognition of all income until age seventy-one. If, however, the individual requires an immediate cash-flow to meet his living expenses subsequent to retirement, he would use the income-averaging annuity option. He may, in fact, split the allowance between both.

The Employer's Tax Position

You might ask why the government tolerates these non-statutory deferred compensation programs. The answer is that the company that pays retirement allowances does not get a write-off for tax purposes until the amounts are actually paid. Since the employer does not get a deduction (that the company would otherwise obtain from salaries) Revenue Canada tacitly agrees that there is no necessity to tax the individual until such time as he actually receives his payments.

The concept of non-statutory deferred compensation works best where an employer-corporation does not need a current deduction in the first place. Such situations would include non-profit or tax-exempt organizations such as universities and hospitals. In addition, there are many real-estate development and oil and mining companies that because of various tax write-offs, don't presently pay income taxes. If a corporation doesn't need a write-off, one gets the best tax treatment. The employer will still get a deduction (if needed) in the year the amount is paid, and the retiring allowance does not have to be taken into income by the individual until such time as he receives it.

For many large corporations, the question of when a deduction of this nature is received is perhaps immaterial. While the tax consequences of, say, $100,000 are certainly important for most individuals, the timing of such a deduction is not really of significance to a Bell Canada or a Canadian Pacific. Thus, deferred compensation programs can be extremely useful even for large corporations which *are* taxable.

Beware of Constructive Receipt

The only problem that one might conceivably encounter with respect to a retirement allowance program is the concept of "constructive receipt". Over the years, tax courts have held that where an individual unilaterally defers his compensation, he is still taxed as if he had received his payments. Thus, for example, if you receive a December paycheque but purposely neglect to cash it until January, you are still taxed in the year that you actually get the cheque.

In order to avoid the doctrine of constructive receipt with respect to retirement allowances, a contract between an employee and his employer usually contains some contingency clause. There must be some element of doubt as to whether the retirement allowance will, in fact, ever be paid. Of course, the contingency cannot be a strict one, such as dismissal for incompetence or for bad moral behavior. If the executive *really* believed that there was an element of doubt as to whether he would receive his money, he would never accept this type of arrangement in the first place.

Thus, the standard contingency clause is usually tied in to something unlikely, such as dismissal for giving away trade secrets to competitors. In the event of being fired for such cause, the retirement allowance would not be paid. This is a contingency sufficient to avoid constructive receipt as each annual installment is segregated out of salaries into the retirement allowance fund. Most of us can live with this kind of contingency. If we give away trade secrets to competitors, the presumption is that the bribe or other payments will be more than sufficient to offset the loss of the retirement allowance.

How Much and When

The term "retirement allowance" is defined in the Income Tax Act to include three types of payments:

1. A payment in recognition of long service,
2. A payment in respect of loss of office, and
3. Certain other termination payments.

Most of the discussion in this chapter involves only the first of these three types of payments. The other two will be dealt with last, in the section on payments for loss of office.

There are, however, no guidelines in the Income Tax Act as to how much can be paid out by a corporation as a retirement allowance. There have not been any tax cases on this matter and it is suggested that *any* amount can be so treated provided it is reasonable. For example, The Canadian Institute of Chartered Accountants in a professional development seminar on tax planning for executives suggests that a payment of up to three-years' salary would be reasonable.

In addition, there are no specific guidelines as to how old the employee must be in order to receive a retirement allowance. *A payment in recognition of long service does not tie in to either a specific age or to a specific length of service with the company.* The significance of these points will be dealt with later, in the section on planning for non-residency.

Protecting the Employee

So far, we have only concentrated on the case of an executive employed by a large public corporation. The major drawback to the concept of a retirement allowance is where a corporation may not be able to fulfill its commitment at the time of the individual's retirement. If, for example, the employer goes bankrupt shortly before an executive is due to retire, the employee does not have any protection beyond that of an unsecured creditor. For that reason, a retirement allowance may not be good planning for employees of medium-sized corporations.

However, the retirement allowance can be extremely useful for a smaller owner-managed business — especially where the executives (owners) have confidence in their own ability to ensure that their company will be sufficiently solvent to meet its future obligations. In addition, a retirement allowance can be an excellent vehicle to assist in passing on the ownership of a small business to other persons, such as one's children or key employees.

Several years ago, I was asked by a Montreal chartered-accountant to assist him in tax planning for one of his clients. The client was a construction company owned by two brothers, each of whom was in his early sixties. Each brother had been drawing a salary of $100,000 a year for the previous five years and the company had earned $500,000 of profits in its fiscal year ended June 30, 1976. Without any planning, the first $150,000 of corporate profits would have been taxed at approximately 25%, while the remaining $350,000 would have been subjected to taxes of about 50%.

The owners of the company were somewhat upset because construction starts in the Province of Quebec had dropped after June 1976, following the completion of the Olympics projects. Then, the industry collapsed completely a few months later when the government changed to the Parti Quebecois following the November election. By the time the accountant called me in as a

42

consultant, it was already early December. I met with him and his clients and at that meeting, the two brothers expressed a desire to retire. They felt that it would be a while before the Quebec construction industry would recover and they really did not want to continue in the business. They decided, however, not to wind up the company but to sell it to a son of one of the brothers.

Given these facts, the first recommendation I made was that the company change its year end to December 31, 1976. It was as of that date that control would pass over to the buyer and an audited financial statement was required in any event. There were no significant construction activities during the six months ended December 31, 1976, and for all intents and purposes, the operations showed a break-even position. However, as of December 31, I suggested that the company pay out $175,000 of retirement allowances to *each* of the two brothers. The brothers legitimately retired as employees, resigned their directorships and offices, and sold their shares.

The retirement allowances totalling $350,000 created a business loss for that fiscal period. The tax rules provide for an automatic one-year carry-back of any business loss which cannot be applied against other income in the current year. By carrying the loss back one year to the fiscal period ended June 30, 1976, the revised net profit became only $150,000 — coincidentally the specific amount which qualifies for the 25% low rate of corporate tax. This resulted in a recovery of $175,000 of corporate taxes otherwise payable.

One of the two brothers took his retirement allowance, bought an income-averaging annuity, and moved to San Francisco. The other brother transferred his funds into a registered retirement savings plan. Both were able to defer significant amounts of tax. In fact, the brother who moved to the U.S. was able to escape Canadian taxes completely. (The next section of this chapter will discuss how this can be done.)

In the case of an owner-managed business, such as in the above example, the retirement-allowance arrangement has one additional benefit. It makes the corporation whose shares are being sold easier to sell. In the above example, the payment of $350,000 reduced the tangible assets of the corporation by $175,000 ($350,000 minus $175,000 of corporate taxes recovered). Whatever price would otherwise have been paid by the son of one of the brothers to acquire the company consequently became that much less. For example, if the value of the corporation before the retirement allowance was $1,000,000 the extraction of these payments reduced the value to $825,000.

A retirement allowance can thus be an integral part of *any* purchase and sale of a private business where the vendor shareholder-manager(s) will also be leaving the employ of the company.

SIMULTANEOUS RETIREMENT AND SALE OF BUSINESS

2 Brothers		June 30, 1976	Dec. 31 1976
$100,000 X 2	Salaries		
	Corporate profit	$500,000	——
2 X $175,000	Retiring allowance		$(350,000)
	Loss	(350,000)←350,000	
	Revised profit	$150,000	

IAAC   RRSP
San Francisco

Retiring allowances make a private corporation easier to sell — they reduce the net tangible assets of the corporation.

Planning for Non-Residency

As I mentioned at the beginning of this chapter, the retirement allowance can be useful not only when one attains normal retirement age but also as a method of tax planning for non-residency. This is because "a payment in recognition of long service" does not tie in to any specific age requirement. To be effective, however, I suggest that there should be a minimum term of service of at least five or ten years *before* the employment relationship is severed.

At this point, it would be useful to review one or two tax-planning ideas which are generally applicable when one is contemplating leaving Canada. First, the Canadian tax system makes a sharp distinction between residency and non-residency. A resident of Canada is taxed on world income. A non-resident is only taxed (at normal graduated tax rates) on employment income from Canadian sources, self-employment income (i.e., business income) and certain Canadian capital gains. However, when property income (such as interest, rents, royalties or annuities) is paid to a non-resident, this is subject to a special flat-rate tax of not more than 25%. A "part-year" resident of Canada is taxed on world income during that portion of the year that the person is resident. During the other portion of the year, there is no Canadian tax obligation as long as the individual does not have Canadian-source employment, business, or (certain) capital gains incomes.

With this background, the first major tax planning idea is to leave Canada, whenever possible, early in a given taxation year. The advantages can best be illustrated with another short case analysis.

In November, 1977, an executive with one of the Calgary-based oil companies came to me for some tax counselling. He was being transferred by his employer to a related corporation operating in Australia. Among other things, the executive wanted to know what tax planning he should do before leaving the country. When he told me that he was booked to leave Calgary in the last week of December, I immediately asked whether or not his departure could be postponed until the first week of January, 1978. The man shrugged his shoulders and indicated that if there were tax advantages, a postponement could certainly be arranged.

I then asked him what benefits he was entitled to by virtue of severing his relationship with the Canadian company. He then began to calculate his accumulated sick leave and vacation pay benefits. In total, these came to approximately $8000. His other income for 1977 was approximately $70,000 — already sufficient to put him into a 55% marginal tax bracket. I explained that adding a further $8000 to the first $70,000 would produce effective taxes of 55% on the incremental income. However, by leaving during the first week in January, the $8000 would then be taxed all by itself and the cost would only be about $1200. I showed my client that by leaving one week later, he could derive an absolute tax saving of $3200:

	1977	1978
Incremental income	$8,000	$8,000
Less: taxes thereon (1977: 55%)	4,400	1,200
Net income	$3,600	$6,800

This particular executive then went so far as to suggest to his employers that they "accidentally" remove him from their payroll as of December 15, 1977. He also suggested that the "mistake" could be found in early January. In this manner, he hoped to move his last two-weeks' salary from 1977 into 1978 in order to compound his tax advantages. The people in charge of payroll were receptive in theory, but they still rejected the idea. Apparently, this company is so large that it is "over-computerized". It was explained to my client that if he were removed from the payroll, the company would never be able to get him back on again. Using the old adage that a bird in the hand is worth two in the bush, my client agreed to receive his normal salary when it was to have been paid in the first place. However, the $8000 of severance pay and other benefits was in fact moved into the following year since he delayed his actual departure from Canada.

This example also explains the importance of retiring early in a given taxation year even if you are not planning to leave the country. Usually, your income in the first year of retirement will be less than your income in the last year of full employment. Therefore, by retiring early in a given year, you can derive substantial tax savings with respect to severance pay, accumulated sick-leave payments, as well as the last year's vacation pay.

Let us now return to the opportunities to use retirement allowances in conjunction with non-residency. Assume that you are an executive employed in Canada by a company that either has or expects to have an affiliated (but legally separate) corporation operating in another country. For simplicity, let's assume the other country is the United States. The president of your company calls you into his office and asks whether you would be interested in moving to Dallas or Denver in about two-years' time as a branch manager for the U.S. company. If you accept such a transfer, there are some excellent chances for tax planning.

You could ask that your present salary be frozen for the next couple of years. Thus, there could be as much as ten or twenty thousand dollars of deferred compensation owing to you at the time you leave Canada. The Canadian company could then pay this to you as a retirement allowance in the year of departure and you could then take the funds and purchase an income-averaging annuity.

Income-Averaging Annuity Payments to Non-Residents

Having "rolled over" your retirement allowance into an income-averaging annuity, your worst exposure to Canadian tax would be a flat-rate withholding tax of 25%. This is the requirement under the Canadian Income Tax Act whenever income-averaging annuity payments are made to a non-resident. However, if you move to a country with which Canada has a Tax Treaty, the rate of withholding tax will be significantly less — generally only 15%.

Where a move is to the United States, you get the best possible tax treatment. If you deregister your income-averaging annuity in favour of a single lump sum once you are a bona fide resident of the U.S., your only exposure to Canadian income taxes is a flat 15%. However, if you decide to receive payments over a period of time, the provisions of the Canada–U.S. Tax Treaty presently in force provide for no Canadian taxes whatsoever. In other words, the payments to you are completely *tax-free* on this side of the border.

In the United States, your receipts of income under the income-averaging annuity contract are considered to be normal annuity payments — i.e., blended payments of principal and interest. The U.S. does not care that payments out of an income-averaging annuity represent income not previously taxed in Canada. The only U.S. tax that you would therefore pay is on the interest element of the annuity. This again means that your principal is recoverable on a tax-free basis.

To summarize, you can either extract your money at a flat 15% immediate tax upon deregistration, or you may receive your retiring allowance over a period of time with no taxes whatsoever. Therefore, if you are aware of an impending transfer out of the country, through which your present employment will cease, there are some excellent tax advantages.

It is important to note that this idea will only work if you are ceasing to be employed by a particular company. If you are going to work for a foreign *branch* of the *same* company, the Revenue authorities will not accept the retiring allowance. This is because, in these circumstances, you would not have retired from a particular employer-company.

Even if you do not have time to plan for potential non-residency several years in advance, the retirement allowance is still feasible. Assume that you are an executive with a Canadian company who receives a salary of $50,000 a year. In January, your superior calls you into his office and asks you to accept a transfer to the U.S. affiliate in Chicago. To keep things simple, assume that your salary for the first year in the United States would be the same $50,000 and ignore the exchange rate difference between the two currencies.

Again, opportunities exist for tax planning. You could ask the Canadian employer to pay you a $25,000 lump-sum retirement allowance. This amount would then be invested in an income-averaging annuity and you would achieve the same tax savings as indicated previously. During your first year of employment with the U.S. corporation, you would be prepared, in such circumstances, to work for a salary of only (the remaining) $25,000. This is because half of what would otherwise have been your salary has already been paid to you before leaving Canada.

With the suggested arrangement you get the best of both worlds. Half your income is taxed at only 15% (or not at all if you are prepared to take your money over a period of time). The other half is taxed at much lower marginal rates in the United States, since your only income for that particular year will be $25,000 and not $50,000. As long as the Canadian company and the U.S. company can make adjustments between themselves, there should be no real problem in setting up this kind of arrangement.

Of course, the Canadian government is aware of the hole that exists in the tax net by virtue of the favourable provisions of the Canada–U.S. Treaty. The Treaty provisions are presently under renegotiation and have been for some time, and it is quite possible that the loophole will eventually be plugged. Thus, I recommend that one seek professional advice before implementing any retirement-allowance program. Even under an amended Treaty, one should be able to get by subject only to a flat 15% tax if one becomes a resident of the U.S.

Finally, the income-averaging annuity is extremely important as a legitimate aid to effective tax reduction where one sells a business or a large portfolio of stock holdings and then proceeds to become a non-resident. The capital gain which arises in these circumstances can be sheltered through an annuity purchase where deregistration occurs after the taxpayer leaves Canada. This will be dealt with more fully in Chapter Twelve.

Definition of a Non-Resident

If you ever plan to become a non-resident, there are certain points that have to be considered. First, the Canadian Income Tax Act does not define the term "resident". Therefore, it becomes a question of fact whether or not an individual is or is not a resident for tax purposes at a particular time. In general, Revenue Canada takes the position that if an individual is not out of the country for at least two years, he will be deemed to have retained residency status if he was a Canadian resident before leaving. In addition, to substantiate non-residency, it is important that members of the taxpayer's immediate family accompany him out of the country. An immediate family would include dependent children as well as a spouse. While you are living outside the country, you are still entitled to visit. Nevertheless, the more time physically spent in Canada, the greater the risk that residency status will be deemed.

In cases that have come before the courts, judges have often looked to the question of whether or not the taxpayer maintains a home in Canada. Thus, whenever a client brings up the idea of "going non-resident", I strongly recommend that he sell his home to strengthen his position. If the taxpayer is unwilling to sell, I recommend that the property be leased out on a long-term (minimum two-year) lease.

Next, you should have a reason for departing the country, such as another job or business opportunity, or perhaps the fact that you have decided to retire to a warmer climate. You should also have a valid residency status in whatever other country you are going to. In other words, if your status in that other country is only that of visitor, it becomes much easier for Revenue officials to deem that you have not ceased to be a Canadian resident.

You should also close out all bank accounts for regular operating expenses. This does not mean that you cannot have Canadian investments. However, you should not maintain bank accounts in Canada out of which everyday living expenses are paid. Finally, club memberships in golf and country clubs should also be surrendered. In some cases, it may be possible to convert a normal membership into a special non-resident status.

While many clients and acquaintances have talked to me over the years about becoming non-residents, I have seen very few who have actually followed through — even where the tax savings would have been extremely substantial. One tends to think long and hard before uprooting an entire family and severing most ties with the past.

Death Benefit Programs

Before leaving the topic of retirement allowances, a few comments on the tax consequences of "death benefits" would be in order. A death benefit is a payment made by an employer to a spouse (or in some cases to other dependants) of a deceased employee who has died while in service. This type of payment can be compared to a posthumous award in recognition of long service.

For tax purposes, the *lesser* of $10,000 or the last twelve months' salary previously paid to the deceased employee is tax-free to the recipient of a death benefit. In most cases, the lesser amount will be $10,000. Although the funds are tax-free to the recipient, the employer still gets a deduction for the payment as a business expense.

However, there is no reason to assume that a death benefit need be *limited* to only $10,000. It must simply be reasonable. Any payment or payments in excess of the base amount would be income to the recipient but would also be subject to a "roll over" into an income-averaging annuity. (See p. 53.) The recipient could thus postpone taxes on the excess amount until such time as annuity payments are received. This would provide the equivalent of a future pension.

Most people think of death benefits as payments that might be made by a corporation such as Bell Canada to the widow of an employee who has died while in harness. And yet, there is no restriction whatsoever limiting the right to pay death benefits to large public companies only. In fact, a death benefit can be extremely useful to tax plan for owner-managed businesses as well. What better way is there to extract a minimum of $10,000 from a corporation and have that amount received tax-free? (To benefit owner-managers, the business must be incorporated since the calculations are made with reference to salaries previously paid.)

Within my own private tax-consulting company, for example, there is a board of directors' resolution which provides that in the event of my death, the company shall pay a minimum of $10,000 to my wife. Similarly, if my wife were to die (she is also an employee of the company) I would receive a death benefit of at least $10,000.

In the same way that a retirement allowance can be used as part of an arrangement to transfer the shares of a business from one taxpayer to another (see p. 42), a death benefit can also be used in conjunction with a buy-sell agreement. If the spouse of a deceased owner receives a large death benefit, it becomes that much cheaper for the surviving owners to buy out their late partner. The value of the business as a whole is decreased by the amount of the death benefit (net of corporate taxes recovered).

All private companies which pay salaries to owner-managers should adopt at least some kind of death-benefit program. There is everything to gain and nothing to lose.

Payments for "Loss of Office"

Although this chapter has discussed retirement allowances primarily in terms of payments in recognition of long service, it should be noted that the definition includes payments in respect of "loss of office" and certain other termination payments. Thus, where an employee is fired or asked to resign, a payment made by the former employer to the individual will be treated as a retirement allowance. Although such a payment is income, it also qualifies for reinvestment into an RRSP and/or an income-averaging annuity.

Note that where a former employee sues his employer for damages for wrongful dismissal, recent amendments to the Income Tax Act provide that most of his receipts (if he wins) will be considered as taxable. Automatically, any award, whether made by a judge or by way of an out-of-court settlement, will be taxed to the extent that the payments do not exceed an equivalent of six-months' salary. Payments in excess of six-months' salary will be tax-free to the recipient provided that the award is a bona fide payment of *damages* for wrongful dismissal. In the absence of a damage suit, all payments received will be considered payments for loss of office and will be taxed as income.

Income-Averaging Annuity Contracts

SUMMARY OF QUALIFIED INCOMES

1. Taxable capital gains.
2. Income from the production of a literary, musical or artistic work.
3. Income from activities as an athlete, musician, or public entertainer.
4. Certain amounts in respect of the disposition of resource properties.
5. A single lump-sum payment from a pension fund upon death, retirement, or withdrawal from the fund.
6. A payment on retirement in recognition of long service.

7. A withdrawal from a deferred profit-sharing plan upon death or retirement.
8. A payment on retirement in respect of loss of office.
9. A death benefit.
10. A "refund of premiums" under a registered retirement savings plan.
11. Recaptured depreciation on the disposition of depreciable property.
12. The taxable portion on the sale of goodwill or other "eligible capital property".
13. Profit on sale of inventory on ceasing to carry on business.
14. Payments in respect of receivables of a "cash basis" farmer on ceasing (or disposing of) all or part of his farming business.
15. The value of certain inventory or receivables of a "cash basis" farmer on ceasing residence in Canada.
16. The disposal of an income interest in a trust.
17. Stock option benefits.
18. The taxable portion of certain prizes for achievement.
19. Amounts withdrawn from a registered home ownership savings plan.

CHAPTER FOUR

RRSPs, Pension Plans
& Other Statutory
Deferred-Compensation Programs

In order to keep as many senior citizens as possible off the welfare
rolls, the Canadian government encourages taxpayers to plan for
their own retirement. The Income Tax Act sets out certain rules
which allow earned income to be exchanged for future benefits.
This deferral is accompanied by specific tax concessions which
make it easier for individuals to finance their retirement programs
by themselves.

The tax rules do, however, draw a distinction between
encouraging realistic savings plans and the tax avoidance possibilities that would otherwise exist if the deferrals were overly
generous.

Registered Retirement Savings Plans

Under the registered retirement savings plan program, an individual is allowed to set aside tax-deductible contributions if these are
made in a given taxation year or within sixty days following the
end of that year. The maximum annual amount is 20% of "earned
income" subject to a dollar limitation of:

- $5500 — where the individual is not a member of an
  employer-sponsored registered pension plan, and
- $3500 minus the individual's contributions to a company
  pension plan (if any).

Earned income is, basically, the sum of net receipts from
employment, self-employment (business), pensions, rentals and
alimony. Where an individual is not a member of a registered

pension plan, the "magic" earned income required for full participation in an RRSP is $27,500. This is because 20% of $27,500 is $5500 — the maximum amount which qualifies for an RRSP in any given year (excluding retirement allowances and other special transfers).

The theory behind the RRSP program is fairly simple. Contributions are made on a tax-deductible (or pre-tax) basis each year. As long as these amounts are invested in qualified investments such as Canadian public company stocks and bonds, Canada Savings Bonds, or mortgages, the income earned within an RRSP compounds on a tax-deferred basis. After several years of ongoing contributions, the available capital starts to snowball and the build-up of capital continues until retirement. At that time, the assets in the plan are liquidated and an annuity is purchased in order to provide a post-retirement cash flow. Although withdrawals from an RRSP are taxable, the individual often anticipates being in a lower tax bracket after retirement than previously.

The benefits of an RRSP are substantial. If, for example, you invest $5500 a year annually at 10% compounded for thirty years, you would have almost $905,000 at the end. This amount could purchase an annuity that would provide a monthly income of $9500 for the rest of your life. It is, of course, an open question of what $9500 a month would buy given current levels of inflation — but that is beside the point, as you will see in the next section.

Should I Have an RRSP?

One of the most common questions posed to me by executives is whether or not an RRSP is advisable, especially because of investment restrictions. Real estate is a non-qualified investment, as are precious metals such as gold and silver, and one cannot invest to any great extent in foreign securities. Notwithstanding the limitations placed on one's RRSP portfolio, my general comment is that an executive really doesn't have a choice. He *must* have an RRSP.

Let's examine the alternatives. For anyone in a 50% tax bracket, it becomes a choice of either having $5500 earning income at a compound rate of, say, 10% each year or having half the capital ($2750) tax-paid and earning income at only 5% (since the unsheltered investment yield would be fully taxable). Having twice the capital returning twice the rate certainly makes an RRSP worthwhile.

If you are one of those who complain that RRSP investments are restrictive and that you would rather acquire real estate or precious metals, I suggest that you can have your cake and eat it too. If you go to a bank to borrow money for investment purposes, the banker is interested in both your earning power and your asset position. If you invest $5500 (pre-tax) in an RRSP, your net worth goes up by that amount. Alternatively, you would have only been able to increase your net worth by $2750 if you were relying upon after-tax capital. Thus, the additional net worth enhances your borrowing power even though the Income Tax Act does not permit an RRSP to be used directly as collateral. I have yet to meet a banker who would discount an RRSP portfolio (as reflected on a net worth statement) for the underlying tax cost to extract the assets. Presumably, this is because the tax is deferred until after the borrower's retirement years.

To summarize then, in dealing with the question of whether or not an RRSP is attractive, simply ask yourself, what better choice is there?

Spousal Plans

If you agree that an RRSP is a valid means of both tax sheltering and building up investment capital, there are additional refinements that should be kept in mind. The first of these is the "spousal" RRSP.

In 1974, the tax rules were amended to allow you to split RRSP contributions between yourself and your spouse. This does *not* mean that you can double up and contribute (up to) $11,000. However, if your annual limit is, for example, $5500, you can channel this entire amount into your own plan, into a spousal plan, or you can allocate in any proportions (for example, 50–50, 60–40, etc.). The only way that a married couple can have more than $5500 added each year to RRSP savings, is where *both* husband and wife have earned income. Thus, if your spouse has an earned income of her own, she too can contribute to an RRSP earmarking the funds either to herself, to you, or in any combination.

Let us examine a situation where a husband has an earned income while his wife remains at home looking after the children. What are the advantages and disadvantages of setting up a spousal plan? The first major advantage of splitting RRSP contributions is that over a period of time, two separate pools of capital are built up. Eventually, each pool will give rise to an annuity. Since tax rates for individuals are graduated, the tax bite will be substantially less if the annuity is split so that the husband only gets part of the income while his wife gets the balance.

The second advantage of a spousal plan relates to another recent tax change. As an additional concession for senior citizens who have had the foresight to save for their retirements though deferred compensation plans, the Act was amended so that the first $1000 of annual private pension income is tax deductible. The $1000 tax deduction generally applies only where the recipient of the pension is over the age of sixty-five. (Receipts from the Canada Pension Plan or the Old Age Security Pension do not qualify for this deduction.) Thus, the second advantage of splitting one's RRSP is to build up two annuities and to double up on the annual $1000 pension-income deduction.

The only disadvantage to a spousal RRSP occurs in the event that a couple gets divorced. Where, for example, a husband has contributed into his wife's plan, the funds belong to her. This disadvantage does not, however, appear to be too serious. In recent years most provinces have adopted family law provisions whereby assets acquired after marriage are divided 50–50 in the event of a marriage breakdown. Thus, a court would presumably take assets held by each party's RRSP into account as part of a property settlement.

My recommendation is that a spousal RRSP should be used — as long as one's marriage is reasonably solid. I don't see much point in being paranoid about what might happen many years in the future. On the other hand, if one's marriage is somewhat shaky, why look for trouble? It might then be best to forgo the tax benefits of this arrangement.

One word of caution. If you place funds into a spousal plan, you must be prepared to leave these dollars for at least a while. The tax rules provide that where a wife withdraws funds from an RRSP, her husband is taxed to the extent that he had made any contributions in his wife's name either for the current year or the two preceding years. This "attribution" of income is designed to prevent a high bracket taxpayer from contributing funds (on a deductible basis) to his spouse's plan where she, in turn, would withdraw the money practically tax-free almost immediately thereafter. You cannot beat the system by causing your wife to withdraw "older" contributions first. Under the above rules, the most recent contributions are deemed to be the first ones withdrawn for tax purposes. Naturally, the converse also applies where a wife contributes to her husband's plan.

Deductibility of Interest

One of the most important planning features with respect to the RRSP pertains to the tax deductibility of interest. Revenue Canada adopts the position that interest on borrowed money is tax deductible where the funds are used for RRSP purposes. This is because the object of the borrowing is to produce income for the taxpayer — even though the income is deferred. However, Revenue's generosity does not extend itself to spousal plans. If one borrows for a spousal plan, one is incurring an interest expense not to earn income for oneself, but for another (separate) taxpayer. Accordingly, the interest expense would not be deductible. Therefore, if you are in a position where you must borrow all or substantially all of your RRSP funds, you would probably be better off investing these dollars into your own plan. It is just too expensive to forgo the deduction of interest, especially with lending rates being as high as they are.

However, if you are borrowing only part of the funds needed for an RRSP, proper "tracking" could allow for the deduction of the full interest. Tracking simply involves ordering your affairs to produce a clear audit trail for Revenue Canada officials. For example, assume that in your family you are the only one with an earned income and you wish to contribute $5500 into an RRSP. You would like to split the RRSP equally between yourself and your spouse, but you have only saved up half the required funds. The proper procedure would be as follows:

First, you would use your savings and purchase an RRSP in the name of your spouse. Then, a day later, you would borrow the remaining funds required from your bank or other lending institution and you would use these borrowed funds specifically for the purpose of purchasing your *own* RRSP. In this manner, you could show Revenue officials that you borrowed for your plan and not for your spouse's. If you are lax and make all the transactions at the same time, the authorities will only allow a portion of the interest. They will argue that since you only invested half of your own capital and borrowed the other half, only a proportionate amount of your interest should be deductible.

RRSP Interest vs. Mortgage Interest

Another important feature of tracking relates to the use of RRSP funds to create tax deductibility with respect to mortgage interest on your own home. In Canada, there is a significant difference between *deductible interest expense* and *non-deductible interest*. This topic will be dealt with in full in Chapter Six. As most people are aware, mortgage interest with respect to one's own residence is not a deductible expense, and even if the previous Conservative government's mortgage interest and property tax credit program had been passed, this still would not have provided much incentive to incur a large personal mortgage.

If, for example, your mortgage is at 13% and you are in a 50% tax bracket, you must earn a 26% return on your invested capital in order to net 13%. Since a 26% return is, at best, rather uncertain, tax planners generally suggest that you use your savings to pay off your mortgage as fast as possible. Most mortgages provide that the home owner may pay off up to 10% each year without penalty. Therefore, the following planning is recommended:

If you can save $5500, which you would otherwise earmark each year for an RRSP, you are better off taking this money and paying down your mortgage. At this point, since your equity in your home would be higher, your borrowing power would be proportionately increased. You could then go to your banker and borrow funds for an RRSP. You would then be incurring tax deductible (RRSP) interest instead of non-deductible (mortgage) interest. If you can work out a flexible repayment plan with your banker, or an open line of credit, you will find yourself able to eliminate all your non-deductible interest over a period of only a few years.

No RRSP Annuity Before Age Sixty

In 1978, the tax rules were amended and now provide that you may not take an annuity out of an RRSP before you have reached the age of sixty. If you wish to withdraw funds before that time, you must make a lump sum deregistration of your plan. You are, however, allowed to reregister those dollars on which you do not wish to pay taxes, subject of course to any handling fees that may be charged by the trustees of the plan.

If there is some possibility that you will require funds before you are sixty, because of unforeseen circumstances or a low income year, you may be best off with one or two smaller RRSPs as well as a major plan which builds for your retirement. If you are in need of a few thousand dollars, you would simply deregister one of the small plans and make use of those funds after having paid your taxes.

Bequeathing Your RRSP to a Spouse

There are also some important new rules which apply on the death of a taxpayer. Essentially, if you die and, at that time, you have rights under an RRSP, the value of these rights is included in your income in the year of death. This rule applies unless you have bequeathed your rights under your RRSP to your spouse. Lack of awareness of this rule can be rather expensive — especially if one dies late in a year and has RRSP income over and above other income earned in that year. Generally, your will should provide for a spousal bequest of an RRSP. If an RRSP is bequeathed to a spouse, the spouse then has several choices:

1. She can pay tax on part of that which she receives and then have tax-paid money left over,
2. She can transfer funds into her own RRSP, and
3. She can transfer a portion of the inherited RRSP into an income-averaging annuity.

For example, if I were to die and my wife had very little income in that year, it would probably be advisable for her to take part of the RRSP which she inherits directly into her income. In fact, she might be willing to pay taxes on as much as $100,000. This concept was dealt with in Chapter Three. The total taxes on $100,000 would amount to only approximately $40,000 and on an after-tax basis, she would have about sixty cents on the dollar of tax-paid money available for reinvestment.

Additional RRSP funds could then be transferred into either her own RRSP or into an income-averaging annuity, depending on her income and cash-flow requirements. While an annuity from an RRSP cannot be taken *before* age sixty, one can nevertheless wait until age seventy-one before making withdrawals. On the other hand, an income-averaging annuity is structured so that payments must commence within ten months following the date on which the annuity is first purchased.

Therefore, whether my wife "rolls over" into an RRSP or into an income-averaging annuity depends primarily on her other income and other assets at the time of my death. If she does not require an immediate cash flow, I would recommend that the RRSP transfer be used. In this manner, the capital can be increased substantially before she turns seventy-one. On the other hand, if she has little other income and few other assets, the income-averaging annuity approach would be advisable. This is because the income-averaging annuity will provide an immediate flow of income which can be used (on an after-tax basis) to meet her living requirements.

Bequests of RRSP's to Other Beneficiaries

If you die without leaving a surviving spouse, there is still an RRSP rollover if you leave RRSP funds to dependent children or grand-children under the age of twenty-six. The rollover is $5000 for each year that the dependent child or grandchild is under twenty-six at the time you die. This particular rule was passed by Parliament in response to a lobby from unmarried or divorced taxpayers who felt that they were being discriminated against. Unfortunately, for most people this amendment is probably not worth the paper it is written on.

Think about how it would apply in your circumstances if you were to die without leaving a spouse to receive your RRSP. In most cases, you would not have a substantial RRSP portfolio until approximately age fifty-five. This is because the compounding effect really only builds up in the last ten or fifteen years before retirement. When you are fifty-five, do you expect to have dependent children or grandchildren under the age of twenty-six? I, for one, hope that I will never have dependent *grandchildren*. In addition, by the time I am fifty-five, my youngest child will be twenty-five and the rollover, if any, would not be material.

Becoming a Non-Resident

Ironically, one of the best benefits that one can derive from an RRSP is reserved for a taxpayer who becomes a non-resident of Canada. The worst exposure to tax on RRSP withdrawals by a non-resident is a flat rate of 25%. If one moves to a country with which Canada has a tax treaty, the rate is generally 15% and as mentioned in Chapter Three, the best advantages accrue under the Canada-U.S. Tax Treaty. Annuity payments made to a resident of the United States are not subject to any Canadian tax whatsoever, while in the United States, only the annual interest element is taxable. On the other hand, a lump sum withdrawal is subject to a flat 15% Canadian tax and is not subject to any U.S. tax at all.

Temporary Residents of Canada

The RRSP can also be an excellent tax-saving device for temporary residents of Canada. Take, for example, the situation of a doctor coming to this country to obtain specialist training. Assume that he takes a hospital position paying $35,000 per annum and that he expects to stay in Canada for a three-year period. During those three years, the doctor should invest the maximum amount possible into an RRSP. He would get a deduction for tax purposes and would save about $2500 of taxes each year. Then, when he returns to his own country, his worst exposure to taxation would be a flat 25%. Any time one can recover fifty cents on the dollar when contributions are made and pay not more than twenty-five cents on the dollar a few years later, the saving is worthwhile.

What Kind of Plan Should I Have?

RRSP's are administered by trust companies, banks, and insurance companies. In addition, you are allowed to have a self-directed plan where you appoint trustees (or a trust company) and the trustees make whatever investments that you as planholder desire. Of course, all investments must fall within the acceptable tax guidelines discussed at the beginning of this chapter.

Traditionally, people tend to wait until the end of February to purchase their RRSP for the preceding year. Many millions of dollars are spent annually by companies trying to promote their own particular plans. To attempt to compare all the different alternative investments is a full time job for a qualified investment counsellor. Contrary to popular belief, most accountants and lawyers are not any better equipped to pick "the right" RRSP than you are. When it comes to selecting an RRSP, one cannot necessarily even rely on past performance. Remember that the performance of a particular plan is only a function of those people employed as fund managers. If a well-qualified investment analyst changes jobs, the plan that was number one last year might very well sink to number ten, while last year's poor performer can end up tops the following year.

The only concrete advice that I give to clients is that they invest conservatively. While purists will probably try to extract every last nickel of income, I tend to believe that a difference in yield of one or two percentage points is not going to make or break the average middle-income and upper-income taxpayer in the long run. It is true that compounding at a return of 10% instead of 12% can result in a significant difference over twenty or thirty years. However, plan performances will often balance out over the long run and you may not even be aware of what you could have realized had you invested differently many years ago. So don't worry about that extra one or two per cent unless you have the time to pursue the top performers even though the list keeps changing frequently.

Insurance Companies vs Banks and Trust Companies

Traditionally, insurance companies that administer RRSP's tend to charge the bulk of their fees for handling your money against the initial contributions. This is called a *front-end load*. By contrast, banks and trust companies tend to charge their fees all along in smaller amounts over the entire life of your plan. I once did a study comparing what I considered (at that time) to be an "average" insurance plan to an "average" trust company plan. Over a period of twenty-five or thirty years, there was only a negligible difference in the assets available towards a post-retirement annuity.

Thus, when a client asks me to comment on the differences, I tend to say that in the long run, there is no real difference. However, if one is a short-term resident of Canada, or non-residency is imminent, I suggest that the taxpayer stay away from any plan with a front-end load. This is because, on deregistration, the taxpayer may find himself getting less money than he actually put in. So if you plan on leaving Canada in a few years, your prime consideration should be directed towards an RRSP that will yield the largest possible income initially, with the smallest administration charges. In addition, you should obtain an undertaking from the trustees that your money will be refunded on demand and if there are any deregistration charges, these should be clearly spelled out in your agreement.

Over the years, two schools of thought have evolved with respect to RRSP investments. The first group recommends investing money in interest-bearing securities or mortgages paying the best current yields. Other advisors suggest that one might be better off by investing in equity funds involving Canadian public company securities. The proponents of equities feel that capital growth will outstrip interest yields over the long run as long as one picks the right securities!

However, equity investments are thought by many to be unattractive because of the fact that all withdrawals from RRSP's are taxable as ordinary income. In other words, one does not get the advantage of the favourable tax treatment accorded to Canadian dividends through the dividend tax credit (see Chapter Seven). In addition, capital gains become transformed into regular income, while ordinarily, one-half of capital gains is subject to tax.

In the December 11, 1979, Budget a very important change was proposed. An exemption from tax was to be allowed for RRSP withdrawals to the extent of one-half of accumulated Canadian common stock dividends received after 1979, as well as one-half of capital gains. Unfortunately, this budget was defeated, and this measure was one of the few not reintroduced into Parliament in April 1980. If implemented, it would certainly have made stocks more attractive than ever before as RRSP investments.

"Cashing In" an RRSP for a Life Annuity

Until just a few years ago, there was only one way to "cash in" an RRSP. The Income Tax Act required that a taxpayer, prior to reaching the age of seventy-one use the funds accumulated in an RRSP to purchase a life annuity from an insurance company. The annuity benefits were then taxable as and when they were received. The only available alternative was to make lump sum withdrawals from the RRSP before you were seventy-one and become liable to pay income tax on all amounts received. In order to protect one's position against an early death, one was also permitted to modify the ordinary life annuity by adding a "guaranteed term" rider. (A guaranteed term means that payments continue for at least that length of time even if the annuitant dies prematurely. However, any time a taxpayer lives beyond the guaranteed term the payments still continue until such time as the taxpayer dies.) The guaranteed term permitted under an RRSP life annuity was always up to fifteen years. In addition, one was also allowed to arrange a joint-and-last-survivor annuity program where payments would continue out of an RRSP until both husband and wife had died. Even the joint-and-last-survivor option could be structured to have a guaranteed term of up to fifteen years.

Over the years, the requirement that one deal only with a life insurance company at the tail end of a program did not appeal to many potential RRSP investors. Actually, the insurance companies have been somewhat unjustly maligned because of a very common misconception. If you are seventy years old and you go to an insurance company with $100,000 in your RRSP, you could probably find a company that would agree to pay you an annuity of approximately $14,000 a year if you do not opt for any guaranteed term. Of course, you would not ordinarily think that this is any bargain. If you are male, you are probably conscious of the fact that your average life expectancy is only seventy-two years. Thus, how would you feel about receiving $14,000 for only two years out of a $100,000 investment made initially?

If you agree with the above reasoning, you have fallen into the common trap. While it is true that the average life expectancy of a male would be seventy-two years, this is only where the person for whom the computation is made is younger than forty years old. Once one passes the age of forty, life expectancy goes up. You will find, if you examine a standard table of mortality rates, that a seventy-year-old male has a life expectancy of another twelve years, and that a female of the same age is projected to live another fifteen years. Thus, an insurance company is not really mistreating you by offering $14,000 a year as an RRSP yield. In preparing calculations, the insurance company must budget for a twelve to fifteen year payout. Since most people are not aware of this, insurance companies have acquired "bad reputations" somewhat unjustly over the years.

Two New Options: Fixed-term Annuities and Registered Retirement Investment Funds

In 1978, however, the government decided to allow trust companies to enter the RRSP annuity field and two new options were introduced:

1. A fixed-term annuity may now be purchased to provide benefits to age ninety and/or
2. RRSP savings may be transferred into a new kind of investment vehicle — a registered retirement income fund (RRIF).

Financial and other institutions that were previously eligible to issue RRSPs are permitted to offer the new options. These include trust companies as well as insurance companies.

Typically, however, the government gave and took at the same time. Above, I indicated that anyone issuing a life annuity to a seventy-year-old must be prepared to pay out over a twelve-year period. Under the fixed-term annuity to age ninety, the same initial capital is paid out over a twenty-year period. Thus, the penalty for taking a fixed-term annuity (over twenty years) is to receive much smaller annual payments than under a life annuity. The fixed-term option may therefore only be attractive to those taxpayers with other incomes and other assets who wish to pass on estates as large as possible to their heirs. Of course, rates of return are subject to change from time to time and it is always necessary to shop around for the best possible deal before making a final decision.

Under the RRIF option, a specific fraction of one's total RRSP assets — capital plus accumulated earnings — is withdrawn each year by the holder to provide an annual income until he is ninety. The fraction is related to the age of the taxpayer in the year and is simply equal to "1" divided by the number of years remaining to age ninety. As an example, for a seventy-year-old purchaser, an RRIF would run for twenty years. In the first year, with twenty years remaining, the holder would be required to take into income 1/20 of the total value of the plan at the beginning of the year. After another year, 1/19 of what is left would be withdrawn, a year later 1/18 and so on, until the final year, when the taxpayer reaches ninety, withdrawal would exhaust the fund. A taxpayer is only permitted to own one RRIF. He may, however, if he so chooses, allot only a portion of his RRSP accumulations to the establishment of an RRIF and invest the remainder in any number of fixed-term or life annuities.

A taxpayer may also base the term of an annuity or RRIF on the age of his spouse, if the spouse is younger, thus securing benefits for the spouse to age ninety. Should a person die before reaching ninety, the benefits under the new options, as well as under life annuities with a guaranteed term, could be bequeathed to a surviving spouse. Otherwise, as indicated previously, the value of any remaining benefits must be included in the deceased person's income in the year in which he dies. The schedule on page 70 shows how an RRIF works, assuming that the taxpayer is seventy years of age and that the interest yield within the plan is 8%. (It is important to note that although the schedule depicts interest at only 8%, the rate is in fact flexible and is tied in with investment yields as they fluctuate both up and down.) As the schedule indicates, the fraction of the plan assets to be paid *increases* each year and the payments received by the taxpayer increase as well.

Presumably, the increasing payments are intended to keep pace with the rise in the cost of living. Thus, in theory, the RRIF is better than both of the other options. This is because there is a flexible rate of return, rather than a fixed rate, and increasing, rather than level, payments. However, the RRIF does break down rather badly in practice. This is because the payments made during the early years are much smaller than the equivalent yield which could otherwise be obtained under either of the alternative two options. It would not be until the taxpayer is approximately eighty-two or eighty-three years old that the RRIF would provide a better annual return than a life annuity. By this time, the taxpayer could easily have starved to death on a much smaller yield!

The RRIF will probably only be useful for taxpayers who have other incomes and other assets. In most cases, however, an individual would be more interested in maximizing his cash flow in

PAYMENTS UNDER A REGISTERED RETIREMENT INCOME FUND
FOR EACH $1000 INVESTMENT BY A TAXPAYER AT AGE 70

Taxpayer's Age on January 1	Fraction of Plan Assets To Be Paid	Balance at Start of Year**	Payments During The Year
70	*1/20	$1,000	$ 50
71	1/19	1,026	54
72	1/18	1,050	58
73	1/17	1,071	63
74	1/16	1,088	68
75	1/15	1,102	73
76	1/14	1,111	79
77	1/13	1,114	86
78	1/12	1,110	93
79	1/11	1,099	100
80	1/10	1,079	108
81	1/9	1,049	117
82	1/8	1,007	126
83	1/7	952	136
84	1/6	881	147
85	1/5	793	159
86	1/4	685	171
87	1/3	555	185
88	1/2	400	200
89	1	216	216

*1/(90 – taxpayer's age)
**Calculated at a constant interest rate of 8%. Note that the actual rate would fluctuate.

70

the decade before he turns eighty. It is during this period that a taxpayer might still be mobile and able to enjoy whatever comforts money can bring.

The problems with the new RRSP options can be alleviated somewhat by legislative amendment. If Parliament were less conservative and would make the payout period under the fixed-term annuity or the RRIF only to age eighty-five, the annual return could be increased significantly. Of course, some taxpayers might then be destitute at eighty-five. At this point, the government would have to step in and support these relatively few people. One would have to ask the question — how many Canadians do in fact live beyond age eighty-five, and of these, how many would have RRSPs in the first place? Without any statistical analysis, it is difficult to answer this question, but I would hazard a guess that the number is relatively small.

Registered Pension Plans

One of the most popular of the deferred compensation plans is the employer-sponsored registered pension plan. Essentially, a pension plan can be one of two kinds. It can be a "non-contributory" plan where the company alone makes annual contributions on behalf of the participating employees; or it can be a "contributory" plan where both the employer and the employees make contributions.

Within the limits described later in this section, both employee and employer contributions are tax deductible. The funds are placed into a trust and they are invested on behalf of participants. As long as the trustees make qualified investments, the income generated on these contributions is not taxable. Thus, there is a compounding of both principal and income from year to year that builds up a lump sum that is ultimately used to provide retirement pension benefits.

Upon retirement, the amount accumulated on behalf of each particular employee is paid out to him, generally in the form of a life annuity, thereby providing funds towards his future living expenses. Although the benefits received at that time are taxable, the employee is likely to be in a lower tax bracket after retirement than previously. As an additional tax incentive to participate in such a plan, there is the annual pension-income deduction, which makes the first $1000 effectively tax-free each year.

An Employee's Allowable Contributions

Most plans are structured so that employees will ultimately receive pensions of between 40% and 60% (usually based on 1½% to 2% for each year of service) of their average annual salaries for their "best" five years. In recent years, because of inflation, the best five years have tended to be the last five years.

The theory behind a pension of 40–60% of the best five years is that after retirement, an average individual's cost of living should be substantially less than it was earlier on (ignoring inflation). Presumably, this is because one's children tend to be grown up and self-supporting by that time, and if one owns a home, the chances are that the house has already been paid for.

Obviously, the benefits of a company pension are dependent in part on the length of time that the individual has been a participant in the plan. The longer one is a member, the greater the amount of annual contributions that have been put aside by the employee (in the case of a contributory plan) and by the company.

The maximum deduction permitted by the Tax Act for current service contributions is $3500 per annum. It is rare, however, to find employees contributing this maximum each year since most employees cannot afford to put aside that much money and still maintain a reasonable standard of living. Accordingly, most pensions plans are designed so that an employee will only contribute from 4% to 7% of his or her annual salary. Using a 6% factor as an example, only employees earning approximately $60,000 a year or more would be contributing the maximum of $3500 per annum. In such cases, the individual would not be able to contribute further amounts into an RRSP. As previously indicated, where an individual contributes less than $3500 to a company pension, he or she is permitted to contribute the difference up to $3500 into a (personal) RRSP.

The Tax Act is concerned with setting out basic rules which are fair and equitable to both employees and employers but which do not provide for undue tax avoidance. Within each plan, there is a certain amount of flexibility and the parties involved can order their own affairs as circumstances dictate. For example, some plans provide for past service contributions (see below). Some might set certain (smaller) limits and some might provide an incentive in the form of supplementary payments for employees who make additional contributions.

Past Service Contributions

In addition to current service contributions of up to $3500 per annum, employees may also make payments of up to an *additional* $3500 for prior services rendered during years in which they were not members of the plan. This is referred to as "past services while not a contributor". There are two major reasons for these provisions. The first pertains to situations where an employee has been working for a company for a certain period of time before the company had set up a registered pension plan in the first place. Second, many pensions plans restrict eligibility until employees have attained several years of service or a certain age.

In general, employers would like to see their long-time employees getting the same benefits as those who join the company at the time a plan is established. Accordingly, it is reasonable that some provision be implemented whereby the more senior employees can, in fact, "catch up" and not be penalized for having worked for a company before the introduction of a pension plan. Thus, the need for past service provisions becomes evident.

In addition to the *annual* limit of $3500 for past services while not a contributor, the Tax Act also prescribes a *lifetime maximum* of $3500 multiplied by the number of years of past service before becoming a member. For example, an employee who had been working for a particular company for five years before the company introduced a pension plan may contribute (in addition to current service amounts), a lifetime maximum of 5 X $3500, or $17,500, between the time the plan is accepted by the Minister and the time the employee retires. These contributions can be made in amounts of up to $3500 in any *given* year. The employee may instead choose to contribute less than $3500 per annum and make up his lifetime limit of $17,500 over a longer period.

In some cases, pension plans are structured so that one is not permitted to join until a certain length of service has been completed. If eligibility is restricted, this would automatically produce a period of past service while not a contributor and would result in an opportunity later on to make additional contributions. There are several reasons why a company would restrict membership into its pension plan until a certain length of service has been attained.

Any contributions made by an employee are automatically refundable to him, even if the employee should leave the service of his employer. The refund might be immediate, deferred until a certain period of time has elapsed, or may be available only in the form of a smaller pension later on. Payments out of an employer's pension plan qualify for the annual $1000 pension income deduction referred to earlier in the discussion of RRSPs — regardless of the recipient's age at the time these amounts are received.

However, *employer* contributions to a plan are *not* necessarily payable to an employee who resigns or is fired. The pension plan regulations permit an employer to adopt "delayed vesting" for up to five years. This means that annual contributions made on behalf of a particular employee do not necessarily have to "belong" to that employee at the time the money is put in. Thus, contributions made by an employer in the first year only become the property of the employee at the start of the sixth year. Similarly, the second year's contributions may only vest at the beginning of the seventh year, and so on. Eventually, if the employee stays with the employer long enough, the contributions for the last five years vest in time to provide a full retirement pension.

The fact that a plan can provide for delayed vesting is an important incentive for employers since it can help in reducing staff turnover. This is because an employee knows that should he leave his employer, he stands to lose all unvested pension rights. For many executives, the amount can be substantial. If an employee leaves anyhow or is dismissed, the employer may not recover amounts contributed into the plan on the employee's behalf — even if these amounts have not yet vested. The unvested contributions are reallocated instead to the remaining employees. This ultimately allows senior executives to derive even larger pensions than what their own contributions and amounts contributed directly on their behalf would otherwise have purchased.

While most employers are pleased to provide additional benefits to loyal employees, they must also consider their own budgeting controls. Thus companies often impose membership restrictions against new employees who are likely to leave during the early (high turnover) period. The past service provisions then allow employees who have remained to catch up later on.

Increasing Contributions for Past Service

The third and final type of deductible payment an employee can make is in respect of contributions for past years during which the individual *was* already a contributor to the pension. The maximum amount is $3500 minus the amount claimed for *both* current services and past services while not a contributor.

At first glance, this may not appear to make much sense. It is not (apparently) logical that the maximum sum of contributions for current service and past service while not a contributor should be $7000, while the sum of all three types of contributions, including those for past service while a contributor, should only be $3500. This apparent anomaly can, however, best be explained by using an actual situation.

Take the case of a middle-management executive who joined a company three years before it inaugurated a pension plan. The executive is now earning $30,000 a year and is fifty-five years old. He is making contributions of 6% of his salary for current services, or $1800 per annum. He has decided (now that his children are grown up and he has sufficient disposable income) to make up his

$10,500 of allowable past service contributions while not a contributor (three years at $3500 per year). He will accomplish this by making additional annual contributions of $1050 each year over the next ten years. Thus, the sum of his contribution for current services ($1800) plus the contribution for past service while not a contributor ($1050) will be $2850 per annum. If this executive finds that he has surplus funds available at the end of a given year, he may then decide to put in up to *another* $650 for past services while a contributor, thereby making a total of $3500 for the year. The advantage of the additional contributions is, of course, the expectation of larger pension benefits, especially if the employer matches these further contributions.

On the other hand, if this same executive were earning $60,000 a year and was already contributing 6% of his salary (maximum $3500) for current services, he would not be eligible to make any contributions for past services while a contributor.

Your Own Pension Plan

It is important for each individual to understand the pension plan of the employer with which he or she is associated (if that company does in fact have such a plan). Usually, there are various options available that are unique to each particular plan and while we have discussed the general operation of company plans, proper investment planning cannot be accomplished without an understanding of what the specific options are. For example, if your benefits are fixed at 2% for each year of service, you may not wish to make optional contributions — especially if you anticipate a lifelong career with the same employer.

However, if you are a member of a company pension plan, and your total contributions are less than $3500 per annum, it would generally pay for you to make up the difference by contributing to a personal RRSP. In addition, if you are already involved in a company pension, you should be more inclined to use a spousal RRSP. This is so that both husband and wife can ultimately split post-retirement annuity incomes.

Deferred Profit-Sharing Plans (DPSPs)

Some employers have rejected the registered pension as a fringe benefit since it ties them into fixed annual contributions regardless of profitability. Many of these companies have opted in favour of deferred profit-sharing plans instead. Under a DPSP program, contributions by an employer depend on profitability. There are no minimums and the company is not locked into guaranteeing employees pensions that are tied to a percentage of their average final (or best) earnings. As is the case with other deferred plans, contributions are deductible by the employer although employees do not pay tax until they withdraw the funds. Investment income also compounds on a tax-deferred basis.

A deferred profit-sharing plan is different from the plans that we dealt with earlier in this chapter, because employees cannot make tax deductible contributions. The employer may, however, contribute up to the lesser of $3500 or 20% of the salaries or wages paid for each participating employee. Again, delayed vesting is permitted. Of particular note is the fact that membership in a deferred profit-sharing plan does not curtail the *individual's* ability to contribute into his *own* RRSP. Thus, an executive may find his employer contributing up to $3500 to a DPSP while the individual contributes $5500 to his own RRSP. Between the two plans, up to $9000 can be invested each year on a tax-deferred basis. (The above rules apply in all provinces other than Quebec. For Quebec tax purposes, membership in a deferred profit-sharing plan does limit one's eligibility to contribute to an RRSP to only $3500 per annum.)

A DPSP is especially important in tax planning for smaller businesses since it can be set up for owner-managers and selected personnel only. On the other hand, the authorities may not accept a company pension plan for registration if that plan is primarily for the benefit of shareholders owning alone, or in combination with relatives, 10% or more of the voting shares of the company. Thus, a registered pension plan is restricted to those companies that truly wish to have a retirement plan for their (arm's length) employees.

As is the case with the other deferred plans sanctioned by the Tax Act, there are strict investment controls for DPSPs and purchases of non-qualified investments or foreign investments (in excess of allowable limits) may result in penalty provisions. Nevertheless, the ability to combine a corporate DPSP with a personal RRSP is extremely attractive. Business owners should speak to their professional advisors about incorporating deferred profit-sharing plans into the overall tax planning structure. This will be dealt with more fully in Chapter Nine.

Registered Home Ownership Savings Plans

An outline of deferred income plans would not be complete without a short review of the rules for registered home ownership savings plans (RHOSPs).

For a long time, Canadians had been complaining because mortage interest incurred with respect to the purchase of one's own residence is not deductible, in contrast to the situation that exists in the United States. The Trudeau government maintained, however, that the Canadian treasury could not afford to allow the deductibility of home mortgage interest without quite a significant restructuring to make up for lost revenues. In all fairness to Mr. Trudeau's position, one should realize that it is very difficult and indeed misleading to try to compare certain isolated aspects of the tax systems of different countries. For example, although the U.S. system with respect to mortgage interest appears to be much more liberal, keep in mind that our basic personal exemption in 1980 is $2890 while the equivalent personal exemption in the United States is only $1000. This shows how wrong it is to take selected items out of general context.

In 1974, as a concession to first-time homebuyers, the government introduced the concept of the registered home ownership savings plan. The RHOSP is available for any taxpayer eighteen years old and over who does not own a home and is also not married to a spouse who has an interest in residential real estate. Where an individual is qualified, up to $1000 a year can be contributed until $10,000 (plus interest) is accumulated. The maximum length of time that one can keep an RHOSP open is twenty years.

If funds are withdrawn from this plan and are used towards the acquisition of an owner-occupied home, the withdrawal is tax-free. It should be noted that home furnishings do not qualify (although they used to) and contributions are only deductible for a given year if made before December 31. One is permitted to contribute in the year of acquisition of a home although the contribution should be made before taking title to that residence.

Whenever funds are withdrawn and are not used during that year or within sixty days thereafter to purchase an owner-occupied home, the withdrawal becomes taxable. Proceeds withdrawn and not used to acquire an owner-occupied home may be rolled over into an income-averaging annuity. Although funds may be moved from one RHOSP to another, once a withdrawal is made, a taxpayer may never reinstate. In this respect, you are only allowed one RHOSP in a lifetime. Since the intention of the program is to provide tax-free income towards the acquisition of a home, Revenue Canada adopts the position that interest on money borrowed to contribute into an RHOSP is not deductible.

Analysis of RHOSPs

So much for the rules. Unfortunately, the effectiveness of the RHOSP breaks down for several reasons. First of all, human nature appears to be such that one does not think about saving towards the purchase of a home too many years before the home is actually bought. Thus, it is unusual to find a taxpayer who has had the foresight to put more than two or three annual contributions into his plan. Even between husband and wife, it would be unlikely to find more than $5000 or $6000 in total.

In addition, even if a taxpayer waits ten years and contributes $1000 per annum, he could only expect to have approximately $18,000 (with interest) available at the end of that time towards the acquisition of a home. However, over that same ten-year period it is likely that house prices would have doubled or even tripled. Thus, the individual is no closer towards the acquisition of his residence than he would have been ten years previously. It is my opinion, therefore, that the RHOSP will not make a home significantly more accessible to the average Canadian taxpayer.

Certainly, however, the RHOSP should be used for its short-range benefits. If a couple decides in November, 1980, that the following spring would be a good time to buy a first home, and if both husband and wife have income, it would certainly pay for each to contribute $1000 in 1980 and again in 1981. That way, there would be $4000 of tax-free money available towards the purchase. Certainly this is better than having no subsidy at all.

The RHOSP as a Gifting Program

For many middle-income and upper-income taxpayers, there are some unintended benefits with respect to their children that can be derived from the home ownership savings program. With escalating housing prices, it is not uncommon to find parents providing the downpayment for their children's homes. Let us take an example in which the parents are willing to provide $10,000 to their twenty-eight-year-old son towards the acquisition of his home. As we will see in more detail in Chapter Six, a gift of cash between parents and children is not taxable. In this case, the parents do not get a tax deduction and their son does not have to take anything into income. The reason for these rules is that cash simply represents income on which taxes have already been paid. Presumably, the parents (if they are in 50% tax brackets) will have had to earn $20,000 by that time in order to have $10,000 of after-tax capital available for their son's purposes.

With a little advance planning, however, the gift of the downpayment for the home *could have been tax deductible*. Let's assume the parents start a gifting program in the year that their son turns eighteen. If that year is 1980, the exemption that the father would get for his son would be $990. This is provided that the son's net income is not in excess of $2000. What if the son is still going to school, but has earned a net income of $3000 after tuition fees? At this point, his father will have lost a personal exemption of $990. If the father is in a 50% bracket, the additional tax cost to him would be almost $500.

On the other hand, if before December 31 the father gifts $1000 to his son, the son could take these funds and purchase an RHOSP. The RHOSP contribution would be tax deductible and would reduce the son's net income to only $2000. This would reinstate the father's deduction of $990 and would consequently result in a $500 tax saving. Thus, the cost of having made a $1000 gift in the first place becomes only $500. In this manner, the RHOSP can be used to provide a very efficient Christmas gift.

If the father is concerned that his son might withdraw the funds from the home ownership plan, he can explain that every taxpayer is only permitted one RHOSP in a lifetime. Thus, a withdrawal of funds without the father's permission effectively ends any further contributions. In most cases, the child will cooperate for his (or her) own good.

In cases where the child is not a student but is in his (or her) late teens or early twenties and is working, the gifting program still has merit. If, for example, a son is twenty-two years old and is earning $14,000 a year, even at this relatively modest income level, he is still in approximately a 35% tax bracket. In addition, the son is not likely to be thinking seriously about the possibility of buying a home in several years. However, the father can still make the annual gift of $1000. Even in the son's tax bracket, if the gift is reinvested into an RHOSP, there will be a tax saving to him of $350. These dollars could then be *gifted back* to his father and the net cost of the gifting program for that year becomes only $650.

To summarize, an RHOSP can be used very effectively to reduce the cost of providing a downpayment for a home to one's children. This may have not been intended by the legislators, but it nevertheless works.

CHAPTER FIVE

A Tax Shelter Update

A tax shelter may result when a tax deductible loss from a particular source is offset against other income. In Canada, there are three popular tax shelters: real-estate investments, motion picture films, and oil and gas exploration ventures. With rising incomes, tax shelters have become increasingly popular in recent years. Unfortunately, coupled with the high demand, the quality of available shelters has, in general, diminished.

Too many people place shelter aspects ahead of investment considerations. They forget that a "tax shelter" is not the same thing as a "tax loss". An effective tax shelter only occurs when there are write-offs (such as depreciation) that produce losses for tax purposes, but where the *value* of the investment has not diminished and there has been no loss of cash. Just because a loss is deductible, does not make it a tax shelter. Someone in the 60% tax bracket who actually lays out one dollar is still out of pocket a minimum of forty cents — even if his expenditure is deductible.

Tax Shelters in the Real Estate Industry

The "Good Old Days"

Before the Tax Reform of 1972, the acquisition of rental buildings was a popular tax deferral and avoidance technique. At that time, the Tax Regulations divided buildings into two "classes" for depreciation purposes. Class 3 (with a depreciation rate of 5%) included concrete and steel reinforced structures, while Class 6 (with a depreciation rate of 10%) contained wood frame, stucco on frame, and brick veneer buildings. In each case, capital cost allowance (tax depreciation) was claimed on a diminishing balance basis. Thus, if the cost of a Class 6 building was $100,000, the first year's depreciation was 10% of $100,000, the second year's depreciation was 10% of $90,000 ($100,000 − $10,000) and the third year's depreciation was $8100 (10% of $100,000 − ($10,000 + $9000)). In any acquisition of real estate, the tax rules required that land and building costs be segregated or apportioned. As is the case today, land costs were neither deductible nor depreciable.

The shelter aspects of real-estate acquisitions stemmed largely from a special provision of the tax depreciation rules. If an individual bought a rental building late in the year, he was still permitted to claim a *full year's* capital cost allowance. This would produce a "property loss" deductible from other income. In other words, tax depreciation in the year of acquisition did not have to be prorated in the same way as accounting depreciation is treated. Thus, if one's downpayment was low enough, the first year's write-

EXAMPLE 1: A TYPICAL REAL-ESTATE SHELTER BEFORE 1972

1. The taxpayer's marginal tax rate is assumed to be 60%.
2. The example ignores land costs for purposes of simplicity.

Cost of Class 6 building — acquired on last day of taxation year	$100,000
Financing:	
By way of mortgage	$ 95,000
Cash investment	5,000
	$100,000
Statement of rental income:	
Gross rents net of operating expenses	Nil
Less: Capital cost allowance (10% X $100,000)	$ 10,000
Rental loss	$ (10,000)
Tax saving on $10,000 rental loss (60% X $10,000)	$ 6,000
Less: Cash investment recovered	5,000
Net "shelter"	$ 1,000

off often resulted in a tax saving that fully offset the actual cash investment. This is illustrated in Example 1.

The first example is somewhat oversimplified because it ignores land costs, which are not depreciable and consequently erode the shelter. In addition, the example overstates the amount of financing usually available against a project. One would not ordinarily get 95% mortgage financing, and even if such financing were obtainable, a property would probably not carry itself with that amount of debt.

The key point, however, is that the depreciation loss of $10,000 does *not involve an outflow of cash*. In addition, the property is presumably worth the same amount *after* the tax write-off as it was *before*. Since there has been no decrease in value and no loss of funds, this investment is a true tax shelter. In every year after the first, as long as the building carried itself from a cash-flow standpoint, further capital cost allowances could be claimed to produce for each year (before 1972) a tax loss deductible against other income. If the project was a good investment, it eventually ended up paying for itself.

Under the pre-1972 tax system, there was no "day of reckoning" until the property was sold; and, even then, proper planning could achieve a further postponement. To illustrate a typical situation, let's suppose the $100,000 building in the first example was then sold.

EXAMPLE 2: DEFERRAL OF RECAPTURED DEPRECIATION BEFORE 1972

Cost of building	$100,000
Less: Accumulated capital cost allowances (over several years)	40,000
Undepreciated capital cost (u.c.c.)	60,000
Less: Proceeds from eventual sale	(90,000)
Recaptured capital cost allowances	(30,000)
Purchase of other building in year of sale	200,000
New "base" for future capital cost allowances	$170,000
Recaptured capital cost allowances — revised	Nil

The second example assumes $40,000 of cumulative capital cost allowances for tax purposes. For an individual in a 60% bracket, this would have resulted in accumulated tax savings of $24,000 (60% X $40,000). If the property were then sold for $90,000, it would become apparent that in fact, the property had only depreciated by $10,000. The tax rules therefore provided that excess (unwarranted) depreciation was to be recaptured or brought back into income in the year of sale. In this case, the excess depreciation is $30,000.

However, whenever a rental building was sold before 1972, the tax on recaptured depreciation could be deferred through the acquisition of another property of the same class in the same year. The second example also assumes that a building costing $200,000 was purchased as a replacement. The recaptured depreciation was thus eliminated and the only penalty was a smaller new base for *future* capital cost allowances (that is, $170,000). In addition, if the replacement building were acquired at the very end of the year (before any revenue could be generated), the taxpayer, instead of having recaptured depreciation as *income*, could then claim a tax *loss* of 10% of $170,000 or $17,000.

Generally, buildings tended to appreciate and not depreciate in value. Thus, a capital gain, which was tax-free under the "old" system, could also be used to pyramid one's tax-deferral structure. Over a period of time, the astute investor was often able to build up a sizeable portfolio of real estate holdings subsidized, to a large extent, by tax savings from capital cost allowances.

If one practised tax deferral by sheltering recaptured depreciation with other acquisitions throughout one's lifetime, the deferral became an absolute tax saving. Before 1972, death did not result in any disposition of property being deemed for tax purposes and there was no recaptured depreciation. To further compound the advantages of dying with depreciable property in one's portfolio, the heirs were allowed to take over inherited depreciable property at *current fair market values* and could begin to claim their capital cost allowances on that (inflated) amount.

1972 Tax Changes

Major changes to the rules were made in 1972. The deduction of capital cost allowances on rental buildings and leasehold interests was, from that time on, limited to the net cash income from these properties after deducting operating expenses. Thus, in general, capital cost allowances can no longer either produce or increase rental losses.*

If one owns property and operating expenses such as mortgage interest, taxes, heating, insurance and repairs and maintenance exceed gross rental income, the *cash* rental loss continues to be deductible. However, this loss cannot be increased (or created in the first place) as a result of tax depreciation.

Of course, in most cases, one would not want to own a rental property where there is a large negative cash-flow over an extended period of time. The only exception might be where there is a substantial anticipated appreciation in the value of the property itself which, when realized, would more than offset the prior operating losses.

The opportunities that existed before 1972 to defer tax on recaptured depreciation were blocked as well. A separate capital-cost-allowance class must be created for all rental buildings acquired or built after 1971 at a cost of $50,000 or more. Thus a taxpayer might have many Class 3's or Class 6's, and when a property is disposed of, the negative balance in the capital cost allowance pool resulting from the sale cannot be offset against the costs of another rental property.

Furthermore, one can no longer avoid tax on recaptured depreciation by retaining a rental building until death. The Income Tax Act now provides, at that time, a deemed disposition at a value halfway between undepreciated capital cost and fair market value — unless the property is bequeathed to one's spouse or to a

---

*The limitation restricting the deductibility of capital cost allowance losses does not apply to corporations whose principal business is leasing land and buildings or property development. Such corporations may continue to offset rental losses created by capital cost allowance against miscellaneous other income.

"spousal trust". Even such a bequest only postpones the inevitable, since the regular deemed disposition rules would apply when the spouse, in turn, dies. The rules are further designed so that any heir who acquires depreciable property on which there has not been a full recapture becomes ultimately liable for taxes when he himself makes a sale. As well, one-half of capital gains are now taxable. These matters will be dealt with more fully in Chapter Twelve.

Multiple Unit Residential Buildings

The federal government's attack on real estate as a tax shelter produced some rather interesting consequences in 1972 and the following two years. Investment capital flowing from the private sector to the construction industry quickly dried up. Many wealthy individuals no longer maintained the same interest in real estate as they did in previous years, because they felt that the rewards would not be commensurate with the nuisance factor of having to administer properties. By 1974, the construction industry was clamoring for a reintroduction of tax concessions, and there already existed an acute shortage of residential housing in Canada. This, of course, accelerated the rise in rental costs with a corresponding increase in the rate of inflation.

Finally, in its November 1974 Budget, the federal government retreated somewhat from its previous position. Two new classes of depreciable property were created — classes 31 and 32 — to contain the costs of multiple unit residential buildings where construction commenced after November 18, 1974. A multiple unit residential building (MURB) is defined as a building where not less than 80% of the floor space is used towards providing self-contained domestic establishments and related parking, recreation, service, and storage areas. Class 31 parallels Class 3, both as to depreciation rate (5%) and also as to the type of construction (concrete and/or steel reinforced buildings). Class 32 was set up to parallel Class 6 (10% depreciation for wood frame or brick veneer construction). Capital cost allowance on these qualifying properties *is* permitted to create or increase a rental loss.

Since 1978, however, the government has started to phase out the rules allowing *any* building to be depreciated at 10%. Thus, all MURBs where construction commenced after December 31, 1977, are automatically classified as Class 31 properties, and whenever a (pre-1978) Class 32 property is acquired by a new owner after the end of 1979, the depreciation rate to the buyer reverts to 5% only. Existing Class 32 properties are still depreciable at 10% to their current owners. All other building acquisitions of wood frame and similar construction (such as older apartment buildings, office buildings, shopping centres, warehouses) now automatically fall into a buyer's Class 3. It is no longer possible to buy or build a Class 6 property.

The rules pertaining to "separate classes" for all rental properties acquired after 1971 have not, however, been amended or repealed. Thus, although capital cost allowance on a MURB may create a rental loss, such capital cost allowance is subject to ultimate recapture in the year of sale without the relief that might otherwise be obtained if additional property is acquired (unless replacement properties cost less than $50,000).

The intention of the MURB rules was to stimulate taxpayers to buy or build new residential construction. The depreciation loss on an "end of the year" acquisition could then be offset against other income. The tax incentive has already been illustrated on page 84.

Soft Cost Write-Offs for Real-Estate Developers

In retrospect, this modest opportunity to shelter against taxes through MURB acquisitions was only the beginning of the revival of the construction industry. If one is a developer of real estate, rather than only an investor, a good deal more than merely a capital-cost-allowance loss can be derived as a tax shelter benefit. This is because there are several significant costs associated with real-estate construction which are capital in nature but which may be written off for tax purposes in the year or years incurred. These components are called "soft costs" and include:

1. Interest paid on borrowed money during the construction period.

2. Expenses of borrowing money (such as mortgage application and commitment fees and appraisal costs).
3. Landscaping of grounds.
4. Expenses of representation (for example, the costs of obtaining proper zoning approvals and building permits).
5. Costs of site investigation to determine suitability for a project.
6. Utilities service connections (such as the costs of obtaining power, telephone and water services).
7. General overhead expenses:
    a) office expenses
    b) offsite supervision during the construction period
    c) advertising for tenants

From an accounting standpoint, the above soft costs help to make up the total value of any project under construction. Thus, they are capitalized on financial statements and are only written off through normal depreciation over the life span of a building. However, for tax purposes, soft costs are subject to an *immediate* write-off because of specific tax legislation.

The term "soft costs" originated to distinguish these particular components of a construction project from the "hard costs" of construction — the bricks, mortar, and direct labour. Another tax term has also evolved with respect to these costs which in its own way is just as descriptive. Soft costs are also known as "first-time write-offs", a term which indicates that these particular costs are incurred only *once* — during the construction period.

The Tax Position of Real-Estate Developers

Are soft costs useful to real-estate developers? If one is in business as a developer constructing buildings for resale, these properties become *inventory* for tax purposes. In other words, a developer's project bears the same relationship to him as a book does to a book store or an automobile to a car dealer. For tax purposes, this means that a profit on sale is *fully taxable* as business income and is not a capital gain.

Assume, therefore, that a builder builds a construction project to sell to an investor for $100,000. Assume as well, that the actual costs of the project are only $70,000 out of which $20,000 are categorized as soft costs. If a sale takes place in the same year that the project was constructed, soft costs do not have any tax value to the developer. He must simply record the difference between his total costs of $70,000 and his selling price of $100,000 as income. Even if the sale takes place one year later, the soft costs are, in this case, of only limited value to the developer. In the first year, he may claim a $20,000 tax write-off for these soft costs but his inventory value for tax purposes then becomes only $50,000 ($70,000 minus $20,000 written-off).

Then, in the second year, when the building is sold to an investor for $100,000, a $50,000 profit would have to be recorded. This $50,000 would represent the actual profit of $30,000 plus a recapture of $20,000 of soft costs previously written off. In other words, soft costs are not of much use to a developer who is constructing a project for resale. They are only of value to someone who is building a project to *retain it* for rental purposes. Where this is the case, there is an immediate write-off while the recognition of income can be deferred for perhaps many years until a sale is eventually made. The effects of soft-costs are illustrated in table form on page 92.

Around the same time as the MURB legislation was introduced, a number of developers came up with a rather interesting concept concerning soft costs. They decided to sign up their investors *before* beginning a construction project. Under the new arrangements, the investors would themselves become developers. The "real" developers would then become "subcontractors" who would supervise the actual construction activities. However, since the investors would be the owners of the project from the very outset, the "subcontractors" could break down their billings into both hard-cost and soft-cost components.

In other words, instead of paying $100,000 for a completed project, the investor-developer would incur hard costs of, say $80,000 and soft costs of $20,000. The soft costs of $20,000 could then be written off immediately and, if the project qualified

APPLICATION OF SOFT COSTS TO REAL ESTATE DEVELOPERS (IGNORING LAND COSTS)

Note: Real estate projects are inventory.
The profit on sale is ordinary income.

	If sale takes place in year of construction	If sale takes place in subsequent year Year 1	Year 2
Selling price	$100,000		$100,000
Cost of project			
Hard costs	50,000	50,000	
Soft costs	20,000	20,000	
Total cost of project	70,000	70,000	
Soft cost write-off	(20,000)	(20,000)	
Inventory value for tax ($70,000 − $20,000)	50,000	50,000	50,000
Profit on sale ($100,000 − $50,000)	$ 50,000		$ 50,000
Soft cost write-off loss	(20,000)	$(20,000)	
Profit on sale	50,000		$ 50,000
Net profit (Selling price − total cost of project)	$ 30,000		$ 30,000

If a project is built for resale, soft costs are of limited value.

as a MURB, capital cost allowances could also be claimed on the remaining $80,000 of costs. The investor-developer would ordinarily be expected to retain his interest in such a project. He would thus benefit from an initial tax write-off, while any recapture could be postponed indefinitely until a sale took place.

A number of projects were marketed along these lines across Canada in the past few years and the initial reaction of Revenue Canada was very unfavourable. Revenue officials contended that a construction contract does not necessarily make somebody into a developer if his ordinary business is not related to that industry. Many reassessments disallowing these expenses were issued by various District Taxation Offices, although to date, no cases have come before the courts. In some instances, compromises were made in the interest of expediency.

Investors' Soft Cost Write-Offs

In order to make peace with Revenue, someone eventually prepared a detailed analysis of the tax rules pertaining to soft cost write-offs. It was found that only expenses of representation, site investigation costs, and utilities service hook-ups are restricted for tax purposes to taxpayers carrying on a *business*. In all other cases, however, it appears that soft costs are a valid deduction whether one is classified as a real estate developer *or* one admits to being merely a passive investor — as long as the investor has an interest in the project "from the ground floor up". Again, the soft costs are also first time write-offs — meaning that they are only valid as deductions if the investor is an owner of the project during the construction period.

The next step in the evolution of tax shelters was to come up with a comprehensive list of soft cost write-offs available to real-estate investors. The list of these includes

1. CMHC mortgage insurance fee: The fee paid to obtain a guarantee by the Canadian Mortgage and Housing Corporation of payments with respect to the first mortgage (usually 1.5% of the first mortgage).
2. Second mortgage guarantee: A fee paid to the project

manager (usually the developer or general contractor) to guarantee payments of the investors on account of their second mortgages.

3. Legal fees re:
   - First and second mortgage documentation.
   - Construction and management agreements.
   - Tenants' leases.

4. Initial services fee (administration and supervision)
   - Offsite administration and management of project.
   - Providing accounting services and reporting to investors.
   - Guarantee of timely completion.
   - Undertaking to pay net operating costs including maintenance, taxes and interest due to construction delays after scheduled date of completion.

5. Initial leasing and marketing fee
   - Undertaking of project manager to develop, prepare and review policies and procedures with respect to the marketing of rental units during the initial rent-up period, including advertising for tenants.
   - Commissions paid to rental agents.

6. Costs of obtaining financing
   - Standby charges.
   - Appraisal costs.
   - Commitment fees.
   - Commissions to brokers (after November 16, 1978).

7. Insurance on project during construction.

8. Cash-flow guarantee: A fee to compensate the project manager for undertaking to guarantee at least a break-even cash flow for a certain period (e.g. two years) after substantial completion of the project.

9. Landscaping costs (deductible when paid).

10. Real-estate taxes during construction.

11. Interest on mortgages (interim financing) during the construction period (at actual costs).

Deductibility of the above soft cost write-offs for real estate investors has, in fact, been reviewed and accepted by Revenue Canada as long as the actual amounts are reasonable. As a general rule, most developers appear to be working with soft cost percentages of approximately 20%. In other words, the total soft costs tend to be around 20% of the costs of each particular project — including land, building and soft costs together.

Recently, however, there appears to have been a tightening in the attitude of Revenue officials. It now appears that certain of the soft cost expenditures will not be deductible "up front" but will be required instead to be amortized over a reasonable length of time. For example, it is Revenue's view that the costs of advertising for tenants should only be written off over the length of the initial leases. Similarly, rental guarantee fees paid by an investor should be prorated over the guarantee period. The April 21, 1980, Budget introduced special legislation dealing with prepaid expenses, presumably to strengthen Revenue's position. This means that the full soft-cost tax-shelter may not be obtainable immediately (as in the past), although essentially the same write-offs will be claimable over only a few years.

The Future of Real-Estate Tax Shelters

The MURB legislation was repealed for all construction commencing after December 31, 1979, although in 1980 one will still be able to invest in some of these projects where ground was broken before the end of last year. However, new MURB construction may not necessarily be such an attractive investment in any event. Many projects are somewhat overpriced (this will be discussed a little later), and also the only significance of a project qualifying as a MURB is the 5% capital cost allowance. Since the repeal of the 10% depreciation factor, one must make a very substantial investment in a project in order have a worthwhile capital cost allowance to claim.

The important thing for investors to note, however, is that *soft costs are still claimable on new construction* — even after 1979. In addition, to be eligible for soft cost write-offs, a project does *not* have to qualify as a MURB. None of the soft costs deductible by investors pertain specifically to residential property. In other words, one can also have a completely viable tax shelter through *commercial* property construction. This would include office buildings, medical/dental (professional) buildings, warehouses, hotels, as well as duplexes, town houses, and apartment buildings where construction begins after 1979.

Moreover, there are no restrictions which would require that a tax shelter project be situated in Canada. Participation in a real-estate construction project outside Canada will give the Canadian investor the *same* soft cost write-offs as a project in this country! Since a Canadian is taxable on world income (less losses), a loss from foreign property is readily tax deductible against other income.

Usually, if a project is situated in a foreign country, the soft costs would be capitalized for foreign tax purposes as part of the building. This would facilitate larger future depreciation claims to offset taxable income generated for foreign tax purposes on that particular project. As with any other construction project, one would hope that the foreign property is a good investment and that, after the construction period, it would carry itself.

Although such a project would not provide any Canadian tax shelter after the year of completion (since maximum capital-cost allowances in future years are restricted to those sufficient to bring the rental income down to zero), all that the investor must do is find further new projects in which to invest.

Specifically, the acquisition of an interest in one new construction project each year can, for many taxpayers, provide an adequate shelter while one builds up an impressive real-estate investment portfolio over a period of time. These concepts are illustrated on page 97. The reader should note that the example assumes that a taxpayer invests in a project (in Canada or elsewhere) from the outset before actual construction begins and that the project is completed at the very end of the year without generating any rental income. So far, however, no operating expenses are incurred either. The soft cost write-offs of $20,000 produce a loss that is deductible for tax purposes. The fact that capital cost allowance cannot be applied to make that loss bigger

Note: 1. The taxpayer's marginal rate is assumed to be 60%.
2. The example ignores land costs for purposes of simplicity.

Actual cost of building materials, labour and contractor's mark-up (i.e., "hard costs")	$ 80,000
"Soft costs"	20,000
	$100,000
Financing:	
By way of mortgage	$ 95,000
Cash investment	5,000
	$100,000
Statement of rental income:	
Gross rents net of operating expenses	Nil
Deduct:	
Soft cost write-offs	$ 20,000
Capital cost allowances	Nil
	20,000
Rental loss	$ (20,000)
Tax saving on $20,000 rental loss (60% X $20,000)	$ 12,000
Less: Cash investment recovered	5,000
Net "shelter"	$ 7,000

does not really affect the viability of the project as a shelter to any great extent. If you compare the figure for the net shelter in this case with that of the first example discussed earlier in this chapter, it becomes evident that tax shelters in real estate are still alive and well into the 1980s.

Evaluating Real-Estate Shelters

It should again be stressed that soft cost write-offs only belong to an investor who has title to a property (or an interest therein) during the construction period. However, one must always evaluate a project first as an investment and then only secondarily as a tax shelter. The key question you must ask is, will the property carry itself? If future projected operating expenses exceed anticipated rental incomes it may be a bad investment. (See the real-estate case study later on in the chapter.)

Another problem centers around the question of ordinary income vs. capital gains upon the sale of a real estate project. Ordinary income is, of course, taxable in full while only one-half of a capital gain is taxed. From cases that have come before the courts, a number of criteria have evolved in order to deal with this contentious issue. These include:

1. The taxpayer's intention and course of conduct. Did he intend to hold a project over a long term to derive rental revenue or was the property purchased primarily for resale at a profit?
2. Secondary intention. Even where the primary intention may have been to derive rental revenue, was there a secondary intention to sell in the foreseeable future?
3. The number and frequency of transactions. The more frequently one transacts, the more likely it is that Revenue authorities will deem real-estate properties to be inventory and not capital property.
4. The relationship of real-estate transactions to the ordinary (earned income) activities of the taxpayer. If, for example, one is a real-estate broker by profession, it is likely that one's profits would be assessed as ordinary income. Even professional advisors such as accountants and lawyers who have real-estate clients are likely to be assessed as traders, at least after a few transactions.

What, then, is the position of someone who has invested in one or two tax-shelter properties with soft cost write-offs and, at some future time, decides to sell? So far, no cases have come before the courts. However, it is unlikely that Revenue officials would permit someone to write off soft costs amounting to as much as 20% of a construction project and then later on (at the time of sale) to recapture these write-offs into income as capital gains. There would be no logic in such a tax treatment. This matter is, however, unclear.

Whenever you deal with a grey area, you have the right to adopt the reporting that would produce the smallest tax if such reporting is accepted by Revenue for assessment purposes. In other words, if you sell an investment, and don't report your gain at all, this would be tax evasion. However, if you take advantage of the grey area and (at least) report your profit as a capital gain, you are complying with the letter of the law. Your worst exposure is that your tax return could be reassessed to reflect the gain on sale as (fully taxable) ordinary income. You are certainly no worse off (except for interest costs) than if you had reported the profit as regular income in the first place.

My general advice is that you report all real-estate gains as capital until reassessed by Revenue. However, when making your own private projections of internal rate of return on investment, I suggest that you calculate on the basis that your ultimate gain could be assessed as ordinary income. If the project is *still* viable from an investment standpoint, then by all means, go ahead. On the other hand, if the success of the project is dependent primarily on tax advantages, then I recommend that you think twice before investing.

The tax uncertainties relating to real-estate dispositions create serious problems for many Canadians. For example, I have a friend who has held two apartment buildings for about twelve years. During the last few years, he bought and sold a few small tax-shelter projects. Recently, he received an offer for the two apartment buildings at over one million dollars in excess of his cost for each. He was afraid to sell because of the lack of clarity in his tax position. Since he is already in a top tax bracket, it makes quite a difference whether he pays an effective tax of 65% on his profit or only 32½% (if it is a capital gain). No one knows for certain whether or not transacting in shelters taints a taxpayer's position with respect to his other real-estate holdings. It is also impossible to get an advance ruling on this subject from the Revenue authorities.

Type of Investment

In evaluating real-estate tax-shelters, the next point to examine is the type of investment being contemplated. Is the buyer getting a percentage interest in an entire project or does he obtain title to a specific unit? Certainly, a specific unit would be more readily saleable than a small percentage interest in a large project. However, what if that specific unit happens to be the only one which is vacant during a given year? The exposure is certainly larger than an investment where the risk is shared. In some projects, one can maximize benefits if one obtains title to a specific unit while all the rents generated by the project are pooled together.

Quality of construction is also an important investment criterion. You must attempt to assess the builder's reputation and you should also have some familiarity with real-estate values and growth potential in the area in which the project is being constructed. The fact that real-estate shelters do not have to be restricted to residential construction or, for that matter, to Canadian projects provides a tremendous flexibility in doing your shopping. Basically, your investments should be in those places where there is political stability and a hot real-estate market.

You should also keep potential recaptured depreciation and exposure to capital gains in mind — especially in estate planning. Real estate is not a liquid investment. Therefore, you should make an overall attempt to balance your portfolio with holdings that could be readily disposed of if dollars are needed to pay taxes arising on death. As an alternative, you should consider sufficient life insurance to discharge your tax liabilities so that your heirs do not have to dispose of your real-estate holdings under forced sale conditions.

Finally, beware of "over-sheltering". Always remember that the bigger your loss, the smaller the tax advantage becomes as your marginal tax bracket decreases. On the other hand, if the shelter proves to be a good investment and generates income upon its sale, taxes are always levied at increasing marginal rates. For example, there's not much point in sheltering so that you save forty cents on the dollar if you anticipate that a year or two later, enough income will be realized from the sale of a project to put you into a 65% bracket. As a general guideline, I try to keep my clients from sheltering below $25,000 of taxable income. As long as one saves at least forty-five cents on the dollar today, he should be willing to accept higher taxes later on, considering that these will be payable with dollars that are worth less because of inflation.

A Real-Estate Case Study

In order to expand on the concept of examining real estate primarily as an investment, here is a specific study that I made in October 1978. While relevant interest rates have changed somewhat, the method of analysis is still valid.

Two years ago, a group of friends came to me and asked if I wished to join in a small real-estate venture. The idea behind this "partnership" was for each of us put up $10,000 or $15,000 and to try to find properties that would carry themselves out of rental revenues with minimal downpayments. Conceptually, the idea was very appealing and I agreed to participate.

Several weeks later, a real-estate agent brought me a listing describing a small apartment building which was for sale in one of the nicer sections of Calgary. My friends had inspected this property and were impressed by its excellent condition and the fact that it was fully rented. I was asked to review the numbers. The first thing I did was to prepare the schedule which appears on page 102.

What I wanted to do was to determine the probable cash flow from property before mortgage repayments. In my projections, I used a 3% vacancy allowance. Of course, a vacancy factor varies from time to time and place to place and the 3% is for illustration only and should not be construed as being reasonable in all circumstances.

Gross rents projected on an annual basis		$70,000
Less: 3% vacancy factor		2,100
		67,900
Less: Expenses:		
Taxes	$5,000	
Insurance and Heating	3,000	
Light and power	1,500	
Garbage	700	
Janitor	2,200	
Management fee	3,400	
Maintenance and Supplies	2,400	18,200
Cash flow before mortgage		$49,700

My next step was to calculate how much financing the property could carry. There was an existing first mortgage of $282,000 which had recently been placed on the building at 10¾%. I determined the cash flow after first mortgage as follows:

Cash flow before mortgage	$49,700
First mortgage $282,000 at 10¾% — annual payments from amortization tables	32,400
Cash flow after first mortgage	$17,300

The next question was how much capital one should invest in order to earn $17,300. To answer it, I reasoned that either my friends and I had investment capital or we did not have the funds necessary to acquire the property. At that time, if we had cash, we could have invested in second mortgages at a 13% rate of return. Alternatively, we could have pooled our borrowing power to obtain a second mortgage at that same 13% rate. In either event, money was "worth" 13% at that time.

I consulted my mortgage tables and I then determined that a cash flow of $17,300 would provide a 13% yield on an investment of $130,000. In other words, if we invested our own money, $17,300 would provide a 13% rate of return to *us* while, on the other hand, if we borrowed $130,000 instead, the property could absorb this debt and still break even. I therefore computed the value of the property as a whole to be $412,000, being the sum of first and second mortgage financing ($282,000 + $130,000).

The asking price was $589,000, and I told my friends to forget about this property as an investment since it was greatly over-priced. However, a few weeks later, I was informed that the property had, in fact, been sold for $567,000. My friends were somewhat upset and suggested rather dryly that I review my calculations. I checked my figures and found that I had made no arithmetic errors. Being somewhat curious as to the buyer's motives, I went on to do some additional analysis. I first concluded that whoever had bought this property had overpaid $155,000.

Actual selling price	$567,000
Break-even price	412,000
Excess cost	$155,000

I then reasoned that the purchaser must either have had funds of his own or substantial "borrowing power". If he had capital, I concluded that he was willing to invest $155,000 at a zero rate of return instead of the 13% that he could otherwise have obtained in second mortgages. Conversely, if he borrowed the additional funds at 13%, my tables told me that the annual cash-flow loss would be $20,500. My first inclination was to doubt the sanity of the purchaser. He was either giving up $20,500 a year that he himself could otherwise have earned, or he was willing to pay *out* this amount each year to a lending institution.

However, I decided to carry the calculations a little further. In the first years of ownership, whenever a rental property produces a cash-flow loss because of financing, most of that loss (as much as 99%) is as a result of interest expense. Accordingly, the loss is deductible. This loss *cannot* be made *larger* through depreciation, but in my example, the *after-tax* cash-flow loss would be consider-ably less than $20,500. In fact, if one assumes an investor in the 65% bracket, the *after-tax* cash flow loss is only $20,500 X 35%, or $7175.

Against this loss, one would then have to balance a projected appreciation in value. Historically, real estate in Calgary has tended to appreciate by 8% per annum. Eight per cent of $567,000 is $45,000. Even after taking off (for simplicity) a 50% provision for real-estate commission costs and taxes on the gain, there is still an anticipated after-tax appreciation after only one year of $22,500. If one compares the after-tax cash flow loss of $7175 against $22,500 of probable appreciation, the investment starts to appear more and more attractive. The only problem, however, is that the cash-flow loss is *definite* while the appreciation in value is *speculative*.

The Risk Factor

A good friend of mine has what he calls a "greater fool theory" with respect to real estate. My friend's argument is that real estate is overpriced in many places in Canada because everyone appears willing to lay out a substantial amount today, figuring that there is a "greater fool" somewhere who will automatically overpay an *extra* 8% one year later! As long as there is no recession, everyone makes money. However, if hard times should arrive, those who are left holding overpriced properties will find themselves in financial difficulties.

You should never pay too much for property unless you can accept the risk of a potential loss. Ironically, real estate investments tend to favour those who have made money in the past. If you are wealthy, you can afford to subsidize a property that is losing money and still hang on until market conditions improve. As long as there is no sacrifice in your standard of living, then the investment might be worth the gamble. However, if you buy property subject to heavy debt and you are relying on capital appreciation in order to quickly "bail out", then you are treading on dangerous ground.

I would be remiss if I didn't admit that the case study in the previous section is probably somewhat oversimplified. Anyone with a degree of sophistication when it comes to real-estate analysis would not begin to chart a property over only a one-year term. Usually, five-year projections are made and the sophisticated analyst brings back all future cash flows or deficiencies (including after-tax profits on eventual sale) to a present value for purposes of his calculations.

If you are contemplating a specific real-estate investment you should deal with advisors who are capable of assisting in the preparation of these more technical calculations. Of course, keep in mind that the further you go from the present time in your projections, the more likelihood there is of significant errors entering into the picture.

Film Investments

Another popular tax shelter is the Canadian certified feature-film production. With respect to Canadian films, the government must again walk a tightrope, wending its way between the "evils" of tax sheltering on the one hand and the benefits of promoting a particular industry on the other. In order to subsidize the industry, some excellent tax benefits have been introduced for investors.

A certified feature production must run at least seventy-five minutes and generally involves the use of a Canadian producer. In addition, to qualify for tax write-offs under the Income Tax Regulations, there are other "Canadian content" rules. Points are awarded for the use of Canadian directors, screen writers, actors, actresses, and so on. Most of the processing costs must also be incurred in Canada.

If a production qualifies, 100% of a taxpayer's investment is deductible as long as the film is completed before December 31 or within sixty days thereafter. Technically, if a film is not completed by the end of the calendar year, the tax-shelter benefits must be prorated in proportion to costs incurred over the two-year period.

As with most tax shelters, the advantages stem from using leverage. The taxpayer puts up a portion of the required funds, while the balance is subject to financing. The example below depicts a typical investment:

Cost of interest in film	$ 40,000
Bank loan (financing)	30,000
Cash invested	$ 10,000
Tax saving on cost at assumed tax rate of 60%	$ (24,000)
Cash invested	10,000
"Shelter" in year investment is made	$ (14,000)

Of all the different tax shelters, a film investment is the "cleanest". You invest your money and the tax shelter is practically immediate. There are no administration worries and there is no complex bookkeeping or accounting. Any revenues received subsequently are fully taxable — unless sheltered through other future investments.

On the other hand, of all shelters a film is probably the most risky. Revenue Canada will not accept a shelter where the write-off is based on one's total cost (including financing) unless the investor is personally at risk for the amount financed. In the above example, the shelter only "works" if the taxpayer is liable for the $30,000 borrowed.

Technically, the financing is budgeted to be repaid out of proceeds generated by the film — from the box office, television rights, and foreign sales. However, the amount of revenues which will be generated to the investors is usually, at best, uncertain. At the worst possible extreme, a film may be so unappealing that it never gets to the movie theatres in the first place. If this happens, the following eventually results:

Financing repayment required even if no revenue	$ 30,000
Less: Shelter previously obtained	14,000
Net cash loss to the investor	$ 16,000

In the above example, the exposure is clear. An investor in the 60% bracket can suffer as much as an absolute loss of 40% of his investment (40% of $40,000 = $16,000). Of course, if the shelter is obtained in the current year and the loss is not incurred until several years later, the impact may not be as great. This is because the repayment of financing is made in dollars which will presumably be cheaper because of inflation. The loss may be *higher*, however, as a result of (after-tax) interest costs.

Evaluating Movie Investments

As with any other shelter, you should attempt to evaluate a film as an investment first. Of course, this may be somewhat difficult because there are very few concrete guidelines that can be applied. Statistics released in January 1979 by the Canadian Film Development Corporation indicate that only one out of every twenty Canadian films in which the CFDC participated returned a profit to the investors.

However, in the last year or so, it appears that this ratio may have improved somewhat. Perhaps Canadian producers and film promoters are now afraid of scaring off the investors who help to subsidize movie making in the first place. It is possible that the deals now being offered to investors are becoming better than before.

When compared to its counterparts in other countries, the Canadian feature film industry is still in its infancy. Over a period of time, Canadian producers, directors, actors and actresses will develop track records which should be reliable indicators to prospective investors of what their chances might be. Unless one is extremely adventurous, one would then generally stick with those people with good past performances.

One of the important considerations in film investments is whether or not the costs of a particular motion picture are reasonable. Actually, this is very difficult to assess. In late 1979, I reviewed three movie film prospectuses. The first had a total budget of $450,000, the second had a budget of $2,500,000 and the third was a "package" of three films with a total budget of $11,500,000. Which of the three investments is most likely to return a profit? Your guess is as good as mine. Unfortunately, there are situations where no common denominators can be used for measurement. Would you invest in a film where Paul Newman is being paid $1,000,000, or would you rather have your share of the cost increased because that same film would then star Robert Redford, who is asking $1,300,000? Of course, these matters are somewhat subjective and it is difficult to form any specific judgements.

Finding a Common Denominator

When it comes to real-estate investments, one can often find a common denominator against which to compare one project to another. In construction, the common denominator is cost per square foot. With respect to films, I suggest that you try to find another common denominator. In this case, ask yourself how many people must see this film at the box office in North America for you to get back at least your original investment? You could then compare the answer to available statistics for other recent films, both successful and unsuccessful. In this way, you can at least begin to assess your chances. For example, if your potential investment requires a viewing audience of two million to break even, while your "favourite" recent movie only attracted 1.5 million, then perhaps, the risk in this case is too great.

Finally, one of the investment indicators that should be used is the question of whether or not the participants are investing their own funds. This criterion must, however, be used cautiously. For example, if a movie producer is entitled to a fee of $50,000 for his efforts, he could just as easily structure the deal so that he gets a fee of $80,000 and then reinvests $30,000 back into the film. *Remember that the producer would obtain the same tax write-offs as you would.* From a cash-flow standpoint, he would still be receiving $50,000 of income — even if the film is a bust.

To summarize, films can be valuable as a tax shelter if you have the mentality of the high roller and also don't want to be burdened by any administration. Extreme caution is, however, advised.

Oil and Gas Exploration Shelters

Also popular as tax shelters are Canadian Resource Properties. The shelter aspect revolves around the fact that Canadian Exploration Expenses are fully deductible in the year incurred, while Development Expenses are depreciable at between 10% and 30% per annum on a declining balance basis. If financing is arranged to subsidize a portion of these costs, the investor can again write off more than what he has put into a project in a given year.

Broadly speaking, Canadian Exploration Expenses include the following:

1. Viability expenses. (Costs incurred to determine whether or not a drilling program is feasible.)
2. All costs associated with dry holes where drilling has been unsuccessful.
3. Costs relating to a first well capable of commercial production in a new area.
4. Costs of wells successfully drilled, where production will not begin in commercial quantities within twelve months following the completion of drilling.

All other deductible costs are classified as development expenses.

As with other shelters, the taxpayer must be "at risk" for his financing. The risk factor is not, however, as great as it is in movie films. Recently, I was quoted statistics showing that over the last few years, approximately one out of every three drilling attempts has yielded gas in commercial quantities. In addition, a further one out of every ten attempts produced oil. Thus, overall, the opportunity to obtain a return on one's investment dollar appears to be approximately 43%. If the drilling program is diversified, this is not too risky.

The reason for this type of shelter's relatively low risk factor is that drilling is based on geological and geophysical expertise. Certainly, this is far different from film productions which are based on a subjective consideration of what the viewing public might want to see.

In the case of drilling ventures engaged in "frontier exploration" (such as in the Beaufort Sea) additional incentives were also available over the past few years. For every $100 invested, it was possible until recently to write off a minimum of $166. Investors in high marginal tax brackets could receive tax benefits which often exceeded the original investment — even if a project was completely unsuccessful! These special incentives have recently expired, but may be reintroduced (perhaps with modifications) in 1980.

In addition to exploration projects, one has the opportunity to purchase a "working interest" in an already producing field. This opportunity arises where an oil exploration company has already done the drilling work and has found natural resources in marketable quantities. Instead of waiting until these resources are tapped, the geologists and geophysicists determine the present value of the future cash-flows. An interest in the well is then sold to an investor (or a group of investors) for this present value. The investor is fairly well assured of a sufficient cash flow so that he will recover his investment along with a reasonable rate of return. The oil company, on the other hand, uses the cash generated from the sale of the working interest to engage in further exploration activities.

Because the value of the underground resources may be reasonably estimated, the purchase of a working interest can generally be accompanied by a fairly substantial ratio of debt to equity. Even with only a 10% – 30% Development Expense write-off (as opposed to 100% for Exploration) the high leverage can result in a good tax shelter. The greatest exposure facing the investor is the possibility of the well "blowing out". If there is a blow out at the well site, the investor could find his assets literally disappearing in smoke while the liability owing to his financiers remains outstanding.

Complex Accounting

Of all the tax shelters available, oil and gas is certainly the most complex from an accounting standpoint. One must determine how the invested capital is spent in the first place — whether for exploration, development, or for drilling machinery and equipment.

There are also special rules — written in what sounds like fancy jargon — pertaining to Crown royalties, lease rentals and earned depletion. In addition, there are special provincial rules which apply in all of the provinces in which exploration activities take place. Therefore, anyone who invests in oil and gas projects must employ the services of a qualified accountant to handle the reporting function. Since oil and gas accounting and tax is highly specialized, there are relatively few professionals who have an in-depth knowledge of this particular topic.

If you are dealing with an accountant who has not had sufficient exposure to resource activities, I suggest that you tell your accountant outright to subcontract that portion of your tax work to someone who is qualified in this area. Failure to do so can be costly; it is not your errors of commission which would necessarily come back to haunt you, but your errors of omission — such as failure to take advantage of some obscure provincial incentive to which you may be entitled.

Whenever I speak to business owners and executives, I suggest that anyone investing in oil or gas projects be prepared to budget a minimum of $300 or $400 a year *extra* for additional accounting and reporting services.

Evaluation of Oil and Gas Projects

The key factor to evaluating oil and gas exploration shelters appears to be the track record of the major participants. In addition, always find out whether or not the promoters are investing their own funds.

I have been living in western Canada for three years and have actually had very little direct experience inside the "oil patch". One thing that I have learned, however, is that it is not what you know but *who* you know that counts. In other words, if you are invited to participate in ventures with people who have shown a good success ratio in the past, your chances of not only obtaining a tax shelter but also of making a profit are greatly enhanced.

Summary

The foregoing was only a general analysis of what to look for with respect to tax shelters. If you are still interested, take two aspirins and call your accountant, lawyer and investment counsellor in the morning.

CHAPTER SIX

Maximize Your Investment Yields Without Incorporating

Planning around Earned Income

The first step to maximizing investment yields is that which I call "planning around earned income". In all probability, your earned income by itself is sufficient to put you into a fairly high tax bracket. You may find that it is not feasible for you to defer some of this income through a deferred compensation program and that your employer may not be willing to accommodate you with a significant range of fringe benefits. You may also find that incorporating your own activities as a consultant (as outlined in Chapter Eight) is just not possible. In addition, you may not be too interested in tax shelters because of the risks involved.

If you fall into this position, you should at least direct your efforts towards effective tax planning for investments. My concept is very simple: The last thing anyone with a high *earned* income needs is investment income. If you are already in a 50% tax bracket because of your salary or business income, then one-half of your investment yield will immediately be eroded by additional income taxes. How, then, do we go about planning effectively? The place to start is with the investment income deduction.

The Investment Income Deduction

In order to encourage middle-income and upper-income taxpayers to save more and spend less, the Income Tax Act provides each year an exemption from tax of the first $1000 of arm's length Canadian interest, taxable dividends, and taxable capital gains from Canadian securities. The theory is that it takes approximately $8000 or $10,000 of investment capital to produce an annual yield of $1000. Thus, the middle-income and upper-income taxpayer is encouraged to save that amount of capital and to invest conservatively. Of course, the more one saves, the less he has to spend and overall, the idea is to control inflation.

The interest, dividends and capital-gains deduction (known here as the "investment deduction" for simplicity) is a feature of the tax rules that everyone should take advantage of. There is certainly no harm in investing conservatively where the yield is tax-free. If you invest in term deposits at 12% or 13%, you are still going to be ahead, even after considering the decrease in the purchasing power of your dollar, which tends to devaluate by 8% or 10% each year.

Pay Off Your Home Mortgage

After having saved up enough capital to use the investment deduction to its fullest extent, the next step to proper planning is to discharge your home mortgage as quickly as possible. As was already mentioned in dealing with RRSPs, there is a tremendous difference in Canada between taxable and non-taxable interest income and also between deductible interest expense and interest which is not tax deductible.

Assume that you have a mortgage of $50,000 on your home at an interest rate of 12%. Assume, as well, that you *also* have $50,000 of cash which you have recently inherited. Your mortgage costs you $6000 a year in interest, and this amount is not deductible. If, however, you take your $50,000 inheritance and invest it at the same interest rate of 12%, you will receive $6000 of interest income. On the surface, there is an offsetting income and outflow. However, (ignoring the investment income deduction) the $6000 received is fully taxable. If you are in a 50% tax bracket, you will only keep $3000 on an after-tax basis. There is certainly very little merit in retaining $3000 while paying out $6000.

In fact, if your mortgage payable is at 12% and you are in a 50% tax bracket, you must earn a 24% pre-tax return on investment capital to make it worthwhile to carry the mortgage on your home. If anyone can show me how to earn a guaranteed 24% per annum on my money *with no risk*, I would appreciate a telephone call (collect) or a letter!

Thus, I recommend that a home mortgage be paid off as fast as possible. In the hypothetical case above, you should use the inherited capital of $50,000 to immediately discharge your debt. (The only exception might be if you are one of the lucky ones with a low interest "locked in" mortgage which dates back to the pre-inflation era.)

After Burning the Mortgage...

Once your home is paid for, that is when you have some room to manoeuvre. If you find an appealing investment, you may *then* borrow the capital that you need against your paid-up home. If you borrow *specifically for the purpose of making investments*, your interest expense becomes tax deductible. Even if you are forced to borrow at an interest rate of 18%, remember that, for someone in the 50% bracket, this represents a net after-tax outlay of only 9%. If the investment that you purchase appreciates by more than 9% per annum, you will be ahead of the game. But the key point is get your house paid off *first* before you borrow against your *equity* for investment purposes.

Note that there is no shortcut to be taken. If you inherit money and use those funds for investment purposes without having first paid off the mortgage on your home, you will *not* be permitted to argue that you *could have* paid off the mortgage in the first place and then borrowed for investment capital. In tax cases that have come before the courts, the judges have insisted on a proper "tracking". If you take a shortcut, be prepared to suffer tax penalties. As long as your interest expense is deductible, I fully agree with what Dr. Morton Shulman said in his book *How to Invest Your Money & Profit from Inflation:*

> When buying a house, don't worry about the interest rate on the mortgage so long as you can meet the payments. Interest rates always lag behind the inflation rate. More important, the

mortgage rate remains constant throughout the life of the mortgage even though the inflation rate will continue to climb.

Shulman's thesis is that a debt obligation costs you less and less each year because of the devaluation of the dollar. On the other hand, a home tends to appreciate over time as inflation causes replacement costs to spiral upwards. Unfortunately, I don't think that Dr. Shulman goes far enough. He does not distinguish between deductible interest expense and non-deductible interest.

If an interest cost is halved for taxpayers in marginal tax brackets of 50% (or higher) the drain on cash flow is not nearly as great as the payment of non-deductible interest. Certainly, where your *net* interest expense is no more than the annual inflation factor, chances of coming out ahead on your investments become quite good.

To summarize:

1. Buy as expensive a home as you can afford to carry in the first place. No doubt, this is a good investment.
2. Second, pay for it as soon as you can.
3. Then, borrow as much as possible against your equity in the home (if you have the guts to do so) for investment purposes.

For most of us, there will never be another opportunity to latch on to a large sum of dollars with which to pyramid investment holdings. If the $50,000 home you bought in 1970 is now paid for and is worth $200,000, you could probably borrow $150,000 using the house as security. In turn, a $150,000 down payment could (for example) permit you to purchase another real estate project for between $500,000 and $600,000.

Transactions with Family Members

Once you have maximized your investment income deduction by setting aside $8000 or $10,000 of investment capital, and once your home mortgage has been paid off, the next step in effective planning is to try to split investment income with family members. The idea is to take advantage of other persons in the family who are in lower tax brackets than yourself.

While this section will consider transactions with both one's spouse and with children, the reader should note that the Income Tax Act simply differentiates between a spouse and anyone else. Consequently, any references in either this chapter or the next to a taxpayer's "children" can be interpreted as broadly as you wish. A child can therefore mean a grandchild, a niece, nephew, brother, sister or even a close friend. The same tax rules also apply to transactions with one's parents.

The purpose of this chapter is to discuss how to maximize the yield from reasonably finite sums of investment capital. The examples used will incorporate figures of up to $100,000. The point is that a *direct* transaction with another party can often result in significant tax savings when one deals with a certain amount of investment capital. In other words, it may not be necessary to over-complicate one's affairs by setting up corporations, trusts and other similar vehicles.

Transactions involving substantially greater investment capital are discussed in Chapter Seven. In such cases, the use of corporations and trusts is not only advisable, but in many cases, is practically mandatory.

Husbands and Wives

One of the many differences between the Canadian tax system and that of the United States is that Canada taxes a husband and wife separately, whereas the United States permits the filing of joint tax returns. Since Canada treats husbands and wives as separate taxpayers, the Tax Act is therefore somewhat concerned with the potential that might exist for income-splitting between spouses. We have already seen that tax rates for individuals are graduated. Accordingly, the tax on a single taxable income of, for example, $40,000 would be significantly higher than the tax otherwise payable on two taxable incomes of $20,000 each.

In order to prevent splitting of investment income, there is a tax rule which states that where a taxpayer transfers property to a spouse, or to a person who subsequently becomes a spouse, the income generated by the transferred property reverts back to the transferor. In addition, the rules also provide that if the transferee disposes of the property and substitutes something else, the income on the substituted property *also* reverts back to the transferor. These "income attribution rules" apply as long as the transferor is alive, is resident in Canada, and the transferee is his spouse.

The attribution rules apply whenever property is either gifted or sold to a spouse. Note, however, that an actual gift of cash itself does not have any tax consequences at the time the gift is made. This is the case no matter whether the recipient is a spouse *or* anyone else. The donor does not get a tax deduction, nor is the donee taxed. While at first glance this may be surprising, the rationale is apparent if one stops to examine the nature of cash. Cash is simply income on which taxes have already been paid. (There is exception for residents of the Province of Quebec only, who are subject to *provincial* gift-tax legislation.)

For example, if I give my wife $100,000, the gift itself will not have any tax implications. However, if she invests the money at 10%, the interest income of $10,000 will be taxable in *my* hands notwithstanding the fact that my wife received the actual funds. Moreover, if my wife takes "her" capital of $100,000 and acquires shares in a public company, receiving in a subsequent year a dividend of, say, $7000, that dividend will be taxed to me as well. In this case, the public company shares would comprise "substituted property".

There are, however, some interesting omissions in the tax rules that apply to transfers between spouses. The courts have held, for example, that the income attribution rules only apply to income generated from the transferred property itself (or from substituted property). The rules have no bearing, however, on what is referred to as "second generation", or compound income. Thus, if my wife were to take the $10,000 of interest earned in the first year and invest this sum separately, deriving additional interest of $1000 in the second year, this latter amount will be taxed in her hands and not in mine.

Of course, if we put the dollars into proper perspective, it becomes evident that in spite of the "second generation income" advantages, a gift between husband and wife will not result in significant savings. Even if I am in a top tax bracket of 65%, and my wife is not otherwise taxable at all, the most I can save out of having made the gift of $100,000 at the beginning of the first year, is 65% of $1000 or $650, at the end of the second year. Certainly, the tax saving is not material when compared to the initial gift.

Overcoming the Rules

Fortunately, the planning opportunities are significantly greater. Approximately twenty years ago, an important tax case came before the courts. This case, even today, has a tremendous impact on the tax implications of transactions between husbands and wives. In this specific situation, a husband *loaned* a substantial sum of money to his wife. In exchange, the wife gave her husband a note payable, promising to repay the loan on demand but without any interest. The funds were invested by the wife, who then reported the income earned on her own tax return.

At that time, as is true today, there was no legal or tax requirement that interest be charged on any loan between one individual and other. (Again, the only exception is in Quebec, where under provincial gift-tax rules, failure to charge interest results in a deemed gift for tax purposes. No other province has legislation of this nature.)

In this case, the Department of National Revenue applied the income attribution rules in assessing the transaction. The husband appealed. The judge held that the term *"transfer* of property" as used in the Income Tax Act includes transactions involving sales or gifts, but that a "transfer" does not include a loan. Furthermore, the court concluded that there is no restriction against one spouse lending money to the other in order for the recipient to derive income. Surprisingly enough, the Tax Act has never been amended and this case still serves as a valid precedent.

Accordingly, it is recommended tax-planning to split income between spouses by simply making *loans* of investment capital between spouses. However, if taxpayers do split income by using this method, documentation should be prepared evidencing the transaction as a loan. Again, the loan would generally not be interest-bearing and would usually be repayable on demand. One should also keep in mind that a loan could afford to the transferor (in certain jurisdictions) much greater protection than a gift in the event of a marriage breakdown. A gift is never recoverable, whereas a loan, repayable on demand, is.

The after-tax income which is built up by the spouse in the lower bracket can be used for various purposes such as the repayment of a home mortgage or just to provide funds for further investments.

Income attribution will not apply to funds reinvested out of a salary paid by a taxpayer to his spouse who is an employee of his unincorporated business or partnership. In addition, if a wife and husband enter into a legal separation or get divorced, income attribution will cease.

Transfers of Capital Property between Spouses

After dealing with the income generated from property transferred by one spouse to the other, there are also some important capital-gains implications to consider. When one transfers capital property such as stocks (in both public and private companies), corporate bonds or real estate to a spouse, the transfer of property is deemed automatically to have taken place at the transferor's tax cost. In other words, no matter what the current value of that property is, no capital gain or loss is recognized at that time.

However, when the transferee subsequently sells the property, the capital gain or capital loss reverts back to the transferor. The computation of this gain or loss is based on the transferor's original cost for tax purposes. Basically, one accomplishes absolutely nothing in the way of reallocating capital gains or losses by making gifts or sales of capital properties between spouses. There is a full capital attribution rule whenever the gain or loss is ultimately realized on a sale to a third party. This can be illustrated by an example in which:

1. The cost of capital property (e.g., land) to husband is $10,000.
2. The fair market value at date of gift or sale to wife is $20,000.
3. The property is subsequently sold by the wife for $70,000.

Regardless of the fact that the fair market value of the property is $20,000, the husband will be deemed to have disposed of it at his cost of $10,000. However, when his wife subsequently sells the property, the entire capital gain of $60,000 (one-half of which is taxable) will revert to the husband.

When dealing with capital property, one cannot overcome the system by lending this property to the spouse who is in a lower bracket. The courts have held that if a transaction cannot be accomplished on a commercial basis, it cannot be done for tax purposes either. There is no such thing as "lending" real estate or lending stocks or corporate bonds to another person.

There is a new rule that will permit a taxpayer, after 1979, to transfer capital property to a spouse at fair market value. While the recipient will get the benefit of the future growth in value, the transferor will pay the penalty of accrued gains at the time of transfer. This election will probably only be of use where there is a division of property in preparation for a separation or divorce.

Beating the System

With proper planning, however, the rules can be beaten. All it takes is a little bit of foresight. If a husband, for example, wishes to transfer *both* income *and* growth to his wife (in a lower bracket) he would first have to lend her cash. The cash would then be taken by the wife and invested in the capital property in question — whether it is land, shares or corporate bonds. In this manner, the capital growth would accrue to her benefit for tax purposes. In addition, any income generated on the property during the ownership period would also be taxed in her hands. One then gets the best of both worlds. (Under most provincial jurisdictions, in case of a divorce, the assets would be divided equally in any event.)

If one wants to take advantage of these tax-planning provisions, it is important that no shortcuts be taken. It is insufficient to simply register the ownership of a property in whole or in part in the name of a (low bracket) spouse. One would have to be able to show Revenue Canada that a loan was made in the first place and that these funds were used for purposes of making the investment. In addition, one should stay away from backdating transactions. Creating documentation to evidence a loan after the fact is fraudulent, and if the taxpayers are found out, the penalties can be very severe. To summarize, *make loans first and buy the property after.*

Transactions with Persons Other Than Spouses

There are other significant provisions in the Tax Act that are also designed to prevent income splitting. Whenever a taxpayer transfers property to a minor, the income from the transfered property reverts back to the transferor until the minor reaches the age of eighteen. This provision is designed to prevent anyone from splitting income with his children or grandchildren while they are still below the age of majority and then making use of the income generated from the property for the taxpayer's own advantage.

If one does wish to transact with minors, one should go through the formalities of using a trust, for reasons that will be discussed in Chapter Seven. In general, this would be accompanied, as well, by the formation of an investment company and would only be suitable where the taxpayer has substantial investment assets.

 In passing, I raise the somewhat rhetorical question of whether or not it would really be advisable to make large gifts to children under the age of eighteen, regardless of the tax consequences. Even if there were no income attribution rules, would you really want your children to have sizeable investment capital of their own at the age of eighteen?

Unlike the situation between husbands and wives, one cannot circumvent the rules by making loans to children or grandchildren where the recipients are under eighteen. The restriction again stems from legal problems. A child under the age of eighteen has no legal power to contract anywhere in Canada. When something cannot be done under common law, the courts have held that it cannot be accomplished for tax purposes either.

Loans to Older Children

However, where children (or grandchildren) are eighteen or over, it may be extremely advantageous to split income by making loans (as in the case of husband and wife). The following example depicts a typical situation where a parent, by making a $50,000 loan to a child, can save up to $1805 using 1980 exemptions.

EXAMPLE OF TAX SAVINGS RESULTING FROM A LOAN TO A CHILD

Assumptions:

1. Parent has $50,000 of investment capital bearing interest at 10%, *over and above* $10,000 needed to utilize his annual $1000 "investment income deduction". He is in the 50% tax bracket.
2. Parent has a child over age 18 attending university. The child has no income and the parent uses his after-tax investment income to pay tuition fees ($600) and to provide support.

Note: Tuition fees are only deductible by a student, although the $50-a-month education deduction is transferable to a supporting individual whenever the student does not need it to reduce his own taxable income to nil.

Alternative 1: No Loan to Child

Interest income to father (10% X $50,000)	$5,000	
Less: Income taxes thereon (50%)	2,500	
Net interest income		$2,500

123

Add: Tax savings from:
    Personal exemption for child (in 1980)   990
    Transfer of education deduction
      (assume 8 months X $50)   400
                                 $1,390

$1,390 X 50% tax saving		695
Net cash flow		$3,195

Cash flow utilized:
    To pay tuition $ 600
    To pay expenses $2,595
                     $3,195

Alternative 2: A $50,000 loan is made by father to his child. (The loan is non-interest bearing, and is repayable on demand.) A term deposit is purchased by the child.

Child's tax position:	
Interest income (10% X $50,000)	$5,000
Less: Tuition fees paid by student	600
Net income for tax purposes	4,400
Personal exemption (1980)	(2,890)
Investment deduction	(1,000)
Optional standard deduction	
for medical and donation expenses	(100)
Education deduction (8 months X $50)	(400)
Taxable income	$ 10
Taxes payable	Nil
Cash flow utilized:	
To pay tuition	$ 600
To pay expenses	4,400
Net cash flow	$5,000
Advantage of loan ($5000 – $3195)	$1,805

    This saving, which results from capitalizing on the child's lack of income, is certainly significant in comparison to a total investment income of $5000. Multiply this amount by the number of years that the child attends university, and there is a substantial advantage. The savings can be used to provide additional support for the child *or* for the benefit of the family as a whole. The demand loan feature should protect the parent in the event that the child decides to use the dollars for anything other than the purchase of a term deposit or similar investment. Presumably, one's bank manager would witness the note and in the event that the child tried to "cash in", it would be incumbent upon the manager to inform the parent of these developments. Of course, if the child is unreliable, one would not jeopardize one's asset position even for the tax advantages.

Family Planning

If a person has planned a family properly, and the ages of the children are such that one is finishing university just as the next one is starting, you can see that the benefits of the above plan can be compounded. As one child graduates, the parent can demand that the money be returned, and the funds are then available to lend to the next child. Of course, if several children are in university at the same time, then a parent would need more money in the first place to compound the advantages.

Transfers of Capital Property to Children and Others

With respect to capital gains, as opposed to the cash transactions just discussed, there is a significant difference between transfers made to a spouse and transfers made to anyone else. A transfer of capital property to anyone else must take place for tax purposes at *fair market value*. The illustration below shows how this is the case whether the property is sold or gifted.

EXAMPLE OF CAPITAL PROPERTY TRANSFER TO CHILD

Cost of capital property to the father (e.g. land)	$10,000	Father's capital gain
Fair market value at date of transfer	$20,000	
Sale by child subsequently	$70,000	Child's capital gain

As indicated in the example there is a tax trade-off. Where father's land has a cost of $10,000 and a fair market value of $20,000, gifting or selling that property will result in an immediate gain on which he must pay tax. The advantage of the transaction, however, is that the child receives the benefits of future growth. There is no way in which the gain up to the time of transfer can be eliminated. However, with proper planning, this gain can at least be postponed almost indefinitely without restricting the ability of the child to obtain the future growth.

Tax Planning to Defer Capital Gains

The Use of a Tax Reserve

Postponing capital gains involves making a sale and not a gift. If a gift were made, the tax consequences resulting from a gain are triggered immediately. However, whenever a sale is made, the tax rules provide that a *reserve* can be claimed *against* one's gain as long as at least some part of the proceeds is deferred beyond the end of the taxation year. These rules apply with respect to land and securities (public and private) as well as any capital gain on a building. (It should be noted, however, that there is no reserve for recaptured depreciation. The reader is cautioned to consult his own advisors if he wishes to transfer both land and building under the deferred payment plan described below.)

For our purposes, let us assume that the property in question is a piece of vacant land, such as recreational property which is personally owned, on which no depreciation has been (or can be) claimed. If a portion of the proceeds is not due before the end of the year, the formula for the tax reserve is

$$\frac{\text{Amount not received}}{\text{Total selling price}} \quad \text{X} \quad \text{Capital gain}$$

The capital gain is reduced by the reserve and thus each dollar collected represents a partial recovery of the vendor's cost as well as an element of profit.

126

For example, a father could sell the above property to his child in exchange for a non-interest-bearing note due *"30 days after demand"*. As long as no demand is made by the father before the end of the year, no part of the proceeds is due. Consequently, a *full* reserve against the gain may be claimed.

Cost to father	$10,000	
Fair market value on date of sale		
(note due 30 days after demand)	$20,000	
Capital gain		$ 10,000
Less tax reserve:		
$\dfrac{\$20,000}{\$20,000}$ X $10,000		(10,000)
Net capital gain		$ Nil

What is the significance of a note due "30 days after demand"? In general, if a father intends to pass on the benefits of growth to his child (or children), he would not want to earn interest from them either. If he therefore sold the property for a non-interest-bearing note due, say, in twenty years, Revenue officials would argue that father did not sell at fair market value. They would apply present value techniques and deem this note to be almost worthless.

However, a note due 30 days after demand can technically be called at any time. Thus, the fair market value of that note is approximately equal to its face amount. On the one hand, the note cannot be discounted and yet the reserve is still available as long as the father does not actually make any demands.

If the father retires and his tax bracket decreases, he can always demand payment over a period of time. In this manner, he could recognize his capital gain slowly. No reserve is permitted by law in the year of death or in situations where a taxpayer becomes a non-resident of Canada. However, the capital gain can actually be postponed until the last of both father and mother die. This is in cases where the debt receivable is left by will from father to mother (on the assumption that he dies first).

In summary, the foregoing tax plan provides the best possible situation — an indefinite deferral of accrued capital gains to the present time, with future growth being passed on for the benefit of the next generation.

Estate Freezing

In general, and as mentioned previously, the use of direct transactions between individuals is far easier than forming holding companies and trusts. This is especially so when one deals with relatively finite assets and family relationships are good. If the property in the above example was a recreational facility, such as a summer cottage, it would not be unusual for the agreement to provide for a sale from parents to children in order to freeze the potential capital gain, but that the parents would still have the opportunity to use the property in their lifetimes. The sale coupled with a note taken back is one of the simplest "estate freezes".

The term "estate freeze" is often bandied about and you might find a definition useful. An estate freeze occurs when an asset with growth potential (such as real estate or shares) is *exchanged* for a frozen asset which has no growth potential. In the previous case, the frozen asset is the note receivable which can never be worth more than its face amount of $20,000.

Additional Use of Tax Reserves

The tax-reserve provisions can also be used to defer the income of a seller when property is sold (even in an arm's length transaction) and the vendor does not wish to pay immediate taxes on his profits. With proper planning, a purchaser can obtain a clear title while still passing on tax deferral advantages to the vendor.

There was a case in November 1978, where a client came to me with what he thought was a rather complex tax problem. He owned a piece of vacant land in downtown Calgary and had just received an excellent offer from a developer. His profit was substantial and he was somewhat concerned with his potential tax liability. The client indicated that it was too late in the year for him to find adequate shelter to reduce the tax burden.

I suggested that he sell the property under an agreement for sale which would provide for payment to be deferred in full until January 1979. I explained that as long as the proceeds are not *due* before December 31, a reserve can be claimed against his profit.

Initially, the client's reaction was that this arrangement would not be feasible — the purchaser needed an immediate clear title so that he could start developing the property before the end of the year. Of course, my client was not prepared to release title without adequate security. I asked my client how payment would be made and was told that the purchaser had sufficient cash for the full amount.

I then simply recommended that the purchaser take the available cash and place the money into a term deposit due some time in early January with his *own* bank. I also suggested that with this term deposit as collateral, the purchaser's bank could then guarantee to my client that the debt owing by the purchaser would in fact be paid at that time. I explained to my client that an irrevocable guarantee from a Canadian chartered bank is just as valid as having the security of a mortgage against a piece of property. If the buyer were to default, my client would have immediate recourse for the full price from the purchaser's banker. There would also be no risk to the banker, since he would have the security of the purchaser's term deposit.

The transaction took place as I suggested, and to the best of my knowledge, my client obtained the one-year deferral that he was looking for.

An Opportunity for Adventurous Planning

In theory, the preceding tax plan could be taken one step further. The transaction could perhaps have been structured so that the buyer's payment would not be due for ten years (instead of only after two months). The purchaser would again take the cash and buy a term deposit to serve as collateral for the bank guarantee. The agreement with the vendor would provide that the balance of sale would bear interest at the same amount that the purchaser would be getting on his term deposit. In this respect, the purchaser could not possibly be adversely affected. His interest income and expense would simply offset each other.

Again, with the term deposit as collateral, the chartered bank could promise to guarantee payment to the vendor at the end of ten years. However, since the note would not be due until the tenth year, the vendor would not have to take any of his gain into income *until that time*.

If he wanted to, the vendor could receive interest income throughout the period on the full balance of the purchase price. This is substantially more than he would have had if he were simply to have collected his cash, paid taxes on his profit, and reinvested the difference.

However, let's carry this one step further. What would happen if the vendor took his note receivable from the purchaser's bank and went to his *own* banker to get a loan in an amount equal to the debt receivable? Presumably, the vendor's banker would lend dollar for dollar on the security of a guarantee from another chartered bank.

In this manner, the vendor could have the full *use* of *all* his capital in any way that he so desired with no taxes payable until the end of the tenth year! His interest income on the balance of sale owing by the purchaser would offset the interest expense on the bank loan taken out. Having the use of profits and postponing taxes is effective planning. Of course, with inflation, one shouldn't worry too much about the impact of a tax which is deferred for ten years.

ADVENTUROUS PLANNING CAN POSTPONE CAPITAL GAINS

Problem

Vendor owns land with a cost of $5000 and a fair market value of $100,000.

Development Company wishes to purchase the land and needs clear title to build.

Vendor wishes to sell but does not wish to pay *any* tax for ten years.

Solution

1. Development Company puts $100,000 into a term deposit.

The company obtains a letter of guarantee from its banker with the deposit certificate as collateral.

2. Development Company purchases the land from Vendor for $100,000 and signs a note (at current interest) due in ten years. Development Company gives Vendor the bank letter of guarantee to secure the note.

3. Vendor, with the letter of guarantee assuring his $100,000, releases *clear title* to the land.
   Because the note is due in ten years, Vendor may claim a full reserve against his gain.

4. If Vendor wishes to make use of the *entire* capital, he may then borrow $100,000 from his *own* banker pledging his "letter of guarantee receivable" as collateral.

I have discussed this arrangement with several tax accountants and lawyers. Naturally, this planning is somewhat adventurous but it certainly falls far short of being fraudulent. Presumably, if many people start to defer their gains in this manner, the Department of National Revenue will push The Minister of Finance to plug the loophole. Of course, as is so often the case, as one loophole is plugged, others usually arise. This is what makes tax planning so much fun.

General Tax Planning for Capital Gains

While on the subject of tax planning for capital gains, it is worth emphasizing that taxes on gains do not have to be paid until there is a disposition accompanied by proceeds. One of the most popular methods that sophisticated investors use to postpone gains, is simply the concept of *not selling* but *borrowing* instead against increases in values of investments in order to pyramid their holdings. Borrowing with a pledge of property as collateral has no implications for tax purposes.

If the borrowed funds are used for investments, the interest expense is deductible. Even at rates of interest of 17%, anyone in a 50% bracket (or higher) is only paying an effective rate of 8½% (or less) after tax considerations. As long as the investment assets can do better than 8½%, one will profit in the long run.

The ability to borrow is also useful since one can often borrow dollar for dollar against full increases in value. This is better than selling property and having your reinvestment potential eroded by taxes payable. For example, if you own real estate, such as vacant land, and are considering a sale, another good tax-planning technique might be to rent the property instead. Consider the following situation, where an annual pre-tax cash flow of $7750 would result if a property were sold and the after-tax dollars were invested to yield 10%:

Cost of property	$ 10,000
Anticipated selling price	100,000
Capital gain on disposal	90,000
Taxable capital gain	45,000
Taxes at 50%	22,500
Cash available to reinvest ($100,000 – $22,500)	77,500
Available pre-tax return at assumed rate of 10% (per annum)	7,750

As an alternative, a purchaser who is willing to pay $100,000 should be willing to pay a rental under a long-term lease of $10,000 per annum. The agreement would also incorporate an option for the purchaser to buy the property at *today's fair market value* in twenty-five years' time.

From the vendor's position, however, an annual rental of $10,000 per year provides him with a substantially larger cash flow than if he were to reinvest his after-tax proceeds of sale ($10,000 vs. $7750). The vendor is also guaranteed to get his purchase price in any event at the end of twenty-five years.

Tax Planning for Personal Residences

While the general rule is that capital gains realized after 1971 are taxable, a special exemption applies to a gain on the sale of a principal residence. A principal residence is an accommodation owned by a taxpayer (either alone or jointly) which is ordinarily inhabited by him, his spouse, a former spouse or a dependent child at any time during the year — as long as the taxpayer designates the property as his principal residence.

The accommodation can take any form such as a house, apartment, farm, condominium or even a share in a cooperative housing corporation. A principal residence will also include not only the building, but the land on which it is situated, up to a limit of one acre. For any additional land to be treated as part of the principal residence, the owner must establish that it is "necessary to the use and enjoyment of the housing unit as a residence."

So far, there have been no tax cases on the topic of excess land. However, it would appear relatively certain that if one lives in a community where the minimum lot size is, say, five acres, the extra land would fall under the exemption as well. In other cases, it remains to be seen whether or not Revenue officials take a harsh or lenient stand.

If a taxpayer owns two residences, only one of them may be designated as his principal residence for any given year. Where a husband and wife own their home jointly, each of them will have to designate the property as his or her principal residence for the entire gain on eventual sale to be exempt from tax.

In contrast, if one spouse owns and designates a city home as a principal residence, while the other spouse owns another property, the second property may also be designated as a principal residence provided it meets the test of being "ordinarily inhabited" by the owner. A seasonal residence, such as a summer cottage or ski chalet, will apparently meet this test unless the principal reason for owning it is to produce income.

Thus to tax plan properly, it is mandatory for husband and wife to have separate ownership of the two properties. They may start off jointly owning a city house and later on decide to acquire a second residence. Before the latter acquisition, I suggest that one of the two spouses sell his or her interest in the city house to the other. The seller would then be the person who acquires the second property. The gain on the sale by husband to wife (or vice versa) of the interest in the city house would be exempt as a principal residence sale.

Failure to structure ownership advantageously at the time of acquisition of the second property will, however, result in the gain on one of the two properties being at least partially taxable. Technically, one's capital gain must be calculated in the same way as gains on other assets. However, there is a formula exempting a portion of the gain based on the number of years during which the property was designated as a principal residence as a proportion of the total number of years of ownership. For purposes of these calculations, only years after 1971 are taken into account.

Since one's entire gain is normally exempt, Revenue officials do not require any designation of property as a principal residence to be filed from year to year. It is only when property is disposed of and where a *taxable* gain results, that a designation must be filed with one's tax return for that year.

There are also rules that will allow a taxpayer to have up to two sales of principal residences in the same taxation year. Thus, if an individual moves from Montreal to Toronto, and then on to Vancouver, all in the same year, it is possible for the disposition of both the Montreal house and the Toronto house to be tax-free. (Actually, there is no requirement that these houses be situated in different cities.)

A Word of Caution for Habitual Renovators

From time to time, there are newspaper and magazine articles about people who have a rather interesting hobby. They buy older homes, move into them, fix them up, and resell them at a profit. If a taxpayer undertakes such a venture only sporadically, he can still expect to qualify for the principal-residence exemption for his gain on sale. However, if a taxpayer develops the habit of buying, fixing and selling a different house each year, Revenue officials will consider these transactions to be a business. *As such, one's entire gain could become taxable.* There have been a number of tax assessments of which I am personally aware which resulted from investigations initiated from information in newspaper articles. Thus, anyone who practises this rather interesting hobby should either maintain a low profile or be prepared for the possible adverse tax consequences that may result from human interest stories.

Changing the Use of a Principal Residence

To accommodate taxpayers who are subject to temporary transfers, the Act permits a taxpayer to move out of a home and still designate the property as his principal residence for up to four years. In order to make this election, the taxpayer must remain resident in Canada and must not designate some other property as his principal residence during that period. If the designated property is rented out during that time, capital cost allowances may not be claimed to reduce rental income.

There is an extension to this rule which permits a principal residence designation to continue beyond four years in cases where the individual (or a spouse) is transferred by an employer and later reoccupies the home. This is provided that reoccupation occurs no later than one year following the year in which employment with that employer terminates.

These rules are designed to provide tax relief where a property was first a principal residence and then later becomes a rental property. Unfortunately, no similar alleviating provisions exist for a reverse situation. If a property starts off as a rental property and *then* becomes a principal residence, the taxpayer has a problem. The rules of the Act provide that at the time there is a change of use, there is a deemed disposition of the rental property at current fair market value. *This will trigger recaptured depreciation and capital gains even though there has been no change in ownership.* The taxes payable will have to be paid without any corresponding inflow of cash. The only consolation, of course, is that *future* growth in the value of the property will be exempt from tax under the principal-residence rules.

There is no way out of this dilemma and I simply recommend that you should be aware of the problem. You might still wish to acquire a rental property with the intention of moving in later. This could be a better investment decision than the alternative of waiting until you are ready to buy a house for personal occupancy.

A delay could result in the penalty of having to pay a much higher price for the property in the future.

One step that should be considered to reduce tax exposure would be to refrain from claiming depreciation during the years that the property is a rental property. You would have to equate the tax benefits of having claimed depreciation initially against the detrimental effects of a subsequent recapture.

Whenever a taxpayer occupies part of his property and rents out the other part, the "housing unit" will consist of the portion occupied by him, and the rental portion is subject to capital-gains treatment when a disposition takes place. If a housing unit is used for non-residential purposes, such as where a doctor carries on his practice using a part of his home, only that portion occupied by the owner as a housing unit will be eligible to be treated as a principal residence. Any gain on disposal of the non-residential portion will be subject to normal taxes.

At some point in time, most Canadians must make a decision whether to buy a home or to rent. Certainly, there are many factors that must be taken into account. However, in defense of home ownership, it should always be considered that a personal residence is the only major asset on which profits can be realized without a part being caught up in the taxman's net.

CHAPTER SEVEN

Maximizing Your Investment Yields Through Incorporation

For those Canadians with substantial investment assets, the tax saving that results from income splitting can best be accomplished through the use of family-owned holding companies. Before exploring this avenue in detail, however, a short review of the tax rules for corporate-earned investment income would be useful.

Overview of the Corporate Tax Structure for Investment Income

Investment income, such as interest, rents, royalties and the taxable half of capital gains is initially taxed at approximately 50% (the actual rate varies slightly from province to province) when earned by a corporation. The Income Tax Act then permits the remaining 50% to be reinvested.

The theory behind this structure is that as long as at least a 50% tax is paid initially, the government does not mind if the shareholder would otherwise have paid higher (personal) taxes. Since maximum personal tax brackets rarely exceed 65% (except in a few provinces) the government does not find the deferral of up to 15% of tax to be distasteful.

Thus, even before engaging in any sophisticated tax planning, it is evident that it is generally to the advantage of individuals in brackets higher than 50% to earn their investment income corporately. The opportunity to reinvest excess dollars not otherwise available personally can provide a significant tax advantage.

Although an investment company can only "keep" 50% of what it earns, at any time dividends are paid out to shareholders an amount equal to 16⅔% of the investment income is then *refunded* back to the corporation. In other words, the net *permanent* corporate tax is only 33⅓%, and 66⅔% of each dollar's earnings is eventually available for distribution. These rules are summarized in the schedule below:

Investment income	$100
Corporate tax	50
Net corporate retention (maximum)	50
Refundable tax (16⅔% of $100)	16.67
Available for dividends	$ 66.67

The Taxation of Canadian Dividends Received by an Individual

As odd or complicated as the above rules may seem, the tax treatment of dividends received by a Canadian individual from a Canadian company is even more strange. When an individual receives a Canadian dividend, the dividend is included in the taxpayer's income. In addition, he is then required to include in income a *further* 50% of the amount actually received. This extra 50% is called the "50% gross-up".

The grossed-up dividend (150% of the actual) is then taxed in the individual's marginal bracket for that year. Initially, this appears to create a penalty situation where more than what is actually received is taxed. However, in arriving at the individual's taxes payable, there is a dividend tax credit which is *equal* to the 50% gross-up. (The federal dividend tax credit is 75% of the gross-up, while a provincial dividend tax credit covers the balance.) These rules are illustrated in the schedule on page 139.

If you examine the schedule, it becomes apparent that the tax treatment of dividends does not result in a penalty to the shareholder who receives them. Although one initially pays tax on an amount greater than what is actually received, the dividend tax credit *more than compensates* for this inequity. If, for example, you are in a 40% tax bracket and you receive $100 of additional income from any other source *except* Canadian dividends, you would expect to pay $40 on this *incremental* income. However, on a Canadian dividend, the tax is only $10. Similarly, a taxpayer in

138

SCHEDULE OF TAX PAYABLE ON $100 CANADIAN DIVIDEND

Taxable income level	$18,000	$40,000	$70,000
Individual's marginal tax bracket	40%	50%	60%
Cash dividend	$100	$100	$100
50% gross-up	50	50	50
Additional taxable income	$150	$150	$150
Tax in marginal bracket	$ 60	$ 75	$ 90
Dividend tax credit			
(combined federal and provincial)	50	50	50
Net tax payable	$ 10	$ 25	$ 40

the 50% bracket only pays $25 tax on a $100 dividend, while someone in a 60% bracket pays only $40.

The favourable tax treatment of dividends from Canadian companies takes into account the fact that a dividend is a distribution out of profits on which a corporation has previously paid tax. *The dividend tax credit is intended to compensate the individual shareholder for at least a portion of the corporate tax previously paid.*

Actually, the "gross-up and credit" system is designed to exactly compensate a shareholder for a permanent corporate tax of 33⅓%. Thus, when anyone receives a dividend of $66.67 out of $100 of investment income initially generated through a private corporation, this provides the *same after-tax retention* as would have been the case if the owner of the corporation had received the entire investment income ($100) directly.

As mentioned previously, if the shareholder of a corporation is in a tax bracket higher than 50%, he can use the corporation to obtain some tax deferral advantages. At some future time, when he decides that he wishes to draw out dividends, he is *no worse off* than he would have been had he owned the investment *personally* in the first place. There is an illustration of the two alternative approaches on pages 140 – 141. (The reader should note that this example ignores the effects of the $1000 investment-income deduction.)

COMPARATIVE AFTER-TAX RETENTION ON INVESTMENT INCOME

ALTERNATIVE A — Investment income (e.g. interest, rents, royalties, taxable capital gains) is earned personally

Investment income	$100	$100	$100
Marginal tax bracket of investment holder	40%	50%	60%
After-tax retention on $100	$ 60	$ 50	$ 40

ALTERNATIVE B — The investment income is earned by a private corporation

Investment income	$100
Less: Approximate effective federal and provincial corporate tax*	50
Retained earnings	$ 50

Shareholder's tax bracket	40%	50%	60%
Tax deferral (prepayment) under Alternative B	$(10)	$ Nil	$10

*The company has a potentially refundable dividend tax on hand of $16.67.
This amount is refundable at the rate of $1 for every $4 of dividends paid.

Effect when dividends are eventually paid out

Retained earnings in corporation	$50		
Add: Refundable tax	16.67		
	66.67		
Less: Dividend in cash	(66.67)		
Corporate net retention	Nil		

	40%	50%	60%
Shareholder's tax bracket			
Dividend in cash	$ 66.67	$ 66.67	$ 66.67
1/2 gross-up	33.33	33.33	33.33
Income for tax purposes	$100.00	$100.00	$100.00
Tax at marginal rates	$ 40.00	$ 50.00	$ 60.00
Less: Effective dividend tax credit (equal to gross-up)	33.33	33.33	33.33
Net tax	$ 6.67	$ 16.67	$ 26.67
Net retention (dividend in cash – net tax)	$ 60.00	$ 50.00	$ 40.00
Net retention without corporation (Alternative A)	$ 60.00	$ 50.00	$ 40.00

The Investment Income Deduction

The previous example does not take into account the annual
$1000 investment-income deduction which was discussed in
Chapter Six. The investment income deduction only applies where
qualifed income is received from arm's length sources. Thus, using
an investment company may have one small pitfall. If you channel
all of your investments into a private corporation, and then
proceed to extract dividends, what was previously arm's length
income becomes non-arm's-length. You must therefore "hold
back" at least $8000 to $10,000 of investment capital which
should be invested in your own name. This amount should be
sufficient to yield $1000 of arm's-length investment income from
Canadian sources annually.

Therefore, you would not usually consider an investment
company until you are in at least a 50% tax bracket and also have
significant *additional* capital beyond what is required to maximize
the use of your annual $1000 deduction.

The Use of Investment Companies

The gross-up and credit system, which provides that 50% of all
amounts actually received as dividends from Canadian companies
is first added to income and is then deducted directly off taxes
otherwise payable, has a very interesting by-product. This by-
product is the major factor in tax planning for Canadian corporations and their shareholders.

Specifically, up to $30,000 of Canadian dividends can be
received each year by any individual *totally tax-free* as long as he or
she has *no other income.* This is illustrated in the example on page
143, which uses average tax rates applicable across Canada.

The example shows a dividend of $30,000 that is grossed up
by an extra $15,000. However, after applying personal exemp-
tions and other deductions, the tax otherwise payable is completely offset by the $15,000 dividend tax credit. The net effect is to
reduce taxes to nil.

IF THE TAXPAYER HAS NO OTHER INCOME, $30,000 OF CANADIAN
DIVIDENDS ARE TAX-FREE

Dividend	$ 30,000
1/2 "gross-up"	15,000
Net income	45,000
Less: Estimated personal exemptions	5,000
Taxable income	$ 40,000
Estimated federal and provincial taxes	
On $25,000	$ 8,100
On $15,000 (Tax bracket 46%)	6,900
On $40,000	15,000
Less: Dividend tax credit	
(combined federal and provincial)	(15,000)
Net tax payable	$ Nil

Remember that the concept of tax-free dividends only applies where a taxpayer has no other income. If the taxpayer in our example had an *extra* $1000 from *any source whatsoever*, the taxable income would become $41,000 instead of $40,000. In this case, since the individual is already in a 46% combined federal and provincial tax bracket, the extra $1000 of income would cost $460 of taxes. There would be no further dividend tax credits available to offset this additional burden.

Thus, if you receive dividends as well as other income, the other income "floats to the top" and gets taxed at your highest marginal bracket with no relief. If you have substantial other income, you should be aware that the tax advantages of Canadian dividends are reduced substantially. You should also note that there is no direct relationship between dividends and other income. Therefore, you could *not* receive, for example, $15,000 of salary and a further (tax-free) $15,000 of dividends. The interaction of various dividend and other income mixes must be determined on a trial and error basis with the aid of your own accountant in your particular province.

Opportunities for Income Splitting through a Corporation

The tax rules for investment income were designed to produce an equitable treatment where income is earned and is then passed on as dividends *to the person who injected the capital into a corporation in the first place.* It is probable that the legislators failed to adequately consider the opportunities which exist to use a corporation as a vehicle to collect income and then *deflect it to family members in low tax brackets.* This is illustrated in the form of a diagram (below), and in the example on page 145, which outlines the magnitude of the tax advantages obtainable by simply putting together the investment income rules explained previously.

INCOME SPLITTING THROUGH A CORPORATION

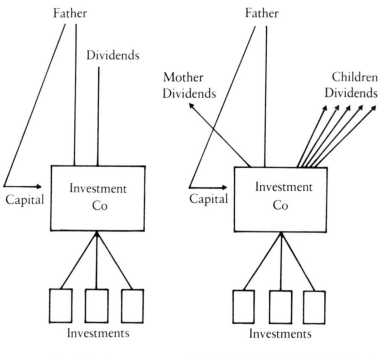

INTENTION OF RULES   OPPORTUNITIES FOR TAX PLANNING

ADVANTAGES OF A FAMILY-OWNED INVESTMENT COMPANY

Assumptions:

Father is in the 65% bracket and has $2,000,000 of investment capital earning interest at 10%. He is married and has four dependent children. His wife and children have no income.

ALTERNATIVE 1 — Investment income is earned personally

Interest on $2,000,000 at 10%	$200,000
Less: Income taxes thereon at 65%	130,000
Net retention (35% of total)	$ 70,000

ALTERNATIVE 2

- A corporation is formed and $2,000,000 is loaned by Father to the company on a non-interest-bearing basis.
- Father subscribes to preferred shares with voting powers sufficient to control but with no "growth potential".
- Mother and the children subscribe to common shares.

Interest on $2,000,000 at 10%	$200,000
Less: Corporate tax at 50%	100,000
Retained earnings	100,000
Add: Refundable tax to corporation when dividends are paid ($16\frac{2}{3}$% X $200,000)	33,000
Cash available for dividends	133,000
Less: Dividends to wife and four children	(133,000)
Remaining cash available for dividends	Nil
Dividend to each of wife and four children ($133,000 ÷ 5)	$ 26,600
Net tax payable by each	Nil
Net retention by family (5 X $26,600)	$133,000
$133,000 ÷ $200,000	66.5%

In the example shown, Father incorporates a private company to hold the investments which he would otherwise retain personally. He exchanges his investments for a non-interest-bearing loan owing by the corporation to himself. Outside of the Province of Quebec, there is no requirement that Father charge the corporation interest on funds which he has advanced. In addition, if Father does not charge interest, there are also no tax requirements that interest be imputed. (For Quebec tax purposes, one would have to transfer the assets into the corporation in exchange for some sort of non-dividend or low-dividend-bearing preferred share. These shares would have to be structured so as not to involve substantial future growth or income potential).

At the time of incorporation, Mother and the four children simultaneously invest a relatively nominal amount of money and subscribe to the common shares. Growth and dividend benefits would attach to these shares. In order to avoid "income attribution" (as discussed in Chapter Six) it would be important for the family members to invest their own funds or use money borrowed from outsiders. If necessary, Father could guarantee their loans without creating any adverse tax situation.

Since the investments are now held by the corporation, the company would begin to earn the interest income which would otherwise have been Father's. Initially, the corporate tax rate is approximately 50%. Even if no further steps are taken to split income, there is a $30,000 after-tax advantage, since the corportion would retain $100,000 (50% of $200,000) as compared to the $70,000 that would otherwise have been retained by Father personally. This illustrates the tax deferral advantages for individuals in brackets over 50% who use corporations to limit their tax exposure on investment income.

In addition to the fact that the corporation can retain 50% of its investment earnings, the company also has the ability to pay out 66⅔% of its profits by way of dividends. This is because of refundable tax considerations. In this case, at the time dividends are paid, $33,000 out of the (previously paid) corporate tax of $100,000 is refundable to the company. This would enable the company to pay Mother and the four children dividend payments of approximately $26,600 each. If none of them has other income, the net tax payable after gross-up and credit will be nil. Thus, $133,000, or 66.5% of the total earnings, is available for reinvestment purposes.

To reiterate, an investment corporation is therefore a vehicle for collecting income that would otherwise be taxed in one person's hands at high marginal rates. The income is then recycled and reallocated to other family members who are in low brackets to achieve significant absolute tax savings.

Sheltering Capital Gains

While the previous examples in this chapter assume an interest yield, income splitting through a corporation is viable for all sorts of investment activity. If, for example, the family corporation holds marketable securities, the tax burden of capital gains can also be reduced greatly. This is because the taxable half of the capital gain is taxed as investment income, while the tax-free half of a gain is not only tax-free to the corporation, but also can be extracted by the shareholders personally, with *no tax payable*, on a special dividend basis. The example below illustrates how a *taxable* capital gain of $50,000 may be sheltered where investment assets are held through a family corporation.

TREATMENT OF TAXABLE CAPITAL GAIN MADE BY
AN INVESTMENT COMPANY

Assumptions:
1. Father makes a capital gain of $100,000 of which $50,000 would be taxable. He is in the 65% tax bracket. Without the benefits of a corporation, his tax would therefore be $32,500.
2. Father is married and has four children — none of the other family members have any income.

If a family investment-holding company had made the gain instead:

147

Taxable gain	$50,000
Less: Corporate tax at 50%	25,000
Retained earnings	25,000
Add:Refundable tax to corporation	
when dividends are paid (16⅔% X $50,000)	8,333
Dividend to other family members	$33,333
Dividend to each ($33,333 ÷ 5)	$ 6,666
Net tax payable by each	Nil
Final corporate tax ($25,000 – $8,333)	$16,667
Father's tax — if no corporation	$32,500
Corporate tax	16,667
Tax saving	$15,833

Sheltering Public Company Dividends

Investment yields in the form of public company dividends can also be sheltered by funnelling these earnings through a private corporation. When a private holding company receives dividends from Canadian public companies, these dividends are taxed at a flat rate of 25% *instead* of the regular 50% tax which applies to other forms of investment income. However, this 25% tax is completely refundable as soon as the holding company in turn pays out these dividends to its shareholders. Thus, where Canadian public corporation dividends are received by a private company and are simultaneously paid out, there is *no tax whatsoever* at the corporate level.

Again, given a spouse with no other income and four children, the opportunity exists for each one to receive $30,000 of dividends tax-free. On a combined basis, this amounts to $150,000 per annum. If the average Canadian public company pays a dividend of 5% (computed as a percentage of the cost to acquire the shares in the first place) it is therefore posssible to *completely shelter* the income yield from $3,000,000 of share investments! (5% X $3,000,000 = $150,000).

Of course, the potential to tax shelter all kinds of investment income will vary from case to case and depends primarily on the number of family members that one has available for this purpose. The opportunities are, however, astounding. The idea that taxes should be paid by those who are best able to absorb them is clearly a myth. Ironically, if one has two or three million dollars of accumulated capital, the (net) tax rate on investment yields may be less than the rate that would apply against a small pay increase received by a grocery clerk.

Control of the Investment Corporation

The previous examples have assumed that Father would control investment policies and dividend payment decisions through his voting preferred shares in the family company. The family members would own the common shares, which would participate in growth and which would facilitate income splitting.

How can Father ensure that his family members will reinvest their dividends back into the company, short of using violence or other unsavory methods of coercion? Actually, he has several alternatives. First, he can cause the corporation to be capitalized with a special class of shares — non-voting redeemable preferred shares. Then instead of causing the company to pay cash dividends to trigger a refund of taxes, he could have the company pay stock dividends to his family members in the form of these non-voting redeemable preferreds. The corporation would still obtain its $16\frac{2}{3}\%$ refund of tax, but all that the family members would receive is pieces of paper. Although a stock dividend from a private company is technically taxable, as long as the amount is less than $30,000 per person, the tax payable would be nil. Since Father would always have voting control of the company, it is he who would decide if and when these special preferred shares would be redeemed.

As a second alternative, the shares owned by Mother and the children could be of different classes. In other words, Mother could receive Class A common shares, child "number one" could

149

receive Class B, and so on. The share structure could be designed so that dividends may be declared on *any class* to the exclusion of any of the other classes. Thus, if one of the family fails to reinvest funds as Father dictates, Father could then cut off the dissident shareholder from future income by refusing to cast his vote in favour of dividends on that particular individual's shares.

As a third alternative, a trust could be created to hold the shares of the children while Father continued to control the flow of income and all investment decisions. Although establishing a trust is the most complicated method and involves the greatest amount of legal and other documentation, it is the preferred route to take — especially if the children are minors.

The Formation of Discretionary Trusts

Usually, a family trust involves three trustees, including Father, Mother and a close family friend, relative, or advisor. Generally, if it is Father who is providing his capital to the investment corporation, he would have the right to replace either of the other trustees although they would not be able to replace him.

The trust would use borrowed funds to subscribe to the common shares of the investment corporation. This is done to avoid income attribution — especially where one or more of the children are minors. Dividends would then be paid by the corporation to the trust as illustrated previously.

When the trust receives a dividend, the trustees have two choices. First, they could have the trust pay taxes on the entire dividend. Obviously, this would not be a good choice since, on dividends in excess of $30,000, there are significant taxes payable. As a second option, however, the trustees are permitted to enter into what the Tax Act calls a "preferred beneficiary election". The preferred beneficiary election is simply a decision to *allocate* the dividends to the children for tax purposes. The allocation makes the children taxable instead of the trust. Of course, as long as the allocation on a per child basis is under $30,000, there are no personal taxes payable. In fact, however, no amounts are actually paid out. The trustees are then in the position of holding tax-paid money and they can reinvest the funds back into the holding company to compound future growth.

If a trust is set up as being "discretionary", this provides even further scope for tax planning. The discretionary feature means that the trustees are permitted to eventually distribute capital (generally upon the dissolution of the trust) to whichever of the preferred beneficiaries (and in whatever proportions) the trustees, at their discretion, may at *some future time* see fit. Thus, Father may freeze his estate and pass on growth, even if he is unsure of exactly where he wishes such growth to go! Perhaps the children are relatively young and their capabilities and personalities are still not known.

The key point is that there is no requirement that the preferred beneficiary election (which allows for equal allocations of income between the children) be tied in to ultimate distribution ratios. As an extreme, for example, even though income may have been allocated to four children for many years, Father may decide that only one child should eventually receive *all* the funds. In fact, the rules permit a decision on distributions to be deferred for up to twenty-one years.

In order to discourage long-term "inter vivos" trusts, (that is, trusts formed by living persons) there is a deemed disposition of trust property at fair market value if the trust is still in existence on its twenty-first anniversary. The deemed disposition would ordinarily trigger capital gains and this should be avoided. Avoidance can be accomplished by simply winding up the trust shortly before the twenty-first anniversary and distributing its assets (the common shares of the investment corporation) to some or all of the children. Of course, if Father is still alive, he could continue to control the company and its portfolio through his voting preferred shares. However, within twenty-one years, he should be in a position to know which of his children are "worthy" of an (eventual) inheritance.

Discretionary trusts giving the trustees the power to make annual preferred beneficiary elections are becoming more and more popular in tax and estate planning. Care must always be taken to comply with the particular laws of the jurisdiction in which the trust is being set up. Accordingly, it is advisable at all times when one is contemplating such a trust to have the arrangement documented by lawyers and accountants who have had experience in such matters.

Capitalization of the Investment Company

A question usually arises in setting up an investment corporation as to how much money each of the shareholders must contribute in exchange for their shareholdings. For example, can a family member invest only one dollar in the common share capital of a company and thereby receive dividends of up to $30,000 a year?

There has been only one reported tax case on this subject. The case involves two Alberta optometrists who incorporated a management company in 1970 to administer their practice. The company was controlled by these two individuals through voting, non-participating shares, but their wives also held shares which were non-voting but fully participating. The company paid management fees to the doctors and declared dividends to the wives which were very substantial in relation to their original investment. In fact, it appears that the wives literally invested pennies and, over a three-year period, received over $90,000 in dividends.

The Minister of National Revenue contended that an indirect benefit had been conferred by the doctors on their wives and that the whole set-up was a sham. The Tax Review Board upheld the Minister's treatment on the basis that although there was a business purpose for the incorporation of the company, the declaration of these dividends to the wives was not a sound business practice.

The judge showed no distaste for income splitting and estate planning as a *concept*, but, in his judgement, he gave the opinion that acceptable limits had been exceeded. He concluded that the scheme was simply intended to avoid income tax and that the dividends were rightly assessed as being income of the doctors.

This case was appealed and eventually settled out of court.

In spite of this one case, many accountants and lawyers are still not overly concerned and investment companies are often set up with only nominal share capital. However, I personally recommend extreme caution in this area. If, for example, one is forming an investment corporation with the expectation of paying $30,000 a year of dividends to family members (either directly or through a trust) I think that the capitalization per person should be at least $10,000.

Thus, in a family corporation involving a wife and four children, common shares should be issued for a total consideration of, say, $50,000. To avoid income attribution, the father should not gift these funds to the family members. Rather, they should take a bank loan which, if necessary, could be *guaranteed* by him. The interest on the borrowed money would be tax deductible since the borrowings would be incurred for the purpose of earning income in the form of dividends from the corporation. In addition, the infusion of an extra $50,000 of capital into the corporation would result in additional income being earned by the company. There would be no economic loss. Finally, the bank loan could always be repaid by the family members out of dividends over a period of one or two years.

The advantage of taking all these steps is that the Minister of National Revenue would probably be hard pressed to allege that a transaction is a sham where $10,000 is invested for the purpose of earning $30,000. Unfortunately, there are no guidelines within the Canadian tax structure and any final decision as to capitalization of an investment company is a matter that must be resolved by the taxpayer in conjunction with his own advisors.

Interest vs. Dividend Income

Retreating somewhat from the rather rarified atmosphere of investment corporations with portfolios of two or three million dollars, let us look at the tax implications of receiving either interest income or dividend income in Canada. There are two

153

distinct areas which should be compared: (1) The relative yields of both interest-bearing and dividend-bearing investments, and (2) The effectiveness of both kinds of investments in counterbalancing the ravages of inflation.

As of June 1980, it would not be unreasonable for an investor to expect a return of around 13% where funds are placed to earn interest. On the other hand, if one invested in Canadian public company securities, one would encounter great difficulty in finding investments that pay dividends of more than 6%. On the surface, therefore, there would be a 7% differential in yield between interest-bearing securities — such as term deposits, mortgages or Canada Savings Bonds — and Canadian public stock investments.

Although most people are aware that an investment in term deposits, mortgages or bonds may produce what appears to be a superior yield, part of the advantage is offset by the decreasing value of the dollar which accompanies the inflationary process. However, many people are still somewhat security conscious and feel that a 7% spread in yields is too large to warrant an investment in the stock market. It is recognized that over the long term, stock market investments could appreciate and may therefore be a reasonable hedge against inflation, but there is still the "down side" risk of potential declines in value.

Unfortunately, most investors do not have enough information when it comes to making proper policy decisions. Much of the problem stems from exposure to our American neighbours. In the United States, there is no difference between the receipt of interest and the receipt of dividends by an individual. Both are taxed at regular personal rates. In Canada, however, there is a very important distinction between these two kinds of income. Dividends are subject to the gross-up and credit treatment, while interest income is simply taxed at ordinary marginal rates. A comparison of *after-tax* retention for individuals in various brackets is shown on page 155. The example ignores the first $1000 of annual investment income, which is tax-free whether the $1000 is comprised of interest, (grossed-up) dividends, or any combination of the two.

A COMPARISON OF AFTER-TAX RETENTION
CANADIAN DIVIDENDS VS. INTEREST INCOME
(Ignoring the $1,000 investment income deduction)

Individual's marginal tax bracket	40%	50%	60%

ALTERNATIVE 1 —
   $100 Canadian dividends

Cash dividend	$100	$100	$100
1/2 gross-up	50	50	50
Taxable income	$150	$150	$150
Tax in marginal bracket	$ 60	$ 75	$ 90
Dividend tax credit			
(combined federal and provincial)	50	50	50
Net tax	$ 10	$ 25	$ 40
Net retention:			
(Cash dividend minus tax)	$ 90	$ 75	$ 60

ALTERNATIVE 2 —
   $100 Canadian interest

$100 interest	$100	$100	$100
Tax in marginal bracket	40	50	60
Net retention	$ 60	$ 50	$ 40

RATIO OF AFTER-TAX RETENTION —			
Dividends: Interest	3:2	3:2	3:2

As the comparison shows, the after-tax retention on dividends for taxpayers in *all* brackets is 1½ times as high as the corresponding retention on interest. Thus, for anyone who is taxable, a 6% dividend will yield as much after tax as a 9% (pre-tax) interest yield. Similarly, an 8% dividend is comparable to interest at 12%.

Therefore, the difference between earning interest at 13% or dividends at 6%, is really only a difference of four percentage points (13%–9%). In addition, the 4% differential is really a *pre-tax* difference. *For a taxpayer in the 50% bracket, a 4% difference in pre-tax yield translates to only 2% after tax.*

Let's put this into proper perspective using realistic numbers. Assume you have $20,000 to invest and have a choice between a 13% term deposit or a Canadian blue-chip stock paying a dividend of 6%. If you opt for the share investment, you must be prepared to sacrifice 2% of $20,000, or $400 per annum. Then you must ask, what are my chances of the securities appreciating by at least an amount offsetting my $400 loss? Of course, there is some risk involved. The securities could decline in value because of poor market performance overall or because you just happened to pick the wrong stock. On the other hand, if you invest $20,000 in interest-bearing securities, you can be *sure* that your $20,000 capital will only be worth about $18,000 at the end of one year given current inflation rates!

I must stress that the foregoing example is only valid where an individual is taxable in the first place. If one is in a 50% tax bracket (or higher) there just doesn't seem to be much value in earning 6½% *net* interest income when the inflation rate is 10%. On the other hand, I have no objections if my seventeen-year-old son invests his summer earnings in a term deposit. The reason is that my son hasn't reached the point where he is taxable. If that is the case, a 13% *gross* return on a term deposit is the same as his *net* return. For him to invest in dividend-bearing securities would, in fact, involve a difference in yield of about 7%.

I also would not be too upset if my eighty-year-old grandmother had her life savings invested in term deposits. Even if she is taxable, she would be much more concerned with the security element of having the money available at any time than she is about the devaluation of the dollar.

Finally, I am not adverse to interest-bearing investments when they are held by pension plans, registered retirement savings plans or deferred profit-sharing plans. As long as the investment income is tax-sheltered, the after-tax yield and the pre-tax yield are one and the same! I would not, however, recommend an interest-bearing investment for anyone who is taxable unless the after-tax yield was at least equal to the annual inflation factor.

My reasoning is probably no different from that of any other potential, knowledgeable lender who is in a taxable position. I therefore think that it is futile to dream that lending rates will ever decrease substantially as long as inflation continues. If a chartered bank pays 50% tax on its profits, it has to lend its retained earnings out at 16% to 18% just to break even.

CHAPTER EIGHT

Incorporating Your Earnings — The Ultimate Solution?

Advantages of Personal Service Companies

By definition, a personal service corporation is a company which earns fees or commission income. Generally, the income arises as a direct result of the activities of one or a few individuals. Personal service corporations set up in the past include: (1) professional corporations (in the province of Alberta only) for doctors, dentists, lawyers and accountants; (2) management companies for professionals; and (3) corporations for athletes, entertainers, executives, commissioned salespersons and business consultants.

Personal service companies can be utilized for tax-planning purposes in a variety of situations. Perhaps their most common application is with respect to professionals and other individuals who are in a position to contract their services through the use of a corporation. In most provinces, only *individuals* can lawfully carry on certain activities, such as the practice of law, medicine, dentistry, or public accountancy. The exception is the province of Alberta, which passed legislation in 1976 which allows taxpayers in the professions the right to incorporate in full. In other provinces, professionals can incorporate part of their practices though the use of a management company.

The advantages of personal service corporations stem from the fact that "active business income" of a Canadian-controlled private company qualifies for a small business tax rate of approximately 25% on the first $150,000 of profits each year until $750,000 has been earned cumulatively. Although any profits over $150,000 are taxed at approximately 50%, it is unlikely that the profits of most service companies in any given year (after salaries are paid out) would be in excess of $150,000 in any event. Thus, the high rate of

159

tax is not really applicable. Until recently, as will be discussed in Chapter Nine, the Income Tax Act contained no specific definition of the term "active business income" thereby permitting much latitude for interpretation.

Management companies have also been used by taxpayers in an attempt to transform what was previously employment income into income from a business. The advantages of management companies (where they have been successful in avoiding the attack of Revenue Canada) can be summarized as follows:

1. They provide the ability to split income between members of one's family — as long as salaries paid are for services rendered and are reasonable in the circumstances.
2. They create the existence of a new taxpayer (the corporation itself), which may qualify for a low rate of tax of approximately 25% on business income. After-tax dollars retained by the company can then be invested on behalf of its "owners".
3. As retained earnings accumulate, depending on how the management company is set up as to shareholdings, estate freezing and income splitting can both be achieved. These topics were discussed fully in the previous chapter.
4. A management or service company earning business income may be subject to much more liberal deductions for expenses than apply against an individual's employment income. The corporation could pay for such costs as conventions, business promotion expenses, and the expenses of owning and/or operating an automobile.

In the past, one of the major reasons for incorporation has been the inability of a taxpayer carrying on an unincorporated business to pay a salary to a spouse. Starting in 1980, however, this restriction has been eliminated and such salaries will be constitute valid deductions for tax purposes. Of course, the remuneration will have to be included in the spouse's income and the payments must be reasonable in relation to services rendered. The spouse paying the salary must also be carrying on a bona-fide *business* activity.

Professionals, executives and others who employ spouses in their businesses may now find that the advantages of incorporation are reduced considerably. It will now be useful to incorporate only where profits are in excess of their families' spending requirements and where the corporate rate is to be preferred relative to higher personal marginal tax rates, or if there is an advantage in paying dividends, or participating in a deferred profit-sharing program. These matters will all be discussed in Chapters Nine and Ten, which include tax-planning techniques for any Canadian private corporation, large or small.

Professional Corporations

As mentioned previously, Alberta is the only province that allows professionals to incorporate their practices in full. A professional corporation is somewhat of a hybrid between an individual and a corporation. By law, the only shareholder is the professional himself or herself. In other words, no splitting of shareholdings among spouses or other members of the family is permitted. In addition, the professional remains personally liable for all the debts and obligations of the corporation. The "unlimited liability" factor gives the public the same security as if it were dealing with the professional directly. This applies with respect to professional matters, trade debts, and any other obligations. In all other respects, the professional corporation is, however, a validly constituted entity. As such, corporate and not personal tax rates apply.

In general, tax planning for the professional corporation is rather simple. The corporation is set up to handle all billings, and pays all expenses. The professional is paid a salary equal to his (pre-tax) living requirements. Wherever possible, the corporation also pays salaries to members of the professional's family for their assistance. Naturally, where such salaries are paid, the professional himself can thus afford to draw less money thereby remaining in a lower tax bracket.

Corporate tax rates then apply to surplus profits. Usually, the

161

corporate tax rate is significantly less than the marginal rate which would otherwise apply to the professional. Consequently, the corporation becomes an investment vehicle for after-tax profits. Some of the profits are used to finance the costs of business expansion, to pay for equipment, and to carry receivables from clients or patients. The balance can be invested in whatever types of investments the "owner" so desires.

Management Companies for Professionals

Outside Alberta, where professionals may not legally incorporate, many doctors, dentists, lawyers and accountants have formed service companies which perform many of the management functions connected with a professional practice. Revenue Canada has indicated that corporations may be used by practising members of the professions in certain circumstances. The services that such corporations can provide would include:

1. Negotiating and signing leases for the premises from which the practice is carried on, and handling monthly rental payments.
2. Hiring and training of staff and maintaining payroll and other personnel records.
3. Purchasing supplies and the acquisition or leasing of all necessary furnishings, including equipment that may be required by the practitioner to carry on his professional practice.
4. Providing accounting services, including billing and collection of accounts receivable.

In a typical situation, most of these services are provided by the corporation on a cost-plus basis. The corporation computes its costs of performing these services and adds a profit factor which is charged back to the professional. Rates ranging from 10% to 15% have not been considered unreasonable. Ironically, the higher the overhead of the professional's operation, the greater the dollar amount of profit that can be transferred to the corporation.

162

Payment of an agreed fee to the corporation has the effect of reducing the professional's income by the amount of the profit factor. Where the individual is already in a high tax bracket, the result is an immediate tax deferral equal to the difference between his marginal tax bracket and that of the corporation. This is illustrated below.

In addition, if one can justify a salary payable to members of the family there is a tax *saving* equal to the difference between the professional's marginal rate and that of the other family members. Whether earnings are retained corporately or paid out as salaries depends primarily on the living requirements of the professional and his family. A management company can also be used as a vehicle to invest surplus funds not required for living expenses.

MANAGEMENT COMPANIES REDUCE A PROFESSIONAL'S
PERSONAL TAXES

If no management company:

Gross income of professional	$120,000
Less: Expenses to operate practice	50,000
Net profit of professional subject to tax	$ 70,000

With management company:

Gross income of professional	$120,000
Less: Management fees paid	65,000
Net profit of professional subject to tax	$ 55,000
Fee income of corporation	$ 65,000
Less: Expenses "taken over" from professional	50,000
Net profit of corporation subject to tax	$ 15,000

$15,000 is "extracted" from the professional's highest marginal tax bracket and is taxed instead at lower corporate rates.

Choosing Between Professional Corporations and Management Companies

Using the management company concept in your business planning may not be quite as advantageous as having a professional corporation. This is because only a relatively small amount of profits can be transferred out of the professional's hands and into a corporation. The management company does, however, permit one specific form of income splitting which is not available through the professional corporation. The management company may pay dividends out of after-tax profits to members of the professional's family — as long as these family members own shares in the company. This is not permitted in the case of a professional corporation since only the professional himself is permitted to be a shareholder. Nevertheless, the ability to incorporate one's *total* earnings and the opportunity to maintain only one set of records favours the professional corporation. I anticipate that several of the other provinces will join Alberta in passing enabling legislation. Certainly, it would pay professionals across the country to lobby for these priviledges.

Federal Legislation Governing the Use of Service Companies

In 1979, Parliament enacted some important legislation relevant to service companies in order to more closely regulate the types of activity which would qualify for the very low small business tax rate and to curtail abuses.

Starting in 1980, corporations used by doctors, dentists, lawyers, accountants, chiropractors and veterinarians in Alberta and elsewhere will no longer be able to use the 25% low rate of tax. The tax rate for them has been boosted to approximately 33⅓%. This is a compromise rate between the low rate previously available and the 50% corporate tax rate that applies in other cases where the low rate is not available.

While some professionals (though their governing bodies) have voiced displeasure with the new change, the after-tax results are still much more favourable than would be the case where an individual practitioner is unincorporated. It is rare that one would encounter an established professional earning income insufficient to put him into at least a 50% bracket. Thus, where the individual is earning more than what he needs to live, it is certainly preferable to pay a tax rate of 33⅓% instead of paying from 50% upward. The minimum tax advantage would be the ability to reinvest 16⅔% of earnings not required for living expenses. Where the professional is resident in a province where personal tax rates reach 70%, the deferral may be as much as 36⅔%. This does not even take into account the other advantages of incorporation such as profit sharing with members of one's family as well as the opportunity to use the corporation as a vehicle for investment of retained earnings.

In a sense, the new legislation might be a blessing in disguise. In the past, professionals have worried that Revenue Canada would not recognize a valid tax status for their corporations. Senior officials had threatened that they would disallow the existence of these corporations and attribute all income back to the professionals. Alternatively, Revenue Canada had considered deeming these corporations (even if valid as separate entities) not to be earning active business income and, as such, not qualifying for the preferred low rate. Certainly, if a 50% corporate tax were imposed on the income of a professional's corporation, much of the advantage of incorporating would be lost. Now that the tax status of Alberta professional corporations and professional management companies in general is known, many practitioners should reconsider prior decisions to hold off and wait.

The battle of professionals to achieve tax advantages is not, however, over. In the April 21, 1980, Budget, a proposal was made which will curtail the use of even the 33⅓% rate for corporate professional partnerships. Basically, the proposal will require all corporations acting in partnership to share between them one annual business limit of $150,000 which will qualify for the 33⅓% rate. Thus, in the case of a large partnership, the advantages of incorporation on a per-person basis may not be that significant.

I therefore recommend that wherever possible, corporate partnerships be dissolved. Instead, the organization should be structured as independent practices sharing common overheads. In other words, wherever possible each individual company should do its own billings to patients, customers or clients and a formula should be evolved for prorating *overheads only*. Each corporation would therefore be a completely separate entity. This is probably feasible for many medical and dental practices. In addition, this idea may have merit for certain law practices as well. The larger accounting firms may have more difficulty in implementing such an approach since it may not be practical. In the case of accounting firms, different accountants often do work for the same client during a given year and it would be difficult to split the billings.

The Future of Service Corporations

With respect to athletes, entertainers, incorporated executives, commissioned salesmen, and consultants, the new rules provide that beginning in 1980, the small business tax rate will only apply where a service corporation meets *one* of two tests in a particular year. The first condition, is that not more than two-thirds of the corporation's gross revenue from a business can be derived from services performed for or provided to any one entity. This is called the "diversity of income" test. Where a corporation fails to meet the diversity of income test, it will *still* qualify if the company retains more than five full-time employees throughout the year, none of whom own 10% or more of the shares of the company or are related to the controlling shareholders.

Where a corporation meets *neither* of those two tests, the 33⅓% tax rate will apply *as long as the corporation is in fact carrying on a business*. If, on the other hand, the corporation is nothing more than an "incorporated employee", it appears that Revenue Canada will be justified in disallowing the corporation's existence. The question of "what is a business" will still be important within the framework of tax planning. If a corporation has not got a business purpose and its only objective is to reduce taxes otherwise payable, there is ample legal precedent for the Minister of National Revenue to look through the corporation and deem its owners to be earning personal employment income. The following sections examine the effects of the new requirements on specific types of service companies.

Athletes

It will be difficult for most incorporated football or hockey players to meet either of the two criteria necessary to qualify as an active business. It is unlikely that other business income (such as from advertising or endorsements) would comprise at least one-third of the total or that the athlete's corporation would have the minimum six full-time employees.

If the corporation's only income is from a professional football or hockey club, it is quite likely that Revenue will insist that the employee-employer relationship has not been altered. Therefore, the existence of the corporation will be questioned and it is probable that its income will be attributed back to the individual player. However, if the corporation earns at least some (significant) income from other activities such as advertising or endorsements, it is likely that the corporation can show that it has a valid business purpose. If that is the case, it appears that the corporation will be allowed to stand and that the 33⅓% tax rate will apply. Of course, this is not as desirable as a 25% tax rate but it is certainly preferable to high marginal personal taxes.

In my opinion, for a corporation to show that it has a valid business purpose, a minimum of 10% of *gross revenue* (i.e., gross fees or commissions) would have to be earned from outside sources. In other words, if a hockey player's corporation earns $90,000 in fees from a pro hockey club, it is unlikely that the corporation will receive sanction from Revenue Canada unless it can earn at least $10,000 of outside endorsement or advertising revenue. If such revenues are not readily attainable, I would suggest that incorporation may be just a wasted effort.

Another unresolved and related issue is the question of what constitutes "*a* business". If a football player in the Canadian Football League incorporates and his company earns $66,000 of income in fees from the football club, that same corporation would require another $33,000 of "outside business income" in order to qualify for the low rate of tax. Assume that the football player's corporation contracts with a major brewery to provide the athlete's services for public relations. Assume, further, that the annual fee for these activities is $33,000. Would the athlete's corporation then qualify for the low rate? It would appear, at first glance, that the company has passed the "diversity of income test". However, will Revenue officials argue that income from athletics and income from public relations constitutes two separate businesses? At this time, the answer to this question is unknown.

Certainly, any athlete who finds himself in this or a similar position would be well advised to incorporate. One of my personal guidelines in tax planning is something that I call my "no worse off principle". The no-worse-off principle states that if the outcome of a tax plan is in doubt, and the tax advantages are significant, one should take every step possible to follow the plan through. If one is successful the desired benefits will accrue. If on the other hand, one is unsuccessful, the worst outcome is that the taxpayer would be put back in the same position as if he had not sought an advantage in the first place.

In the above example, the worst position in which the athlete could find himself would be where the corporation is disallowed and the income is attributed back to him personally. If this is the case, the athlete is really "no worse off" than if he had not incorporated in the first place. To warrant the costs involved, however, there should be at least some possibility of success.

Entertainers

Canadian entertainers should be able to benefit nicely from the new rules since, in most cases, they will have sufficient diversity of income to substantiate the fact that they are carrying on a business. To illustrate how arbitrary the new rules are, however, consider the position of an entertainer who has a solo act and accepts a long-term contract to perform in one place — his company may become ineligible in that year for the 25% tax rate. However, where that same entertainer performs his nightclub act in several different locations during the year (even within the same city) his company would qualify for the small business incentive.

As another example, any band leader with five people in his band who is considering incorporation should protect his position by hiring a sixth person! In that way, the company would meet the second test of eligibility, and even if the band receives a long-term engagement, the low rate of tax is protected.

Incorporated Executives

For an executive's management company to qualify for the 25% rate, it is imperative that the individual remove all signs of employment. If he is a shareholder, he may continue to retain his stock, but he should resign any directorship and cease to hold a position as officer. Diversity of income is extremely important. In cases where a former employer requires the executive to carry out his activities solely for and on behalf of that company, the use of a personal service corporation is not really viable. Revenue Canada will just look through the company and allocate its income back to the individual.

While the new legislation has not yet been tested, I don't think that an executive will be able to "beat the system" by simply contracting his services to five different subsidiaries of the same employer. This will probably not constitute diversity of income. Similarly, an executive will not be able to take advantage of the tax rules by hiring six secretaries onto "his" payroll who were previously employed the the ex-employer. Revenue Canada will deem this type of an arrangement to be a sham.

In many cases, executives should probably not attempt to qualify for the 25% low rate of corporate tax. Remember, even if diversity of income is not met, a 33⅓% rate is still applicable as long as the corporation is carrying on *a business*. I personally feel that where a corporation earns at least 10% of its gross revenues from outside sources from the same type of activities that the executive furnishes to his past employer, an argument can be made to support the fact that the corporation is validly engaged in a business. Therefore, this is the minimum target that I would suggest for many executives. As long as there is no conflict of interest, it appears that many employers will allow their senior employees to incorporate and seek outside consulting activities — at least to the extent of 10% of all gross revenues. If this is feasible in your case, I strongly suggest that you review these matters with both your employer and your own advisors.

Commissioned Salesmen and Other Consultants

For commissioned salesmen and other consultants the new rules mean that special care must be taken in order to meet the new guidelines. Consider, for example, the case of two incorporated insurance agencies — one selling general insurance and the other selling life insurance. Assume that both employ fewer than six people. Because it sells insurance on behalf of several insurance companies, and derives less than two-thirds of its gross revenue from any one source, the general insurance agency would automatically qualify for a 25% tax rate. On the other hand, a life insurance agency typically sells insurance on behalf of one major insurance company. Since its commission revenue comes primarily from one entity, it will be classified as a business which will not qualify for the low rate — although the 33⅓% rate will apply. Notwithstanding the law, one can argue that this is unfair. This is because both companies are independent agents and have basically similar business activities. Unfortunately, fairness doesn't count.

As a further illustration, a structural engineer whose corporation services one major client in a given year could find his company blocked from the low rate of tax for that year. This may suggest a merger with other unrelated companies within the same field, and if the engineer is not willing to merge, he would have to take into account the cost of higher taxes (at the 33⅓% rate) as a penalty for accepting one major client or contract. (Even a merger may not be advisable since the problem here would be the requirement that the low-rate base of $150,000 be shared among otherwise unrelated parties.)

Organizing the Personal Service Company

For most people, the question of whether or not to set up a personal service company cannot be resolved without the assistance of professional advisors. Your accountant and lawyer should be able to explain your tax position to you, and also *quantify the benefits* which you may hope to derive. Since each individual's income, expenses, family situation, and living requirements are different, one cannot simply rely on what one's friends are doing when it comes to making your own business decisions.

Assuming that such a company is advisable, how is one set up? The steps would include the following:

1. You must decide whether or not the company is to be exclusively concerned with one type of activity only, or whether it will undertake many different kinds of projects.
2. You must then incorporate a company with the appropriate objectives and share-capital — including the right to reinvest accumulated income in diversified investments.
3. The shares must then be issued to the intended shareholders. (At this stage, estate-planning considerations should be taken into account by having, in some cases, the incorporator's spouse and/or children subscribe for shares in the corporation).
4. You must arrange for a management agreement between yourself as the incorporator and the company to be prepared in writing. The agreement should set out in detail the services to be provided by the corporation and the fees to be charged for such services.
5. In the case of a professional practice, the present employees (other than those who are required to be employed directly by the professional) should become employees of the

corporation. The change of employers should not be overlooked when preparing annual T–4 slips.

6. The corporation should then proceed to do everything necessary to enable it to operate. These activities would include opening bank accounts, obtaining a telephone listing, ordering stationery with an appropriate letterhead, arranging with Revenue Canada to make required payroll deductions, and generally carrying out all steps necessary to perform its management contract.

Each step must be carried out in a proper and specific sequence in order to avoid problems at a later date. For example, the corporation should not commence to render services until after its charter has been obtained and until after the management and employment contracts have been duly and properly signed. In addition, if one is setting up a personal service company *following* the severing of one's relationship with an employer, all signs of the previous employment relationship should be removed. For example:

1. The individual should no longer be allowed to sign letters or contracts on behalf of the former employer — especially using the former employer's letterhead.

2. The former employee should be removed from the former employer's group insurance and pension plans.

3. If possible, the service company should operate out of different premises from those where the former employer carries on its business.

4. A company-owned or company-leased car should be surrendered and/or transferred by the past employer to the new service company.

5. Wherever feasible, the executive's corporation should be permitted to carry on outside work as long as it is not in direct conflict with the contractual arrangements with the former employer. Again, if the former employer is unwilling to allow outside revenues amounting to at least 10% of the total, the corporation should probably not be formed in the first place.

CHAPTER NINE

Tax Planning for the Private Canadian Business Where the Small Business Rate Applies

Before 1972, the calculation of corporate income taxes was quite simple. The first $35,000 of annual taxable income was taxed at approximately only 21%. Any taxable income in excess of $35,000 was taxed at around 50%. These were combined federal and provincial rates and although the actual percentages varied slightly from province to province, the concept was clear: a low rate of tax applied initially, followed by a high rate which applied thereafter.

Prior to 1972, no attempt was made to differentiate between large and small companies, and no significant attempt was made to distinguish between business and investment income. In the case of a small company, it was advantageous in many cases, to declare bonuses to the owners in order to keep annual corporate taxable income below $35,000. Beyond that, very little tax planning could be done. Actually, since personal brackets at that time reached as high as 80%, one would not normally recommend large bonuses to avoid the corporate high rate. There was no advantage in "saving" taxes at 50% where the "penalty" was payment of 80% at the personal level.

In trying to refine the corporate tax system, the legislators involved in tax reform came to two conclusions: (1) big companies do not need a low rate of tax to facilitate business expansion, and (2) a corporation should not be available as a vehicle for wealthy taxpayers to shelter investment income from what would otherwise be high rates of (personal) tax.

Under the current system, only Canadian-controlled private corporations are allowed to pay taxes at a low rate. The low rate is also restricted to "active business income". Investment income earned by a private company is initially taxed at 50%, but is subject to the refundable tax rules which were reviewed in Chapter Seven. We have already seen how the tax system for investment income can effectively be beaten through family involvement. In this chapter and the next, we will examine the methods available to optimize after-tax profits from business operations.

The Canadian-Controlled Private Corporation

First, it would be useful to understand the definition of a "Canadian-controlled private corporation" since this is the only kind of company which still has low-rate privileges. By definition, a Canadian-controlled private corporation (CCPC) is a company which is *not controlled* by one or more non-residents *nor* by a combination of non-residents and Canadian public corporations. Because this definition is phrased in the negative, a corporation will qualify for CCPC status even where non-residents or public companies own exactly 50% of the voting shares.

It is not uncommon to find joint-venture arrangements in Canada between Canadian individuals and either public corporations or non-residents. If the joint-venture is carried on through a separate corporation which is owned exactly 50% by each, this corporation will qualify for favourable tax rates. It would often pay the non-residents or public companies to relinquish control for the benefit of the lower rates of tax that would then apply to the joint-venture corporation, since the lower the tax rate on earnings, the greater the ability to pay dividends.

The first $150,000 of active business income earned by a CCPC is taxed at approximately 25% each year. The low rate applies until $750,000 of pre-tax profits have been earned on a cumulative basis for years after 1971. The optimum utilization of the low rate occurs if a company can earn $150,000 each year for five years. If a corporation has the "misfortune", on the other hand, to earn the full $750,000 in its first year of operations, the low rate of tax will only be available in that one year. In subsequent years, having reached the maximum cumulative figure, the low rate will not apply. (In certain cases, if dividends are paid out, the company can again become entitled to the low rate of tax. However, personal taxes would then have to be paid on dividends received by the shareholders.)

Definition of Active Business Income

Until recently, the Income Tax Act did not contain any definition of the term "active business income." Accordingly, by diversifying their activities, taxpayers were able to arrange their affairs so that interest income on mortgage portfolios and rental income on properties could be deemed to be from active businesses. In addition, many individuals took advantage of the generous low rates to incorporate service companies. In late 1979, however, Parliament finally got around to passing legislation tightening these loopholes.

The definition of active business income, which will apply for 1980 and subsequent years, includes manufacturing operations, natural resource activities, construction, logging, farming, fishing, wholesaling and retailing, and transportation. In addition, certain service corporation revenues will qualify, while rental income may be deemed to be from an active business in some cases.

Rental income will only qualify as active business income of a CCPC where the company has a minimum of six full-time employees throughout the year — each of whom owns not more than 10% of the shares of the company and all of whom deal at arm's length with the majority shareholders. Thus, unless a corporation has six or seven rental buildings with full-time janitors, it is unlikely that the income will qualify.

Where the income does not qualify, corporate taxes of approximately 50% will be levied subject to the refundable tax rules which were explained in Chapter Seven. Where a private corporation earns substantially more than $150,000 of profits from rental activities after operating expenses, it pays that corporation to try to carry on with less than six employees. After all, given the refundable tax rules, dividend payments of 66⅔% of earnings are potentially possible. Where the high rate of 50% applies on "active business income" and there is no refundable tax, dividend payments can not exceed the remaining 50% of after-tax profits.

For service corporations, as was discussed in the last chapter, a low rate of tax will only apply if the corporation either has more than five full-time employees or can attain diversification of income. Failing these two tests means a corporate tax rate of 33⅓%, which in itself, is not too bad.

Professionals in medicine, dentistry, law and accountancy will find their corporations paying 33⅓% (on up to $150,000 of profits each year) no matter how much diversification of income and no matter how many employees. These matters have all been discussed in detail in Chapter Eight. For purposes of this chapter and the one which follows, we will therefore deal specifically with income from services which qualifies for the 25% tax rate and with non-service-company income, such as that derived from wholesaling, retailing, construction or manufacturing.

Although the April 21, 1980, Budget introduced a 5% corporate surtax for the calendar years 1980 and 1981, the actual impact of this provision is, at worst, an additional 1.8% of taxable income. Because this amount is immaterial to tax planning, the surtax will be ignored throughout the remainder of this text.

The Meaning of the Small Business Tax Rate

The small business tax rate will allow for after-tax retention of profits by a CCPC of up to 75% on $750,000. This amounts to $562,500. The theory behind the low rate is that the government hopes that these after-tax earnings will be used for business expansion. There are no rules, however, preventing the utilization of this capital build-up, in whole or in part, for investment purposes.

Without the small business deduction, and assuming a tax rate of 50% on all profits, the retained earnings would only be

$375,000 on $750,000. Thus, the small business deduction means approximately $187,500 of potential tax decreases. The actual savings does, however, vary somewhat from province to province. The mechanics of reducing the tax rate from what would otherwise be 50% down to 25% is called the "small business deduction".

Opportunities for Tax Planning

With the foregoing background, (and before exploring CCPCs in detail) one might question whether or not one can tax plan for public companies. For example, what if a public company shows a pre-tax profit on its draft financial statements of $10,000,000?

Since the low rate of tax does not apply to public corporations, one could anticipate taxes of approximately $5,000,000. Can these taxes be avoided? Perhaps. Consider, for example, the declaration of a bonus to the chairman of the board, the president, and five key directors in the full amount of $10,000,000. Naturally, these bonuses would become an expense of the corporation and would reduce the pre-tax profit to nil. This would have the effect of reducing taxes by the $5,000,000 payable in the first place.

Of course, such a scheme would not be feasible. A public corporation is one that traditionally has an ownership that is separate and apart from management. Consequently, the shareholders would be rather upset with any plan along the lines described above. They would certainly rather have $5,000,000 of after-tax profits for themselves than have no profit at all. The purpose of this somewhat ridiculous example is, however, to indicate that tax planning is rather limited for public companies. One can never do anything for the benefit of management that is detrimental to owners, and vice versa.

What about the case of a *non-Canadian controlled* private corporation? Its owner is an American citizen who lives in Florida and never sets foot in Canada. Assume, as well, that the profit of the Canadian company is $100,000. Without any tax planning, it

177

is obvious that taxes payable at 50% (since no small business deduction is available) would amount to $50,000. In this case, could a bonus of the full $100,000 be paid to the non-resident to avoid all Canadian taxes? There would be no complaints from other shareholders because there aren't any. In addition, creditors would not complain as long as their claims are satisfied on time.

The only problem, however, lies with Revenue Canada. There is a nasty little provision in the Income Tax Act which prohibits the deduction of any outlay or expense that is "unreasonable in the circumstances." Faced with the possible loss of $50,000 in tax revenues, the authorities may just try to deem a good part of that $100,000 bonus as unreasonable. Assume that the full bonus were disallowed as an expense. This would result in Canadian taxes of $50,000 — the same amount that one tried to avoid in the first place.

The problem does not, however, end here. In the meantime, for U.S. tax purposes, an American citizen would have received a salary payment of $100,000. This would have to be included in his U.S. income. Assuming U.S. taxes payable of $50,000 on this salary, what would be the result? Out of the original $100,000, there would be Canadian taxes of $50,000 on a disallowed expense and U.S. taxes of $50,000 on a salary. *The net after-tax retention would be zero.*

This scenario is not nearly as ridiculous as the first example involving the public company. The possibility of double taxation is quite real. In fact, the problem could not even be alleviated through an application for foreign tax credits. To obtain a foreign tax credit, one always must be dealing with the *same taxpayer* who is subject to tax under two different jurisdictions. In this case, $50,000 of tax would apply to a Canadian corporation on a disallowed expense, with the other $50,000 being levied against a U.S. individual. When dealing with separate taxpayers, no relief is possible. It is for this reason that accountants and lawyers should be extremely careful in advising their non-resident clients with respect to salary policies. One must be cautious in order to avoid the possibility of severe double taxation.

What about the Canadian-controlled private corporation?

Are there similar restrictions with respect to salary or bonus payments? Fortunately, the situation here is far more flexible. The corporate high rate of tax does not "cut in" until a CCPC has earned over $150,000 of profits. Where a company earns in excess of this amount, the chances are that the owner-manager is already drawing more than, say, $40,000 per annum. The reason for this is simply a function of the owner's standard of living. What good is it to earn a lot of money if one cannot live comfortably?

Assuming, then, corporate profits in excess of $150,000 (and a desire to avoid the high rate of corporate tax), and also assuming that the shareholder-manager is already drawing at least a $40,000 salary (which is deducted in arriving at corporate profits in the first place), I suggest that there is tremendous flexibility. Why should Revenue care about losing 50% corporate tax as long as they are going to get the same dollars (or more) as additional personal taxes? In fact, there have been no reported tax cases on the subject of excessive remuneration of an owner-manager of a Canadian private company.

Remuneration of Spouses

The only time that one raises the possibility of excessive remuneration is where the owner-manager attempts (in an unreasonable manner) to split income with members of his family. In such circumstances, there are two possibilities. Either the excess remuneration will be disallowed, or it will tacked on to the income of the person who really earned it. In practice, the authorities would take the approach that yields the greater tax recovery.

When it comes to dealings with a spouse, you must be careful not to allow your corporation to overpay salaries. Revenue assessors often question the degree of activity of the spouse within the owner-managed business and, based on industry norms, they are often in a position to assess at least a range of values. This range may, of course, be quite broad and, within reason, payments at the top end of the scale should be acceptable. For example, if a husband runs a manufacturing concern and his wife is the office manager, who is to say whether or not she is "worth" $12,000 or $20,000 per annum? Of course, one may even argue that, in some cases, controllers earn over $50,000 a year.

However, accountants and lawyers have evolved a rather interesting method of dealing with such an issue. The concept is called the "chicken threshold". In layman's language, this simply means the point beyond which one is afraid to tax plan aggressively because one is "chicken". While a slight overpayment of salaries may be tolerable, sooner or later everyone reaches his "chicken threshold" — and that's when you should stop. The hard thing to do is to balance your chicken threshold with Revenue Canada's assessment threshold! (The meaning of this latter term should not require any explanation.)

In dealing with spousal remuneration, there are always special circumstances. If, for example, a corporation manufacturers dresses and Mrs. Shareholder is an expert in choosing designs, it may be that she works only the equivalent of three or four weeks a year. Perhaps Mrs. Shareholder is the one who visits London, Paris and New York in order to decide on the styles to be manufactured each season. Clearly, if her choices are good, the company will prosper. Design services of this nature could be worth many thousands of dollars and may not be subject to the normal remuneration criterion which is usually with reference to time spent. Here, the key is the value provided, which is certainly not time-related. Each case is, of course, different and I strongly recommend that the business owner discuss these matters with his own advisors.

Before planning too aggressively, however, there is one particular tax case that is worth mentioning. In this situation, a corporation controlled by a husband paid a salary to the "owner's" wife. The Minister of National Revenue deemed the salary excessive and unreasonable and added it back to the husband's income. The husband objected and the case wound up in court. At that time, the lawyer representing the Minister put the wife on the stand and asked one question: What is the address of your husband's business? She didn't know. Guess who won that case? The moral to be drawn from that situation concerning business involvement is quite evident.

180

Remuneration Guidelines for One's Children

There is also a good deal of flexibility with respect to the role of one's children within the CCPC. If the children are actively involved in the business, reasonable salaries can be paid. Once again, what is reasonable is a matter for conjecture. For example, if my son had just started working for my shoe manufacturing business and I wanted him to learn the operations from the "bottom up", could I cause the company to pay him $50,000 a year for sweeping the floors in the plant? This would not be reasonable. On the other hand, what if my son's title were Vice-President-Maintenance and Director of Sanitary Engineering?

Over the years, I have not noticed Revenue taking too vigilant an approach in auditing remuneration paid to children who are active in the business on a full-time basis. However, a business owner might not wish to overpay in any event because of *non-tax* reasons. Many times, the owner would prefer to avoid the "too much too soon" pitfall and would rather pay higher taxes than overpay his children.

One ploy that is definitely not recommended is the payment of salaries to children where Father then takes back the paycheques and deposits them into his own account. There was, for example, an interesting tax case which was heard a few years ago. In this situation, an Alberta farmer paid each of his ten children $1000 for work allegedly done in that year on the farm. The Minister deemed the payments unreasonable and added them back to the farmer's income. The taxpayer objected and the case wound up in court.

In rendering a decision, the judge found that he had no difficulty accepting the idea that each of the children would have done enough work on the farm to warrant the payment of $1000 apiece. However, the facts showed that the farmer paid each of the children a single lump sum and, on the next day, took the dollars back again into his own bank account. These transactions were alleged to be by way of loans, although no documentation was prepared. In addition, some of the children were minors and could not legally lend money to their father in any event. The judge therefore sided with the Minister and the taxpayer lost. The moral is quite clear. If one pays children, the payments should be bona fide and for services actually rendered.

Where many people fail to take advantage of income tax opportunities is in the area of remuneration to "dependent" children. In 1980, for example, a child eighteen or over qualifies for a personal exemption of $990 as long as that child's net income (after tuition fees, if any) does not exceed $2000. Almost any dependent child has to cost his parents at least $2000 a year for support. If one looks at the owner-managed business as the "golden goose" from which all the golden eggs pass, it becomes evident that if Father is in a 50% bracket, he would personally have to draw $4000 of *additional* pre-tax remuneration to net $2000 for the support of a child.

However, if the child were employed in the business, he or she need only draw a salary of $2000 to net the same amount. There is a potential saving, therefore, of $2000 of "earning power". Also, the salary of $2000 would not even affect Father's personal exemption for that child. Similar provisions also apply with respect to children under the age of eighteen (as long as they make a satisfactory contribution to the business). Thus, there is an opportunity for income splitting and effective tax reduction. Whenever possible, dependent children should become employees of the family business.

The remuneration package should not, however, provide for an annual payment of $2000 on the night before Christmas. Rather, the payments should be made throughout the year commensurate with the services rendered by the child. In all cases, the child should actually work for his remuneration. I would be very unhappy, for example, to try to defend a taxpayer who has paid salaries to a child where the child cannot describe in his or her own words exactly what was done to earn the income. It would also be somewhat difficult to explain away circumstances where payments are made and the parents then take back the money. All salaries paid should, in fact, be deposited to the children's bank accounts and from these accounts expenditures for their benefit should be paid.

Of course, if one is blessed with four teenage children, one may not have enough clerical, office or maintenance work in the business to gainfully employ all four. However, in many circumstances, one can easily justify salaries to one or two children. From an educational perspective, let alone from a tax saving standpoint, employment of the children can be advantageous.

Directors' Fees

There is a common misconception that one can remunerate family members by simply making them directors of the company. Excessive directors' fees are, however, far more vulnerable to reassessment than excessive salaries. This is because there is an established market in Canada for the remuneration of a corporate director.

If a director of a *public* corporation receives between $3000 and $10,000 for his efforts, how can the average Canadian *private* company pay similar amounts on a tax deductible basis? A director of a public company must attend meetings, sit on committees, and is exposed to potential negligence suits. In the case of a private corporation, the meetings are very often a matter of formality only and may not, in fact, really take place.

Remuneration Guidelines for the Owner-Manager Where the Company Qualifies for the Small Business Deduction

Having dealt with salaries to spouses and other members of the family, is it possible to evolve distinct guidelines for the purpose of determining the "best" remuneration package for the owner-manager himself? Actually, such guidelines *can* be established by using simple arithmetic.

For purposes of the examples below, it is assumed that a shareholder-manager of a Canadian private corporation generally operates the business *primarily* in order to satisfy his personal or living requirements. This means that the first "X" dollars earned by the corporation (after paying all other company expenses) must be drawn out one way or another (by salaries, bonuses, or dividends) for the shareholder-manager and his family to live on from day to day. Thus, only dollars *over and above* personal living requirements can be devoted towards savings, and it is these *excess* dollars around which tax planning revolves.

For purposes of illustration, the next example analyses $100 of corporate profits from active business that remains after all operating expenses have been paid for out of revenues and *after* the remuneration needed for living expenses by the shareholder-manager has already been taken. We will examine specifically the sum of $100 and trace the flow of these funds because (1) the amount of $100 is very easy to work with, and (2) we can easily convert from dollars to percentages where our base is 100. However, the *most* important point is that whatever holds true for $100 of business profits of a Canadian-controlled private corporation, also holds true for *any* profits where the small business tax rate applies. In other words, the profit of $100 is representative of a range — all the way from the first dollar of earnings up to the annual business limit of $150,000.

The first possibility is that a shareholder-manager could draw the entire $100 profit by way of salary or bonus, even though he has already satisfied his personal living requirements. As such, depending on how much he has already drawn, we can estimate the taxes payable on an additional draw of $100 as follows:

Amount previously drawn as salary	$18,000	$40,000	$70,000
Combined marginal tax brackets (approximate)	40%	50%	60%
Taxes payable on an additional bonus of $100	$40	$50	$60
After-tax retention on bonus	$60	$50	$40

As an alternative, however, the corporation can retain this profit after paying corporate taxes. Where the small business deduction applies, the corporate tax payable will only be 25% (or

$25) leaving after-tax retained earnings of $75. Thus, *our first conclusion is that a corporation which is subject to the small business deduction can provide to its shareholder-managers the opportunity for a significant tax deferral.* In other words, the company can reinvest significantly more after-tax dollars than the amount otherwise available to the owners themselves.

A COMPARISON OF CORPORATE AND INDIVIDUAL
AFTER-TAX EARNINGS

Corporation

Earnings	$100
Corporate tax	25
Retention	$ 75

Individual

Income level	$18,000	$40,000	$70,000	$108,000
Tax bracket	40%	50%	60%	65%
Salary	$100	$100	$100	$100
Personal tax	40	50	60	65
Retention	$ 60	$ 50	$ 40	$ 35

NOTE: $100 is representative of a range between $1 and $150,000 each year as long as the company is a CCPC and the small business tax rate still applies.

It is evident from the comparison shown above that the minimum tax deferral is 15% based on the underlying income of $100 that was earned in the first place. It is generally unrealistic to assume owner-managers in tax brackets less than 40%. This is because if one anticipates earning below $18,000 per annum for an extended period of time, one would be better off working for someone else. The opportunities for tax deferral do, however, extend to a possible 40% where the owner-manager is in the top tax bracket of 65%.

Meaning of Tax Deferral

In the previous discussion, I have consciously stayed away from referring to the term "tax saving". Actually, there are three possibilities if one opts to allow a corporation to pay tax instead of the owner-manager. Where the corporate tax rate is only 25% and the company has $75 out of $100, it is certainly much easier to subsidize business expansion. Corporate retention would provide many more dollars than if the shareholders were to take out the funds personally and then lend back their after-tax proceeds.

Second, it is important to realize that the accounting concept of a (private) corporation being separate and apart from its owners is a pure fiction. One can never tax plan properly for a private company unless one looks at the owners *and* the company as if they were, in effect, one entity. If, for example, a corporation does not need after-tax profits for business expansion, these same dollars could be used for a build-up of investment capital. The corporation could purchase term deposits, dividend-bearing securities, real estate, gold, silver, or, for that matter, any other kind of investment. All investment decisions would, of course, be those of the owner-managers. Thus, the corporation is simply an extension of its owners. The corporate low rate provides more funds for investment purposes than would otherwise be available to the owners themselves.

However, what if an owner wanted the after-tax profits for personal luxury items? This is the one area where, in a sense, the idea of a corporation being just an extension of its owners breaks down. Soon after a corporation takes its profits and uses them for the personal benefit of its owner-managers, individual taxes must be paid. (See Chapter Two for a discussion of loans to shareholders.) Thus, we do not refer to corporate retention of profits as providing a tax *saving*. It is just a deferral. The advantage of corporate retention lies in *reinvestment* of profits only.

The tax deferral benefits are indefinite as long as the shareholder-manager can afford to leave the dollars inside the company without drawing on them for personal or living expenses. What happens, however, if a shareholder-manager does decide, in some future year, to draw out funds, which have been accumulated by the corporation, for personal or living expenses?

Salaries vs. Dividends

Having caused the corporation to first pay tax on its profits instead of paying out a salary or bonus of $100, the shareholder-manager is now in a position to draw a dividend of *only $75*.

One must never try to compare a $100 salary to a $100 dividend. A salary is paid from pre-tax profits, while a dividend comes out of after-tax corporate earnings. Where the small business deduction applies, one always compares a $100 salary to a dividend of $75.

The example on page 188 illustrates what used to happen when dividends were paid out to shareholder-managers between 1972 and 1977. Unfortunately, we must first deal with some rules that are now obsolete but which should be examined in order to properly understand the evolution of the entire tax system. From 1972 to 1977, the gross-up on Canadian dividends was one-third (instead of the current rate of one-half). This one-third factor applied to a dividend of $75 always produced (for each of the above taxpayers in the example) an income for tax purposes of $100. This income was then subjected to tax in the respective marginal brackets as indicated in the example. However, the tax otherwise payable was then reduced by a dividend tax credit.

The operation of the dividend tax credit was (and still is) the key point to an understanding of how corporate taxes and personal taxes interact when dividends pass through to shareholders.

The Dividend Tax Credit

The federal dividend tax is always three-fourths of the gross-up. Thus, in the following example, the federal dividend tax credit on a cash dividend of $75 (grossed-up to $100) is 3/4 of $25, or $18.75. However, where the example refers to marginal tax brackets, this means not only federal taxes but provincial income taxes as well.

In all provinces, (other than Quebec which has its own tax credit system) provincial taxes are levied as a flat rate percentage of the federal tax otherwise payable. This percentage of provincial taxes is levied *after* the federal income tax has already been

TAX TREATMENT OF DIVIDENDS TO SHAREHOLDER-MANAGERS (1972 – 1977)

Income level	$18,000	$40,000	$70,000	$108,000
Marginal tax brackets	40%	50%	60%	65%
Retention on $100 bonus	$ 60	$ 50	$ 40	$ 35
Dividend in cash = Corporate retained earnings	$ 75	$ 75	$ 75	$ 75
1972–1977 gross-up (1/3)	25	25	25	25
Taxable income	$100	$100	$100	$100
Federal and provincial tax payable	$ 40	$ 50	$ 60	$ 65
Dividend tax credit (combined)	25	25	25	25
Net tax payable	$ 15	$ 25	$ 35	$ 40
Cash flow:				
Cash dividend	$ 75	$ 75	$ 75	$ 75
Net tax	15	25	35	40
Retention on $75 Dividend	$ 60	$ 50	$ 40	$ 35

reduced by the federal dividend tax credit. Thus, in the previous example, if the federal tax otherwise payable is reduced by $18.75, the provincial tax is also reduced by the provincial tax percentage multiplied by $18.75.

In the province of Alberta, for example, the provincial tax percentage is 38.5% of the federal tax. A resident of Alberta who received a cash dividend of $75 in 1977 therefore reduced his federal tax by $18.75 and his provincial tax by 38.5% X $18.75, or by an additional $7.21. The total dividend tax credit (on a combined basis) was therefore $25.96. *In all provinces, (both before 1978 and after) the combined effective dividend tax credit is at least equal to the dividend gross-up.*

Returning to the example on page 188, it is evident that the net retention on a $75 dividend was exactly equal to the net cash retention otherwise possible on a $100 bonus between 1972 and 1977. The effect of the dividend gross-up in those years was to bring the individual shareholder-manager into a position where he was subject to tax on the underlying income that was earned by the corporation in the first place.

The result of the dividend tax credit was then to give that same shareholder-manager an effective credit for the corporate tax that had already been paid on this income. Therefore, the individual shareholder-manager was only responsible to pay the difference between his personal marginal rate of tax and the corporate rate. His after-tax cash flow on a dividend was the *same amount* that he would have received had he taken a bonus or salary of $100 in the first place. This was called an "integrated tax system".

To summarize, the use of a corporation to retain active business income not required by a shareholder-manager for living expenses produced an indefinite tax deferral as long as the small business deduction applied. The deferral ranged from 15% to approximately 40%. The deferral provided excess funds for reinvestment until such time as the shareholder-manager decided to take out dividends. At that point, however, the total tax cost still did not exceed that which would have been paid had the deferral not been chosen.

TAX TREATMENT OF DIVIDENDS TO SHAREHOLDER-MANAGERS (AFTER 1977)

	$18,000	$40,000	$70,000	$108,000
Income level				
Marginal tax brackets	40%	50%	60%	65%
Retention on $100 bonus	$ 60	$ 50	$ 40	$ 35
Dividend in cash = Corporate retained earnings	$ 75	$ 75	$ 75	$ 75
Gross-up (1/2)	37	37	37	37
Taxable income	$112	$112	$112	$112
Federal and provincial tax payable	$ 45	$ 56	$ 67	$ 73
Dividend tax credit (combined)	37	37	37	37
Net tax payable	$ 8	$ 19	$ 30	$ 36
Cash flow:				
Cash dividend	$ 75	$ 75	$ 75	$ 75
Net tax	8	19	30	36
Retention on $75 Dividend	$ 67	$ 56	$ 45	$ 39
OVER-INTEGRATION	$ 7	$ 6	$ 5	$ 4

Effect of 1978 Tax Changes

In 1978, however, the dividend gross-up was raised from 1/3 to 1/2. The new "50% gross-up and credit system" serves to *over-integrate* what was previously a well-balanced system. This is illustrated on page 190. Note that this example starts out with the same numbers as the previous one. The retention on a bonus of $100 has not changed, nor has the corporation's ability to pay a tax of 25% followed by a dividend of $75.

Initially, the new gross-up seems to create a penalty. The taxable income of each representative taxpayer is increased from $75 to $112 — *more* than the underlying income that was earned in the first place. However, while the initial taxes payable are thus higher, the dividend tax credit is *also* larger. Again, the credit is equal to the gross-up. The net tax payable is therefore even smaller than it would have been before 1978. The over-integration is between 4% and 7% of the underlying income ($100) that was earned in the first place.

The purpose of the "new improved" gross-up and credit is apparently to stimulate investment in shares of Canadian companies. Also, if one invests more because of greater after-tax retention, one's spending decreases and this should assist in fighting inflation. In addition, if one invests in one's own private business and the business does well, this benefits the economy overall.

Additional Implications of the New Rules

The effect of the new gross-up and credit has, however, even far more significance. As explained in Chapter Seven, when a Canadian resident has no other income and receives a $30,000 dividend from a Canadian corporation, he will pay *no personal income taxes at all*. (See page 143.)

Although there is no personal tax payable on dividends of up to $30,000 received by an individual, it must be noted that a business would still have to earn $40,000 in order to be capable of paying a $30,000 dividend (after corporate tax). As an alternative to the $30,000 dividend, the corporation could have paid a salary of $40,000, thereby saving the $10,000 of corporate taxes otherwise payable. The individual's tax position would have been as follows:

Salary	$40,000
Less: Personal exemptions and other deductions (estimated)	5,000
Taxable Income	$35,000
On $25,000 tax is approximately	$ 8,100
On $10,000 tax at 46%	4,600
Total taxes	$12,700
Tax saving if *dividend* is paid ($12,700 – $10,000)	$ 2,700
Underlying income earned	$40,000
Over-integration percentage ($2,700 ÷ $40,000)	6.75%

The over-integration of dividends should make one point abundantly clear: wherever possible, almost any business in Canada should be incorporated. This is the case even for the very small family business where the profits are in the $20,000 range and the owners require the entire earnings to meet their personal living expenses. The use of a corporation would enable the owners to convert unincorporated business income in multiples of $100 to dividends in multiples of $75. There would be an absolute tax saving of between 4% and 7%, and one would be foolish not to capitalize on this gift.

In addition, we have seen that there are restrictions on paying wages to family members who have not, in fact, worked and expended sufficient effort to warrant their salaries. However, *the key to receiving dividends is not effort, but share ownership.* Thus for example, if a husband owns a business and his wife is not active, *the corporate structure will allow for effective income splitting, as long as both parties own shares and both receive dividends.*

Tax Planning for a Proper Salary-Dividend Mix

From the foregoing examples, it would appear that salaries are now obsolete — at least where a CCPC is eligible for the low rate of corporate tax. This, however, is not the case. Whenever one tax plans, one must take into account different segments of the legislation contained throughout the Income Tax Act. In this case, specifically, tax planning should include provision for the deferred compensation plans which were discussed in Chapters Three and Four.

For a taxpayer to make use of a registered retirement savings plan, a deferred profit-sharing plan, or even to benefit from the Canada/Quebec pension plan, he requires "earned income". Thus, if a shareholder-manager ceases to draw any salary, he would have to forgo all benefits from the preceding deferred compensation packages. The alternatives of choosing dividends or salaries are compared on pages 194 – 95.

The reason a salary is preferable initially is that the corporation pays a tax rate on 25% on *all* profits (from the first dollar), while an individual does not reach an effective rate of tax of 25% on his income after RRSP contributions and personal exemptions are deducted. The tax saving of a salary over a dividend is, as illustrated, $2025 annually.

Thus in spite of the over-integration of dividends, the first $27,500 earned by a Canadian-controlled private corporation should be paid out to the shareholder-manager as a salary. This amount will make the shareholder eligible for a maximum RRSP contribution and will allow for full participation in the Canada/ Quebec pension plan. The company will then also be permitted to set up a deferred profit-sharing plan to set aside $3500 out of additional earnings.

Since the corporate tax rate on income is 25%, and since the shareholder-manager will then be in approximately a 36% bracket (after his salary) *no additional remuneration* should be paid *unless* the shareholder-manager requires such additional payments for personal or living expenses.

If he does require additional remuneration, all additional

Alternative 1: The corporation pays income taxes on the first
$27,500 of profits (before shareholder-manager remuneration)
and distributes the balance as a dividend. The shareholder then
retains $5500 for investment purposes (to provide ultimately for
his retirement).

Income earned by corporation	$27,500
Corporate income tax at 25%	6,875
	20,625
Less: Dividend paid*	(20,625)
	$ Nil

Cash flow:	
After-tax disposable income	$15,125
Invested for retirement	
(income yield will be taxable)	5,500
Corporate taxes paid	6,875
	$27,500

Alternative 2: A salary of $27,500 is paid, and an RRSP is
purchased (to provide ultimately for the shareholder's retirement).

Salary	$27,500
Less: RRSP	5,500
Net income	22,000
Estimated personal exemptions	5,000
Taxable income	$17,000

On $15,000 federal and provincial taxes are	$ 4,130
On $ 2,000 tax at 36% (combined marginal rate)	720
	$ 4,850

*No personal taxes are payable on the dividend since it is less than $30,000.

Cash flow:
 After-tax retention of salary minus RRSP,
  minus tax; $27,500 – ($5,500 + $4,850) $17,150
 Invested for retirement (income earned on
  RRSP funds will be tax sheltered)   5,500
 Corporate taxes paid (since salary is deductible)   Nil
 Personal taxes paid   4,850
                                                    _____
                                                    $27,500
                                                    =======

Advantage of Salary (i.e., extra disposable income):
 $17,150 – $15,125 = $ 2,025
                                                    =======

payments should be made by way of *dividend* and *not salary* because of the over-integration of dividends. Once one has achieved the full advantage of RRSP's, DPSP's and the Canada/Quebec pension plan, there are no further benefits to be derived out of salaries — as long as the company qualifies for the low corporate tax rate.

Even though personal taxes will have to be paid eventually on withdrawals from an RRSP, the present value of this future liability is significantly less than the initial tax savings of $2025. In addition, the funds within one's RRSP will be able to earn income which compounds on a tax-deferred basis. This is preferable to earning income on investment capital where the income is fully taxed when earned.

Summary

The guidelines for what I consider the best remuneration package for a shareholder-manager of a Canadian-controlled private corporation can thus be outlined as follows where the small-business tax rate applies:

  1. Draw as little income from the corporation as possible and make use of the tax deferral aspects of the small business rate structure.

2. The first $27,500 of gross remuneration should be taken by a shareholder-manager as a salary. $5500 should then be invested into an RRSP.

3. Since the shareholder-manager is then in a 36% tax bracket (after step 2) while "his" corporation pays taxes at only 25%, no additional remuneration whatsoever should be taken out, if possible. This assumes that the shareholder-manager can meet his personal or living expenses on an after-tax retention of approximately $17,150. (The actual dollars will vary from province to province.)

4. If additional remuneration is required for personal or living expenses, any additional remuneration over and above the $27,500 salary should be extracted by way of dividend to take advantage of the 4% to 7% over-integration.

5. $3500 should be invested annually by the corporation into a deferred profit-sharing plan on behalf of the shareholder-manager.

These are general guidelines, and it should be noted that extenuating circumstances may in certain cases, warrant a deviation from the suggested pattern.

Tax Planning for the Family

Logically, if a tax plan is advantageous for one owner-manager, it can provide twice the benefit in the case of two owner-managers. For example, if husband and wife are both active in the business, salaries of $27,500 should be paid to each of them as long as this amount is reasonable. Each would then contribute $5500 into RRSP's. In addition, the corporation could set up a deferred profit-sharing plan for both and contribute $7000 annually. The cash-flow and tax effect of this is illustrated on page 197 (top).

If the illustrated arrangement is feasible, the family's disposable income would be approximately $34,000 and the effective tax cost is only about 16%. *Any time taxes on earnings over $60,000 can be kept to this level, that's tax planning.*

TAX PLANNING FOR HUSBANDS AND WIVES (EARNED INCOME)

	Earnings	Deferrals	Tax	Net Cash
Salary to husband	$27,500	$ 5,500	$ 5,000	$17,000
Salary to wife	27,500	5,500	5,000	17,000
DPSP	7,000	7,000		
	$62,000	$18,000	$10,000	$34,000

Effective tax cost: $\dfrac{\text{Taxes}}{\text{Earnings}} = \dfrac{\$10,000}{\$62,000} = \underline{\underline{\$16.1\%}}$

What happens if husbands and wives do not contribute to a business equally — at least to the point where a salary of $27,500 can be justified for each? Consider, for example, the situation where the husband is active while the wife is at home working hard to bring up children (without receiving any remuneration for this position). They might try this approach to tax planning:

1. Husband should still draw $27,500 by way of salary and make use of the RRSP and DPSP combination.
2. The next $40,000 of pre-tax profits should then be taxed at the corporate level. This would create retained earnings of $30,000 (after 25% corporate taxes).
3. $30,000 could then be paid out as a dividend to the wife. The following example shows how this would work.

AN ALTERNATIVE TAX PLAN FOR HUSBANDS AND WIVES

	Earnings	Deferrals	Tax	Net Cash
Salary to husband	$27,500	$ 5,500	$ 5,000	$17,000
DPSP	3,500	3,500		
Dividend to wife	40,000		10,000	30,000
	$71,000	$ 9,000	$15,000	$47,000

Effective tax cost: $\dfrac{\text{Taxes}}{\text{Earnings}} = \dfrac{\$15,000}{\$71,000} = \underline{\underline{\$21.1\%}}$

In this case, the family's disposable income is $47,000 and the entire tax bite is only 21% on a total income of $71,000. This too is quite inexpensive. Note that the $10,000 tax on the dividend to the wife is *not* really a tax payable by *her* but is the corporate tax payable initially in order to free-up $30,000 of dividends on which no further taxes need be paid.

Separate Classes of Shares

At this point, you might question how one can pay dividends to a wife without also paying dividends to a husband who is (presumably) also a shareholder. The answer is that the company is capitalized by way of several classes of shares.

The idea of using different classes of shares where dividends can be paid on any class to the exclusion of any other has been dealt with in Chapter Seven. As long as the wife in the preceding example has contributed a substantial amount for her shares in relation to anticipated dividends, this technique should pass muster. Of course, if it becomes too popular as a method for income splitting, Revenue may put pressure on the Finance Department for a change in the rules.

Many advisors will still recommend that adventurous planning in this area is in order. Perhaps the key point is my "no worse off" principle. If the family unit *requires* around $47,000 of after-tax income to meet living expenses in any event, there is no better way to meet this objective than that which has just been illustrated. The worst that could happen would be that Revenue could attempt to treat part of the wife's dividend as a deemed dividend to her husband. In such circumstances, one would be no worse off than if part of the dividend had been paid to him in the first place. Thus, there is everything to gain and nothing to lose.

CHAPTER TEN

Maximizing Profits from All Private Canadian Businesses

Taxation Guidelines for Business Income That Does Not Qualify for the Small Business Tax Rate

A Canadian-controlled private corporation that earns active business income in excess of $150,000 in a given year, or which has earned in excess of $750,000 on a cumulative basis, will not qualify for the small business tax rate.* In order to evolve planning guidelines for this group of companies, we will again use an example tracing through $100 of active business income. This time, $100 will represent all amounts that do not qualify for the small business deduction. The range, in this case, is therefore any business profits from $150,001 (in a given year) and up, as well as cumulative profits in excess of $750,000. Again, whatever holds true for $100 will also hold true for all active business income that does not qualify for the low rate. (The exception for manufacturing and processing profits is dealt with later on in this chapter.)

The first example in this section illustrates the alternatives of either paying a salary or bonus currently, or retaining the income in the corporation (and later declaring a dividend). The example illustrates an important point. If the shareholder-manager is in a tax bracket *below* 50%, allowing a corporation to pay taxes on profits at the high rate results in a tax *prepayment*. Of course, one might think that this fact is somewhat academic. It is unlikely that such a profitable corporation (earning in excess of $150,000)

---

*Where a corporation earns in excess of $750,000 of cumulative business profits, it may reinstate its entitlement to the small business rate by paying dividends to shareholders. The shareholders will, however, be required to pay personal taxes on these dividends and the total tax cost becomes quite expensive. This will be explained later in this chapter.

Alternative 1: A bonus of $100 is paid representing active business income that does not qualify for the small business deduction.

Income level	$18,000	$40,000	$70,000	$108,000
Tax bracket	40%	50%	60%	65%
After-tax retention on $100 bonus	$ 60	$ 50	$ 40	$ 35

Alternative 2: The corporation pays tax on its "profit" of $100.

Income of corporation	$100
Corporate tax (high rate applies)	50
Retained earnings	$ 50

Tax deferral (prepayment) where corporation pays the tax	$(10)	Nil	$ 10	$ 15

would have a shareholder-manager content to draw so little income that he does not reach the 50% bracket.

However, one must not underestimate the impact of tax shelters. There are many individuals who forget that they and their companies are really one and the same. There is such an abhorrence towards paying personal taxes that people will apparently go to any lengths to avoid them. Actually, the above example illustrates one of the pitfalls of "over-sheltering" to which I referred in Chapter Five. A taxpayer should never put himself into a tax bracket below that of "his" corporation. *That is a false economy.* If you wish to buy a particular tax shelter because you think it is a good investment, you should either draw additional salary to avoid the tax prepayment or buy the shelter through the corporation in the first place. In fact, there is not only a prepayment in cases where a corporation pays tax at rates higher than personal levels, but there are also severe penalties at the time dividends are later paid out. This will be illustrated next.

Where a shareholder-manager reaches the 50% bracket, the choice between paying a bonus and letting the corporation retain the funds appears to be neutral. In the 60% or 65% bracket, retention by the corporation produces a tax deferral of $10 or $15 for each $100. This is, of course, considerably smaller than the deferral obtained where the small business tax rate applies. Nevertheless, a 10%–15% deferral may still be significant where the earnings are large.

However, to assess the situation completely, we must chart what happens when a shareholder-manager decides (at some future time) to extract dividends. Here, the dividend will be $50 out of each underlying $100 of income and not $75 as was the case in the last chapter. Once again, we must take care never to attempt to compare a $100 bonus to a $100 dividend. Where the small business rate does not apply, the correct comparison is a bonus of $100 against a potential dividend (after corporate taxes) of only $50. The tax consequences when such a dividend is paid are shown in the example on page 202.

The example indicates that there is a substantial tax penalty for individuals in *all* marginal tax brackets for having first allowed active business income to be taxed at high corporate tax rates before dividends are paid out. Actually, the penalty that existed before 1978 when the "old" 1/3 gross-up and credit applied was even larger.

Specific guidelines for tax planning can also be derived from the example. A shareholder in a 40% bracket should automatically draw salaries. This is because of the initial prepayment of $10 per $100, as well as the penalty of 15% which arises upon the payment of dividends. Thus, the example clearly illustrates the disadvantages of oversheltering.

Where shareholders are in 50% brackets, the original choice between personal and corporate tax showed a neutral position. However, at the time of a dividend, there is a penalty of $12 based on each underlying $100 which had been earned initially. Therefore, even an individual in the 50% bracket is better off receiving bonuses in the first place to reduce the amount of corporate tax otherwise payable.

TAX PENALTIES ON DIVIDENDS PAID TO
SHAREHOLDER-MANAGER (NO SMALL BUSINESS DEDUCTION)

Income level	$18,000	$40,000	$70,000	$108,000
Tax brackets	40%	50%	60%	65%
Retention on $100 bonus	$ 60	$ 50	$ 40	$ 35
Dividend in cash = Corporate retained earnings	$ 50	$ 50	$ 50	$ 50
Gross-up (1/2)	25	25	25	25
Taxable income	$ 75	$ 75	$ 75	$ 75
Federal and provincial tax payable	$ 30	$ 37	$ 45	$ 49
Dividend tax credit (combined)	25	25	25	25
Net tax payable	$ 5	$ 12	$ 20	$ 24
Cash flow:				
Dividend	$ 50	$ 50	$ 50	$ 50
Net tax	5	12	20	24
Retention on $50 Dividend	$ 45	$ 38	$ 30	$ 26
Tax penalty	$ 15	$ 12	$ 10	$ 9

For shareholders in brackets of 60% and up, the situation is far more complex. On the one hand, by allowing the corporation to pay tax, there is a 10% to 15% deferral. This means that the corporation has $50 left over (for each $100 that is earned) instead of only $40 or $35 otherwise retained out of a salary or bonus. However, when dividends are paid, there is a 9%–10% tax penalty. The $20 net tax that a shareholder-manager who is in the 60% bracket pays is comprised of:

1. a repayment of the $10 tax deferral previously obtained, and
2. a $10 penalty.

In order to assess what planning methods to adopt for high bracket individuals, one must therefore equate the benefits of tax deferrals

202

against the penalties arising in conjunction with future dividends. Essentially, for purposes of investment decisions, the question reduces itself to: How long does it take money to double? In addition, inflation is also relevant. The tax deferral is in today's dollars while the repayment and penalty can be postponed and paid with dollars that are worth less.

	60%	65%
Tax bracket		
Tax deferral: ($50 – $40); ($50 – $35)	$10	$15
Future tax liability on dividend of $50 after tax credit	$20	$24
The future tax liability is made up of:		
Repayment of tax deferral	$10	$15
Tax penalty	10	9
	$20	$24

Whenever the period of tax deferral is long enough, the advantage to be attained by having additional funds to invest will override an ultimate tax penalty. A decision should therefore be based on the length of time that the shareholder-manager thinks that he can go without drawing funds out of his corporation.

As a general rule, many tax advisors feel that if a corporation is marginally into the top bracket (with a taxable income of, say, $160,000) it is advantageous to be conservative and cause the corporation to pay out a bonus equal to the excess profits (in this instance $10,000). This would reduce active business income to $150,000 — all of which would qualify for the small business rate. (Of course, the corporation would qualify for the small business deduction on the first $150,000 in any event, but in the absence of the bonus, the additional $10,000 would be taxed at 50%.) Paying this bonus of $10,000 does away with any potential tax deferral but also removes a future tax penalty.

On the other hand, if a corporation earns $500,000 in a given year, there are very few advisors who would recommend that the shareholders declare bonuses of $350,000 to "remove" income that does not qualify for the low rate. Why pay at a 65% personal rate just to save 50% corporate tax? If an "owner" is in the 60% bracket or higher and is likely to stay there, and if his corporation is so profitable that it will consistently earn more than $150,000, trying to preserve the small business tax rate becomes impractical. In such situations, the advantages of tax deferral will, over the long run, outweigh the disadvantages of the double tax. In these cases, the shareholder-manager is not likely to require a large amount of additional remuneration in the near future by way of dividends in any event.

Similarly, once a corporation has earned a cumulative total of $750,000 of business profits, dividend payments out of previously taxed earnings (to reinstate entitlement to the low rate) coupled with an ongoing salary program to keep annual profits down becomes costly. Again, if the shareholder is in a 60% tax bracket or higher, it becomes cheaper in the long run to suffer the 50% corporate tax rate.

Other Factors

In making a decision whether or not to declare bonuses, other factors should also be taken into account. These include the following:

1. Will the shareholder-manager retire in the near future and be able to draw dividends while in a lower tax bracket?
2. Are there members of the family in low brackets who are also shareholders and who could derive tax benefits from dividends?
3. Is the company going to be sold or is it going to "go public"? Perhaps, in such cases, the shareholder-manager will be able to derive additional proceeds on the disposition of his shares if he leaves profits in the company. His tax on higher capital gains could be less than his effective tax on dividends.

Income from Manufacturing and Processing

Since 1973, a special incentive provision has had the effect of reducing the *basic* corporate tax rate on manufacturing and processing profits to 40%, with a parallel reduction to 20% where the small business deduction is also applicable.

Although the term "manufacturing and processing" is not defined in the Tax Act, there are several industries such as farming, fishing, logging, on-site job construction, and certain exploration activities which are specifically *excluded* from the incentives. In addition, the rules require that at least 10% of a corporation's gross revenue for the year from all active businesses be from the sale or lease of goods that are manufactured or processed by that corporation in Canada.

Because there is no specific definition as to what is included, one is free to take a very liberal interpretation of the term "manufacturing and processing". For example, the activities of a restaurant should be eligible for this incentive since a restaurant processes food. Similarly, a newspaper or magazine processes paper and even though the major revenue is derived from advertising, it can be said that publishing still qualifies.

Any time a business purchases goods in bulk and repackages them for sale in small quantities, it would appear advantageous to at least try to claim the reduced tax rate. Again, the "no worse off" principle would apply. I had one particular client that was able to save $36,000 in taxes last year by simply mixing with water certain chemicals that had originally been purchased for resale to customers.

Calculating Manufacturing and Processing Profits

Once it is determined that a corporation is engaged in manufacturing or processing, there is a formula to determine what percentage of active business income is deemed to be from these activities. The formula may be expressed as follows:

$$\text{Manufacturing and Processing Profits} = \text{Active Business Income} \times \frac{\dfrac{100}{75} \text{X} \dfrac{\text{Manufacturing}}{\text{Labour}} + \dfrac{100}{85} \text{X} \dfrac{\text{Manufacturing}}{\text{Capital}}}{\text{Total Labour} + \text{Total Capital}}$$

This formula ties in manufacturing and processing profits as a percentage of active business income based on a composite of both labour and capital (fixed assets) employed. The first part of the formula takes into account manufacturing labour and total labour for the year. The formula recognizes that even "pure" manufacturing companies require a certain amount of non-qualifying "support" labour. For example, every business must have sales people, an office staff and executive personnel. The fraction "100/75" allows for a 25% support factor. As long as not more than 25% of the total labour is devoted to non-qualified activities, the gross-up of 100/75 will produce no erosion in the amount of active business income that qualifies for the credit.

"Capital", as used in the formula, includes both fixed assets owned and leased (other than land). The fraction "100/85" means that a corporation can have some non-qualified fixed assets without eroding its manufacturing and processing base — as long as these assets do not exceed 15% of the total. Thus, a capital investment in office and showroom furniture or automobiles will not necessarily reduce the availability of the special rate.

Tax Planning for the Manufacturing and Processing Incentive

Because of the arbitrary nature of the above formula, there are some excellent tax planning ideas that can be adopted. For example, take the situation of a corporation engaged in both manufacturing and non-manufacturing activities. If the corporation's manufacturing profits are high while the non-manufacturing branch operates at just above break-even, one should consider splitting the business into two separate companies. One would transfer as much as possible of the non-manufacturing labour, fixed assets (such as office equipment) and overheads to the non-manufacturing company, and one would keep the manufacturing operations as "pure" as possible. Thus, the non-manufacturing activities would not diminish the use of the special deduction, as could be the case if the two types of operations were combined under one corporate roof.

Conversely, if manufacturing and non-manufacturing activities are carried on by two separate but related corporations, and the manufacturing business is marginally successful while non-manufacturing is very profitable, one should consider amalgamating the two corporations. Because of the arbitrary percentages in the formula, a portion of the non-manufacturing profits may end up qualifying for the deduction.

It is important to note that the manufacturing incentives apply to *all* corporations, even if public or non-Canadian controlled. There is ample opportunity in many instances to obtain absolute tax savings. *This is even better than building tax deferrals*, which has been the subject matter of the greater portion of Chapters Nine and Ten.

Tax Planning for Owner-Managed Manufacturing and Processing Operations — Salaries vs. Dividends

In order to complete our examination of the remuneration guidelines for corporations and their shareholders, we should now review the integration concepts as they apply to corporate tax rates of 20% or 40%.

Logically, if a 25% corporate tax results in deferrals followed by an over-integration of dividends, one would expect to find even better results where the initial corporate rate is only 20%. Also, where the corporate tax rate is 40%, one would expect to find some tax deferrals but, nevertheless, an ultimate tax penalty on payment of dividends. Depending on the brackets of the shareholders and the length of time of the deferral, it may pay to forgo the small business deduction and allow the corporation to pay 40% without worrying too much about double taxation. These points are illustrated by the next two examples.

DIVIDEND VS. SALARY WHERE A 20% TAX RATE APPLIES

		$18M	$40M	$70M	$108M
Income level					
Tax brackets		40%	50%	60%	65%

Alternative 1

		$18M	$40M	$70M	$108M
After-tax retention on $100 bonus		$ 60	$ 50	$ 40	$ 35

Alternative 2:
The corporation pays tax on profit of $100

Income of corporation	$100				
Corporate tax (after small business deduction and the manufacturing and processing tax credit)	20				
Retained earnings	$ 80				

		$18M	$40M	$70M	$108M
Tax deferral where corporation pays the tax		$ 20	$ 30	$ 40	$ 45

Payment of dividend

	$18M	$40M	$70M	$108M
Cash Dividend	$ 80	$ 80	$ 80	$ 80
1/2 gross-up	40	40	40	40
Income for tax purposes	$120	$120	$120	$120
Federal and provincial tax in marginal bracket	$ 48	$ 60	$ 72	$ 78
Dividend tax credit (combined)	40	40	40	40
Net tax	$ 8	$ 20	$ 32	$ 38
Cash flow (cash dividend of $80 minus net tax)	$ 72	$ 60	$ 48	$ 42
Cash flow on $100 bonus	$ 60	$ 50	$ 40	$ 35
Advantage of dividend of $80 over salary of $100	$ 12	$ 10	$ 8	$ 7

DIVIDEND VS. SALARY WHERE A 40% TAX RATE APPLIES

		$18M	$40M	$70M	$108M
Income level		$18M	$40M	$70M	$108M
Tax brackets		40%	50%	60%	65%

Alternative 1
After-tax retention on
  $100 bonus

		$ 60	$ 50	$ 40	$ 35

Alternative 2:
The corporation pays tax on
  profit of $100

Income of corporation	$100				
Corporate tax (after manu-facturing and processing tax credit only)	40				
Retained earnings	$ 60				
Tax deferral (prepayment) where corporation pays the tax		Nil	$ 10	$ 20	$ 25

Payment of dividend

	$18M	$40M	$70M	$108M
Cash Dividend	$ 60	$ 60	$ 60	$ 60
1/2 gross-up	30	30	30	30
Income for tax purposes	$ 90	$ 90	$ 90	$ 90
Federal and provincial tax in marginal bracket	$ 36	$ 45	$ 54	$ 58
Dividend tax credit (combined)	30	30	30	30
Net tax	$ 6	$ 15	$ 24	$ 28
Cash flow (cash dividend of $60 minus net tax)	$ 54	$ 45	$ 36	$ 32
Cash flow on $100 bonus	$ 60	$ 50	$ 40	$ 35
Penalty for not having taken bonus of $100	$ 6	$ 5	$ 4	$ 3

The first example (p.208) deals with income of $100 which qualifies for both the small business deduction and the manufacturing and processing incentives. Again, as in the situation where a 25% corporate tax applies, it appears at first that the remuneration guidelines should only include dividends. This however is not the case. For the reasons given in Chapter Nine, the first $27,500 of shareholder-manager remuneration should still be by way of salary. This would enable the shareholder-manager to take advantage of an RRSP and would allow the company to tax-shelter an additional $3500 through a deferred profit-sharing plan. Any additional remuneration beyond this base salary should be by way of dividends. At this point, a 7%–12% advantage sets in (over the corresponding alternative of additional salaries.)

The next example (p.209) covers the taxation of manufacturing income which does not qualify for the small business deduction. This would happen in the case of a Canadian-controlled private corporation where the profit exceeds $150,000. From the example, it can be seen that only a taxpayer in a 40% bracket or less would not get a deferral advantage by allowing the corporation to pay the tax. Of course, it is very unlikely that the taxpayers would be in brackets below 50% (unless they have "over-sheltered" by other means), considering that we are dealing with income from an active business in excess of $150,000 per annum.

Where the shareholder is in a 50% bracket or higher, corporate retention provides a potential tax deferral of between 10% and 25%. On future payment of dividends, the tax penalty is quite small. An investment of the dollars deferred within the corporation for only a short time will generally override the adverse effects of the penalty.

As a general guideline, therefore, when business income qualifies for the manufacturing incentives, but is substantially in excess of that which is eligible for the small business deduction, the loss of the small business credit is not of serious consequence. Over the long run, if a shareholder-manager does not need to draw large sums of money out of "his" corporation immediately upon (or soon after) earning it, the tax deferral advantages will more than outweigh the negative impact of double taxation.

The Inventory Deduction

A discussion of business income would not be complete without a reference to the special 3% inventory deduction which was introduced into the Tax Act a few years ago. For years, business owners have complained that profits for tax purposes have been overstated as a result of inflation. Assume, for example, that a business sells a product at $20 per unit. If the cost per unit is $16, each item sold gives rise to a profit of $4. Also assume, however, that the selling price is relatively fixed because of competition, but to replace a unit of inventory now costs $18. In such circumstances, the company may have to use its entire profit just for inventory replacement and the "real" pre-tax gain on the first sale should therefore be only $2. If the entire $4 profit were taxable (at full corporate rates) the business would not really be earning anything.

	First Unit	Second Unit
Selling Price (fixed)	$ 20	$ 20
Cost	16 ⟶	18
Profit for tax purposes	$ 4	
Taxes thereon (50%)	(2)	
	2	
Less: Additional cost of Second Unit	(2)	
"Real" profit	Nil	

In order to alleviate this problem, Parliament introduced a 3% inventory deduction in 1977. The inventory deduction applies to the opening inventory of tangible property held for resale by any business. The only excluded businesses are those that are engaged in property ownership and development. (This is because real estate tends to appreciate in any event with inflation.)

The inventory deduction applies not only to finished goods but also to raw materials and work-in-progress. It is a permanent difference between accounting profits and profits for income tax purposes. Thus, if a corporation has a $100,000 profit for accounting purposes while its opening inventory was, say, $600,000, the inventory deduction of $18,000 would reduce income for tax purposes to only $82,000.

The deduction is also not recapturable. It never has to be brought back into income whether or not, in fact, inflation causes an overstatement of profits for tax. Certainly, the 3% factor is somewhat arbitrary and the rules tend to benefit those businesses with low inventory turnovers. A meat packer who turns over his inventory daily may not get much benefit from this deduction, while a jewellery store which might be capable of raising its prices weekly can get an extra advantage.

Planning to Maximize the Inventory Deduction

The arbitrary nature of the inventory deduction lends itself to extensive tax planning. Traditionally, businesses have always chosen year ends when inventory levels are lowest. This is to facilitate the preparation of financial statements where the most difficult task is usually the job of counting stock. Because of the 3% deduction, however, thought should be given to changing year ends (or establishing them in the first place) at the point when inventory is *highest*. Of course, if the costs of stock-taking exceed the tax savings, this is not feasible. However, such a change in policy is definitely recommended for businesses that sell "big ticket" items. Good examples would include dealers in cars or appliances, and jewellery and fur distributors.

For example, a car dealer is likely to have a constant inventory of parts throughout the year. (He never has in stock what you need in any event and it is always on back order.) However, in November, he might only have twenty new cars on the lot, while at the end of May, he might have eighty units. How much longer does it take to count an additional sixty cars? Yet, the effect on the value of inventory and the 3% deduction becomes extremely significant. The same would hold true for a store selling television sets, where inventory would generally be lowest at the end of

January after the post-Christmas sales and highest at the end of November.

If it is not feasible for a business to change its year end, it may still be possible to accelerate purchases so that more goods are held at the end of the fiscal year. This is especially feasible if extended credit terms can be obtained from suppliers. If this "excess" inventory is stockpiled and not even unpacked, one would simply add the dollar value of purchases to both inventory and accounts payable and there is no effect on either profitability or the cost of stock-taking. Consistent use of this method would produce a higher inventory from year to year, with the closing inventory of each year forming the basis of the *following* year's 3% deduction.

In the year that one changes inventory policies, the company's banker must be informed. Otherwise, anyone reviewing the financial statements from a lender's standpoint would see a dramatic increase in inventory and would be somewhat concerned about the liquidity position of the business.

To maximize inventory, it is not even necessary to take delivery of goods. The courts have held that goods belong to an entity as long as legal title passes, even if they are held by someone else. If one has a supplier who is willing to hold goods but still transfer ownership before the purchaser's year-end, the inventory deduction benefits flow. Of course, if the supplier has the same year end as his customer, he should be unwilling to make such an accommodation. This is because increasing the customer's inventory has the effect of decreasing his own.

Finally, in some cases, it may be possible to defer the last day's sales. If a furrier sells a coat on the last day of his year, it is usually possible to arrange to have the sale dated the following day. After all, in almost all cases, there would be some alterations and delivery would not be immediate. In this way, the furrier could get a double-edged advantage. His closing inventory would be that much higher and he could also postpone the recognition of his profit until the following fiscal year.

These are all legitimate methods of maximizing the 3% inventory deduction. Other (not so legitimate) methods come to mind, such as purchasing goods just before the year end and then returning them for a credit note shortly thereafter. One might even consider going so far as to obtain an invoice from a "friendly" supplier for goods that were, in fact, never shipped. A credit note would follow in due course. If one has several corporations within one's "group", each with different year ends, Companies A and B could consider a transfer of their inventories to Company C as of this latter company's year-end. Then, at A's year-end, B and C could transfer their stock to A and so on.

These latter methods are certainly not recommended since they at least border on being fraudulent. Also, the Income Tax Act was amended recently to prohibit artificial schemes conceived to extend the benefits of the inventory deduction. This, of course, does not negate some very real opportunities for effective tax planning, as long as the methods chosen are reasonable.

CHAPTER ELEVEN

The Art of Buying a Business
& the Use of Holding Companies

Introduction

One of worst traps that you can possibly fall into is to buy shares of
a private business in your own name. Proper tax planning almost
always involves the use of a holding company for business
acquisitions. If you take the easy way out and transact directly, you
could end up paying more taxes as a result of this one error than
from all your other mistakes combined.

Holding companies have many other uses beyond being the
ideal vehicle for business acquisitions. In fact, they are the key to
"empire building". However, before we can fully appreciate the
use of holding companies and their role in the tax system, a short
review of some preceding material is in order. As described in the
last two chapters, the Income Tax Act is designed so that corporate
taxes are levied on business income at one of several different
effective rates:

1. Income that is from manufacturing and that qualifies for
   the small business deduction is taxed at 20%.
2. Income that qualifies for the small business deduction but is
   not from manufacturing is taxed at 25%.
3. Income which is from manufacturing but which does not
   qualify for the small business deduction is taxed at 40%.
4. Income that neither qualifies for the small business deduction nor is related to manufacturing is taxed at 50%.

In addition, we have seen that professional corporation revenues
and certain other service company income is taxed at approximately 33⅓%.

When a dividend is received by an individual from an

"operating company" (Op Co) the system of gross-up and credit at least partially compensates for the fact that the dividend is a distribution out of profits that have already been taxed once. The shareholder is credited for at least part of the corporate taxes previously paid and, in some cases, the system even over-compensates.

It is, however, possible that an individual shareholder might not own his interest in Op Co directly but through a "holding company" (Hold Co). In such circumstances, dividends would pass from Op Co to Hold Co before the individual could receive any funds personally.

Mr. X

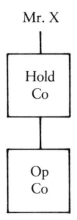

DIVIDEND FLOW FROM OPERATING COMPANY THROUGH HOLDING COMPANY TO INDIVIDUAL

The Taxation of Inter-Corporate Canadian Dividends Out of Business Income

If the system taxed dividends passing from one corporation to another (out of business income), one can visualize that if a *chain* of corporations existed, there would be less and less ultimately available for the person at the "top" of the chain. If that were the case, the individual would suffer double and triple taxation depending on how many corporations stood between him and the source of income in the first place. This is illustrated in the following example, which assumes (for purposes of discussion only) the inter-corporate dividends out of business income were subject to *even one dollar* of tax.

IF INTER-CORPORATE DIVIDENDS OUT OF BUSINESS INCOME
WERE TAXED (ALL NUMBERS REPRESENT $)

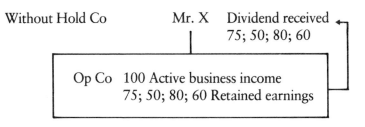

Without Hold Co   Mr. X   Dividend received
                                   75; 50; 80; 60

Op Co   100 Active business income
        75; 50; 80; 60 Retained earnings

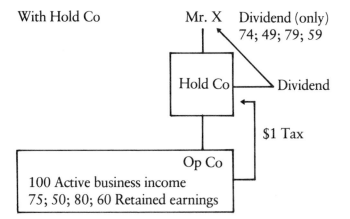

With Hold Co   Mr. X   Dividend (only)
                                   74; 49; 79; 59

Hold Co ——→ Dividend

$1 Tax

Op Co

100 Active business income
75; 50; 80; 60 Retained earnings

To avoid double taxation, the system provides that only the corporation which earns business income (i.e., Op Co) pays tax on that amount and type of profit. If there is any further tax to be paid, the rules are also designed so that this additional tax is not extracted until an *individual* ultimately receives dividends.

Thus, dividends received by one corporation from another out of business income pass *tax-free*. This is the case as long as the recipient corporation has a "substantial interest" in the capital stock of the payer. A substantial interest is defined as *more than 10%* of both the paid-up capital and the voting powers of the other corporation.

An interest of "10% or less" is referred to as a "portfolio investment". Portfolio dividends are subject to a special 25% flat-rate (refundable) tax, which was dealt with in Chapter Seven. Before 1978, a portfolio holding existed where any corporation owned 50% or less of the voting shares of another corporation. Thus, dividends only passed tax-free where the recipient company had control. Of course, in any given situation, it is only possible for one corporation to control another. Under the new rules, however, as many as nine corporations could have substantial interests in the shares of another company. Dividends flowing from that company to all these corporate shareholders would not be taxable.

Tax Planning Opportunities

If a significant interest in an operating business is acquired, the purchase can now be structured through a holding company so that the acquired corporation can end up *paying for itself* by flowing through dividends to its new "parent". (For purposes of this analysis, the term "parent" will refer to any situation where one corporation acquires an interest greater than 10% in another.) The following example illustrates the advantages of using a holding company to make an acquisition of an operating business.

Assume that Mr. X is an investor in the 60% bracket. He would like to acquire an interest in Op Co that is greater than 10%. He negotiates with the prospective vendor, and the purchase price is settled at $100,000. Assume, as well, that Mr. X does not have the necessary cash to make the purchase. He does, however, know of a lending institution that is willing to finance the acquisition.

Effectively, the transaction can be structured in one of two ways: either Mr. X can make the acquisition personally, or he can use a holding company to do so on his behalf. In either case, interest incurred on the borrowed funds will be tax deductible since his loan is for the purpose of earning income.

218

However, what about principal repayments? Presumably, Mr. X would not make an investment in Op Co unless he felt sure that the investment would ultimately pay for itself. In other words, he would expect that dividends from the newly acquired company would subsidize its cost. If Mr. X makes the purchase in his own name, he would have to draw dividends over a period of time so that his after-tax retention is sufficient to pay off the financing of $100,000. As described in the examples in Chapter Seven, an individual in the 60% bracket pays an effective tax of 40% on Canadian dividend income — after the gross-up and credit. Thus, Mr. X would need $166,666 of *gross* dividends to retain a net amount of $100,000 for purposes of discharging his bank indebtedness.

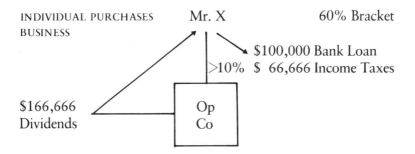

INDIVIDUAL PURCHASES BUSINESS — Mr. X — 60% Bracket

$100,000 Bank Loan
>10% $ 66,666 Income Taxes

$166,666 Dividends

Op Co

60% Bracket

Dividend	$100
Gross up	50
Taxable dividend	$150
60% tax	$ 90
Tax credit	50
Net tax	$ 40

Effective tax on dividends is 40%

Let D = Gross dividends needed to pay off bank
$.60D$ = $100,000
D = $166,666

In contrast, if a holding company is used to structure the purchase, Op Co will only have to generate $100,000 of dividends to its new "parent". As long as the parent holds more than 10% of the shares of the subsidiary, the dividend will be received tax-free and can then be paid over *directly* to the lending institution. To summarize, with proper planning, *it is possible for Mr. X to save as much as $66,666 for every $100,000 of purchase cost.*

Carrying this example one step further, if an extra $66,666 is not needed to pay taxes at the personal level, Op Co "saves" not only the dividend itself, but an even greater amount of "earning power". If Op Co is eligible for the small business deduction, the company can afford to channel $88,888 of pre-tax earnings into other areas. If Op Co is extremely profitable and pays taxes at the high corporate rate, the fact that $66,666 is not needed translates to an earning power of $133,333. This is illustrated below.

With the small business deduction Op Co "saves" $88,888 of earning power		Without the small business deduction Op Co "saves" $133,333 of earning power	
Earnings	$88,888	$133,333	
25% tax	22,222	66,666	50% tax
Dividend (not needed)	$66,666	$ 66,666	

From the foregoing, it becomes evident that one *must* use a holding company as a vehicle to acquire shares of other companies, at least where the share interest is greater than 10%. *To do otherwise would result in unnecessary personal taxes that could be easily avoided with proper planning!*

Although the example assumes that the purchase price is borrowed from a lending institution, the same planning would hold true even if Mr. X acted as his own banker. He would want to be able to recoup his investment on a tax-free basis, without the necessity of extracting dividends subject to personal taxes. This

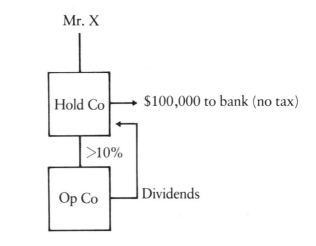

Mr. X

Hold Co → $100,000 to bank (no tax)

>10%

Op Co — Dividends

Only $100,000 is needed to pay off loan
Op Co "saves" $66,666 of dividends

can be achieved by lending his own capital to the holding company, which would in turn acquire Op Co. Dividends could then be paid from Op Co to the holding company and the funds could be used to repay Mr. X's own advances.

Is there a catch? You might ask why the government has been so magnanimous as to have permitted such a wonderful opportunity to structure business acquisitions. Fortunately, there is no oversight in the law and the use of holding companies for such purposes is by no means a sham nor does it constitute undue tax avoidance.

The reason the government has relaxed the rules on the flow of inter-corporate dividends is that for every acquisition there is a corresponding sale. So far, we have only examined the position of a purchaser. For every purchaser there is a vendor who will be paying a "capital gains tax" as a result of having sold his interest in Op Co. If the government gets its capital gains tax "up front" from the vendor, they may as well make it easier for the purchaser to buy.

You might also wonder whether the government is sacrificing substantial revenue by permitting a purchaser to structure his affairs to avoid taxes on dividends. Actually, there is no loss from the treasury's standpoint, as will be discussed in the next section.

The Relationship between Dividends and Capital Gains

Most of us have to reorient our thinking if we wish to use the tax system effectively. Until 1972, everyone preferred capital gains to any other type of "income" because there was no tax at all. Even after 1971, one-half of capital gains are tax-free. However, the 50% gross-up and credit that took effect in 1978 changes the relationship between dividends and capital gains. As strange as it may seem, most Canadians should now prefer receiving dividends to capital gains — even though dividends are *fully* taxable. This can be shown with the aid of the simple example below:

Individual's tax bracket	40%	50%	60%
Effective tax on $100 dividend (after gross-up and credit)	$10	$25	$40
Effective tax on $100 capital gain (taxable gain is $50)	$20	$25	$30

As discussed in Chapter Seven, the effective tax on dividends is only 10% to someone who is in the 40% bracket. Thus, taxpayers in 40% brackets or lower will pay significantly less tax on dividends than they would on capital gains. Where an individual is in the 50% bracket, the choice between receiving a dividend and a capital gain is neutral. For individuals in the 60% bracket, capital gains are still preferable (in spite of the new, improved dividend tax credit) but the difference is very small — only $10 for every $100. Thus, the government has obviously decided that it really doesn't matter whether a tax on capital gains is paid by a vendor or whether a tax on dividends is charged to a purchaser.

Of course, no attempt is made to publicize the advantages of using holding companies for business acquisitions. Presumably, Revenue officials would not be too upset about receiving tax dollars *twice* — once from a vendor when he pays tax on capital gains arising from his sale, and again from the purchaser when he struggles to pay for an acquisition which he has made personally.

Corporate Reorganizations

The use of holding companies also has advantages when it comes to reorganizing existing business situations. Assume, for illustration, that Mr. A, Mr. B, and Mr. C are unrelated parties, each of whom owns one-third of the issued shares of an operating company. The operating company, for purposes of this example, has $75,000 in surplus cash that has been generated from prior operations. While Messrs. A, B, and C get along quite well when it comes to administering the daily affairs of their company, they do not necessarily see eye to eye when it comes to investments. Mr. A is a big spender and would like to draw his share of the surplus funds as a dividend in order to meet his living requirements. Mr. B, on the other hand, wishes to invest his share of the money in term deposits, while Mr. C would like to acquire real estate. Under the existing structure (illustrated below), a problem exists because the diverse objectives could not be realized without paying out taxable dividends.

BEFORE REORGANIZATION

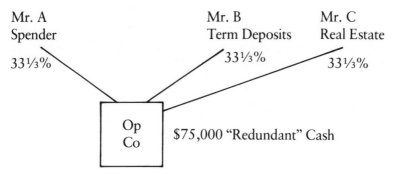

223

If, however, the shareholders each had personal holding companies, the problem could be solved. Using special provisions of the Income Tax Act, each of Messrs. A, B and C could transfer his shares to his own holding company (on a tax-free basis) in exchange for shares of the holding company. Op Co could then pay three dividends of $25,000 to each of the "new" shareholders. Mr. A, in turn, could draw his portion as a further dividend and use the after-tax proceeds for living expenses, while Messrs. B and C could cause their holding companies to invest in term deposits and real estate respectively.

HOLDING COMPANIES CAN BE USED TO MEET SHAREHOLDERS' DIVERSE REQUIREMENTS

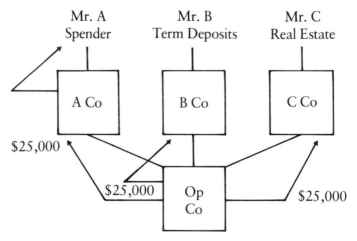

Mr. A could obtain a further advantage by dividing the ownership of A Co among his family. If the Op Co dividend of $25,000 were split between the family members, it is possible that the tax bite could be eliminated completely.

Another advantage of the holding company structure just described is that each of A, B and C would be free to involve their families in the ownership of their personal holding companies without necessarily consulting their other "partners". In cases where the shares of Op Co are held directly, Mr. B might (for example) object to Mrs. A being a shareholder. No similar objections could be voiced by Mr. B with respect to A Co's share structure.

In summary, holding companies can be very effective in segregating the diversified spending or investment desires of business owners from their common operating objectives. There are also other advantages. By keeping Op Co free from excess or "redundant" assets, if business ever turns sour, there is less for the creditors to seize — although this does not mean that a corporation can pay large dividends where bankruptcy is already imminent. In addition, Op Co becomes far more saleable if it does not own assets that a prospective purchaser would not be interested in acquiring. Investments out of excess profits could be made by the holding companies just as easily, and there is no need for any prior payment of personal taxes.

While holding companies have their advantages as a vehicle to reorganize business situations, the complexities of rearranging one's affairs should not be understated. For example, specific tax rules must be followed in order to transfer shares in a business to a holding company without attracting tax. In addition, if Messrs. A, B and C had owned their shares in Op Co before 1972, certain other tax problems could arise with respect to capital gains considerations. These complexities would have to be handled by qualified legal and accounting professionals.

Finally, it should be stressed that the use of holding companies is primarily for the benefit of flexibility. The fact that A Co is owned only by Mr. A, and B Co by Mr. B, etc. will *not* provide for a multiple use of the small business deduction. In other words, for all practical purposes, the entire group of companies will only be permitted to earn $150,000 annually and $750,000 cumulatively at low corporate rates.

Certainly, the use of holding companies for the purpose of reorganizing existing structures is worth exploring, while holding companies should almost always be used in the first place for business acquisitions.

Bringing Buyers and Sellers Together

A comparison of the net tax costs of dividends and capital gains for taxpayers in various marginal brackets lends itself to some excellent planning opportunities to bring buyers and sellers together. An advisor working with both parties and without any personal involvement can help greatly to facilitate business acquisitions.

For example, if a prospective vendor of a business is in a low tax bracket, it would be advantageous for that individual to take a dividend from "his" company *before* selling his shares. Of course, if he takes a dividend, this would reduce the tangible net worth of the company and would result in a corresponding decrease in the purchase price. If the purchase price is reduced by the same amount as the dividend, the vendor's capital gain would become that much smaller and the tax thereon is decreased as well. Thus, a vendor in the 40% bracket could pay ten cents on the dollar on a dividend, instead of twenty cents on capital gains.

Very often, good timing can help a deal progress much more smoothly. If a business sale and purchase is being negotiated towards the end of the year, it may be advantageous for the vendor to take a dividend before December 31. He would then sell his shares (for a smaller price) on January 2, and in this manner, the dividend and the capital gain would be taxed in different years.

Sheltering a Vendor's Tax

Whenever an individual makes a capital gain, he should consider spreading his tax through an income-averaging annuity contract (IAAC). Capital gains is one of the special non-recurring types of income that qualify for these annuities, which were already dealt with in Chapter Three. Of course, the ideal situation is a sale of a business, followed by the purchase of an IAAC and a subsequent non-residency. This is because of the very favourable tax treatment (also discussed in Chapter Three) with respect to annuity payments received by non-residents.

Fortunately for the Canadian government, however, not

everyone who sells a business leaves the country. About three years ago, I was advising a client who was selling a rather large, privately owned business and was planning an immediate retirement. His taxable capital gain was well in excess of a million dollars. The client told me that it was his intention to purchase a condominium in Florida and to spend six or seven months a year basking in the sunshine. I suggested to him that he might shelter his gain through an income-averaging annuity and then move to the U.S. on a permanent basis for two or three years.

Even after I calculated the very significant tax saving, the client surprised me somewhat by flatly turning down my suggestion. I asked him why and he said that he would miss his grandchildren too much if he were living in Florida on a year-round basis. I told him that for the tax saved, he could afford to charter a jet and ship his grandchildren down to visit several times a year. The client was still not receptive. He told me that he had lived and worked in Canada all his life and that there was no way he would ever consider leaving. I finally shrugged my shoulders, folded up my Income Tax Act, and left my client to face his capital gain alone.

The Ideal Corporate Structure

As indicated in the diagram of the "Ideal" Corporate Structure (p.228), Mr. X. should own his shares in Op Co through a holding company. It doesn't really matter whether the holding company has been used to acquire Op Co from someone else, or whether the business of Op Co was *started* by Mr. X in the first place.

As Op Co earns active business income, it should float its after-tax profits up to Hold Co by way of dividends. (If Op Co earns over $150,000, salaries should be paid to Mr. X until he is in a 60% bracket. After that time, corporate taxes of 50% are usually less costly in the long run.) Whether or not Mrs. X is involved in the ownership of Op Co (indirectly through the holding company) is optional. If the family only has one business, it is generally advantageous for both Mr. and Mrs. X to participate in the ownership. If there is a second business operation *unrelated to the*

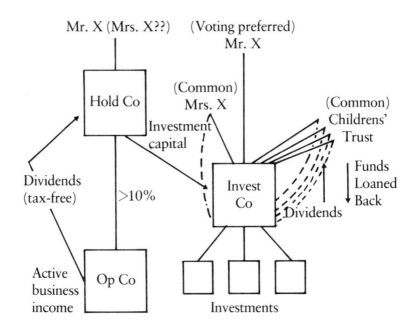

first, it would usually be more advantageous for Mr. X to own all of the shares of the first corporation and for Mrs. X to be involved only in the second business. In this manner, it may be possible to obtain two low-rate tax bases instead of one.

As Hold Co receives dividends (tax-free) from the business income of Op Co, the dollars which are not needed for business expansion should be transferred across as investment capital to a separate investment company (Invest Co). The investment company would be controlled by Mr. X through voting preferred shares, while the family members would own the common shares either directly or through a trust. The income of the investment company would be taxed initially at 50% (as discussed in Chapter Seven) but is subject to refundable taxes. Dividends could then be paid to the family and the funds would then be loaned back.

The capital of Invest Co would increase each year from a combination of Op Co's profits (to the extent that these are not needed for business expansion) and the reinvestment of dividends paid out to the family. No personal taxes need be paid by Mr. X on any dollars other than those needed for living expenses, while Mrs. X and the children can each receive dividends of up to $30,000 a year from Invest Co tax-free. Of course, if Mrs. X is active in the business of Op Co, she too would receive a salary and would participate in an RRSP and a corporate deferred-profit-sharing plan. In these circumstances, she might not participate in dividend distributions from Invest Co.

Expanding the Business Empire

As an offshoot to the "ideal corporate structure", there is also the opportunity to use the profits of Op Co 1 as capital to invest in further business acquisitions. If Mr. X (the indirect owner of Op Co 1) becomes interested in a new venture, the holding company structure would enable him to acquire the new business without any personal tax penalty.

STRUCTURE FOR FURTHER BUSINESS ACQUISITIONS

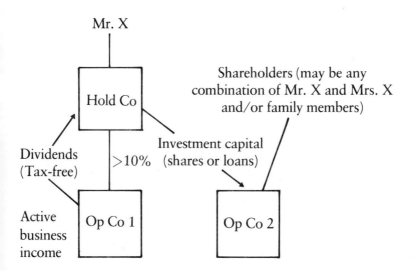

Again, the source of the funds would be Op Co 1, which would first pay (tax-free) dividends to Hold Co. The holding company would then reinvest these funds to acquire Op Co 2. The shareholders of Op Co 2 can actually be any combination of family members. Wherever possible, one would consider creating a structure under which the two businesses are not associated for tax purposes.

The advantage of having the businesses of Op Co 1 and Op Co 2 in separate corporations goes beyond the potential of doubling up on the small business tax rate. This structure also facilitates a sale of *either* business and the retention of the other. If separate businesses are under one "corporate roof", a sale becomes much more difficult. In addition, Mr. X may consider involving key employees in the ownership of one business without necessarily causing them to participate in the growth of the other.

From the last diagram, you should also be able to visualize the benefits where Op Co 2 happens to be a company whose only asset is real estate used by Op Co 1 as business premises. Keeping the real estate in a separate corporation generally facilitates business arrangements. It may be possible to sell the real estate without disposing of the operating business and vice versa. In addition, one can involve key employees in the business activities without also making them equity holders in the real estate.

The Era of the Holding Company

We are just beginning to enter the era of the holding company in Canada. There are many who feel that a multitude of companies tends to be somewhat cumbersome and may diminish the effectiveness of business operations. This could be true. You must always weigh the business advantages and disadvantages of two alternative approaches before making *any* decision. Prior to incorporation, you must determine in each case whether or not the dollars to be saved warrant the existence of a new company.

Where the owners of Op Co are not looking to expand and all profits are needed for their personal living requirements, a holding company may not be useful. On the other hand, for substantial share acquisitions, a holding company is mandatory. In practice, decisions can only be made on the basis of specific facts and with the aid of your professional advisors. Of course, an understanding of the tax system helps.

While on the topic of financial arrangements, here are two new changes to the tax rules that are worth noting: small business development bonds and lease-option arrangements.

Small Business Development Bonds

To assist small businesses, a recent budget amendment will permit Canadian-controlled private companies eligible for the small business tax rate to obtain cheaper after-tax financing from banks and other lending institutions.

The legislation is a temporary measure under which interest payments on up to $500,000 of debt issued after December 11, 1979, and before December 31, 1980, will be treated as dividends. Accordingly, such payments will not be taxable to the lender or deductible to the borrower.

Where the lender is a public corporation, and the interest on these bonds is treated for tax purposes as dividends, this will generally comprise a non-taxable receipt. This will enable the lender to charge a comparatively reduced rate on the loan. Also, the loss of an interest deduction to the borrower will not necessarily be costly if the borrower's corporate tax rate is only approximately 25%. This financing vehicle will be especially attractive to small corporations in the early years when initial losses are often incurred and an interest deduction is not really needed, in any event.

To qualify under these rules, the bond will have to be of at least one-year's duration and not longer than a five-year term. In addition, both parties must elect that the obligation qualify as a small business development bond.

Lease-Option Acquisitions

Where payments of rent under a lease-option agreement are in reality on account of the purchase price under the option clause, taxpayers have, in the past, been able to deduct significant amounts from income for which no recapture has been provided and which has subsequently been recovered at the time the property was acquired and resold.

A typical example of such a "tax avoidance arrangement" is where a business leases a car for a three-year period with an option to purchase at a price well below the fair market value of the vehicle at the end of that time. Under the tax rules before 1980, if the company exercised its option and then sold the car, there were no provisions to recapture the excess rent previously paid. The profit has always been treated as a capital gain — only half of which is taxable.

A special Budget Resolution now makes provisions for the recapture of excess rental payments for options exercised after December 11, 1979. Any decision whether to lease or purchase assets will now have to be rethought to take into account the new tax provisions.

CHAPTER TWELVE

A Common-sense Approach to Estate Planning

The first eleven chapters of this book should assist you in accumulating as much capital as possible during your lifetime. The purpose of this chapter is to show you how your family can retain a reasonable portion of these savings after your death.

Your major concern in estate planning should be to ensure that your assets eventually pass on to your designated heirs — preferably without Revenue taking too large a share. The first step in minimizing taxes is to know what you are up against. The post-1971 system is designed so that wealth is taxed as and when it is accumulated. Each time you realize a capital gain, one-half of your profit is taxed on a pay-as-you-go basis. This is the opposite of the rules prior to 1972, under which capital growth accumulated during one's lifetime was not taxed until death. At that time, the old Estate Tax Act applied, with calculations based on one's net worth.

Under the present system, since capital gains are only taxed when realized, you can always postpone the necessity of sharing profits by not selling your property. In Chapter Six, we explored the idea of borrowing against increases in values and the use of tax reserves where proceeds of sale are deferred.

Can capital gains be avoided completely? In the absence of specific tax rules, there are only three ways that come to mind: gifting property, becoming a non-resident and death. Provisions have, however, been designed to prevent an easy escape. We have seen, for example, that a gift of property to anyone other than a husband or wife is a deemed disposition at fair market value. A gift will thus trigger accumulated capital gains, although future growth will pass to the benefit of the recipient.

Capital Gains Planning for Non-Residency

Technically, rules have also been designed to prevent anyone from avoiding taxes by becoming a non-resident. At the time of departure from Canada, the Income Tax Act deems a disposition at fair market value on many kinds of capital property, such as publicly traded securities. The deemed disposition forces a tax-payer who is leaving to include in his income one-half of the difference between his cost and the fair market value of the property at the time of departure. Small gains (up to $5000) are exempted and taxpayers are permitted to request a postponement until an actual sale is made — provided that they furnish adequate security to the tax collector.

Although the intention of the Act is to block an individual from leaving the country without giving the tax man his due, the rules can be circumvented. However, some good advance planning is required. Assume, for example, that you own shares in a public company with a cost of $10,000 and a fair market value of $40,000. If you simply become a non-resident, there will be a deemed disposition at fair market value resulting in a taxable capital gain of $15,000 (one-half of $30,000). This amount would have to be added to your income in your final year as a resident of Canada. However, if you have advance notice that you are going to be leaving the country, the best thing would be to actually sell the property before you depart. You could then shelter the taxable capital gain through the purchase of an income-averaging annuity. The annuity purchase would reduce the amount that would be included in income on your last tax return. Then once you become a foreign resident, you could commute the annuity in favour of a lump sum. At worst, the tax exposure would only be 25%, but if you move to a "treaty country" (such as the U.S.) the tax rate is usually 15%.

You could then use the tax-free half of your gain as well as the proceeds from the annuity to reacquire the same property. The result is a double advantage! Not only is the Canadian tax reduced substantially, but also the tax cost of the property for foreign tax purposes becomes its current fair market value. In the above example, the tax value of the replacement property would be $40,000 in the foreign country and foreign capital gains (if applicable) would only be measured from that point on.

The importance of advance planning for non-residency cannot be overemphasized. Where an individual passively accepts an immediate job transfer and then returns to Canada the following April just to get his last Canadian tax return prepared, it is already too late to plan. If his property has not been sold and the annuity has not been purchased, the taxpayer is simply stuck with the gain — which is the intention of the tax collector in the first place.

Deemed Dispositions on Death

Not everyone wishes to leave Canada or gift away property. If becoming a non-resident and gifting are not feasible, you eventually encounter the "ultimate" of the deemed dispositions — that which takes place upon death. The tax rules are summarized in the schedule on page 236.

From the schedule, it is evident that the tax consequences of death depend on two factors: to whom is the property bequeathed and what kind of property did the deceased have. For non-capital property such as cash, Canada Savings Bonds and life insurance benefits, there are no income tax implications whatsoever — no matter who one's beneficiary happens to be. This is because cash, Canada Savings Bonds and other non-growth assets represent income on which taxes have already been paid. In the case of life insurance, the proceeds are not taxable since policy premiums are not deductible. (The only exception to these rules is in the province of Quebec where there is still a Provincial Succession Duty based on one's entire net worth immediately before death.)

With respect to all other property, husband and wife are considered as being the equivalent of one person. No tax need be paid until the last of the two dies. Thus, whenever capital property is bequeathed to a spouse, there is a (tax deferred) transfer at cost. No gain is recognized until the recipient spouse either sells the property or, in turn, dies and passes it on to someone else.

235

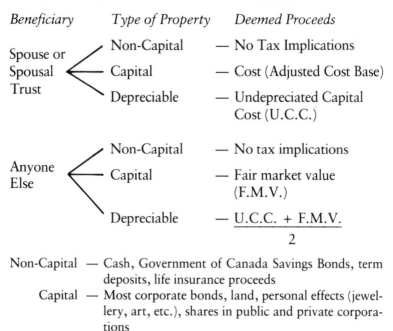

Beneficiary	Type of Property	Deemed Proceeds
Spouse or Spousal Trust	Non-Capital	— No Tax Implications
	Capital	— Cost (Adjusted Cost Base)
	Depreciable	— Undepreciated Capital Cost (U.C.C.)
Anyone Else	Non-Capital	— No tax implications
	Capital	— Fair market value (F.M.V.)
	Depreciable	— $\dfrac{\text{U.C.C.} + \text{F.M.V.}}{2}$

Non-Capital — Cash, Government of Canada Savings Bonds, term deposits, life insurance proceeds

Capital — Most corporate bonds, land, personal effects (jewellery, art, etc.), shares in public and private corporations

Depreciable — Buildings

Similarly, depreciable property passes at undepreciated capital cost (cost minus accumulated depreciation for tax purposes).

If capital property is passed to heirs other than a spouse, there is a deemed disposition immediately before death at fair market value. This will trigger all accrued capital gains on the deceased's last tax return. Whenever *depreciable property* passes to other heirs (upon the death of either or both husband and wife), there is a deemed disposition halfway between undepreciated capital cost and fair market value. The "halfway" rule will cause the recognition of less income than would otherwise be the case on a disposition deemed to take place at fair market value. This is illustrated in the example on the next page.

The reason for having special rules for depreciable property seems to be that this kind of property is less liquid than other growth assets and, as well, is less susceptible to being sold in part.

DEEMED DISPOSITION OF DEPRECIABLE PROPERTY (BUILDING)
TO OTHER HEIRS

Fair market value *(A)*	$120,000	$140,000	$200,000
Cost	100,000	100,000	100,000
Undepreciated capital cost *(B)*	60,000	60,000	60,000
Deemed disposition = $\frac{A + B}{2}$	$ 90,000	$100,000	$130,000
Recaptured depreciation	$ 30,000	$ 40,000	$ 40,000
Taxable capital gain	Nil	Nil	15,000
Total "deemed" income	$ 30,000	$ 40,000	$ 55,000
If sold before death:			
Recaptured depreciation	$ 40,000	$ 40,000	$ 40,000
Taxable capital gain	10,000	20,000	50,000
Total income if sold.	$ 50,000	$ 60,000	$ 90,000

For example, if one dies leaving 10,000 shares of a public company, 2000 shares can always be sold if necessary in order to pay taxes. It is not quite as easy to dispose of a 20% interest in a building.

Although the deceased escapes full taxation, the rules go on to provide that the heirs will become liable to recognize the remaining income at the time they actually dispose of the property. Thus, there is no forgiveness of tax, only a deferral.

The Use of Spousal Trusts

The concept of the husband-wife unit is perhaps the most important factor when it comes to estate planning. To repeat, there is a complete "rollover" (that is, a tax-deferred transfer) when property passes from either spouse to the other. The rollover applies not only to outright bequests, but, as well, whenever property is left to a *trust* for the benefit of the surviving spouse.

237

A "spousal trust" may have two advantages. The first pertains to situations where a taxpayer feels that his (or her) spouse is either not interested in administering property or does not have the necessary expertise. Instead of leaving property directly, the person drawing up his will can create a trust. This gives the "testator" (the person making up his will) the opportunity to appoint outside executors and trustees. In this manner, the responsibility for investment and business decisions can either be taken away entirely from the other spouse or the burden can be shared. The second advantage of a spousal trust is even more important. Leaving property in trust, instead of outright, gives the testator the opportunity to control the *ultimate* disposition of his property — even from beyond the grave.

If, for example, I was preparing my will today, I would start by estimating my current net worth in the event of death. Let us assume, for purposes of illustration, that this amounts to $500,000. Now, before you assume that I am wealthier than you are, note that most business owners and executives are worth much more dead than alive because of life insurance. Estates ranging from a half a million dollars and up are therefore not uncommon. Returning to my situation, I have one wife and four children. My objectives, like yours, are first to protect my wife and second, to provide for the kids. If I were to leave all my property directly to my wife, she could then do whatever she wanted with the assets. She could remarry and give all the property to her new husband. She could spend all the money, lose all the assets in the stock market, gamble away everything in Las Vegas, have children with a new husband and disinherit our children, or conversely she could take the capital and triple it.

The point is, I don't know what would happen. Thus, by leaving my property in trust, I could control the ultimate disposition. I would have the opportunity to appoint trustees and executors so that my wife could not act alone. If I followed standard practices, I would nominate three trustees or a trust company. If individual trustees were appointed, the power to make all decisions would usually be left to the majority.

If I made these arrangements, the trustees would have a dual responsibility after my death — to my wife and to the children. My will would provide for the assets to be maintained for my wife's benefit with the residual amount to be divided among the children upon her death. I would instruct the trustees to pay out capital amounts (in addition to income) upon reasonable request only. For example, if my widow remarried and proceeded to ask the trustees for $200,000 out of the estate to finance her new husband's business, the request would presumably be refused. After all, the trustees could not agree to anything that might jeopardize the position of the children.

On the other hand, if my wife were to approach the trustees after my death for $5000 towards the purchase of a new car, the trustees would probably sanction such a withdrawal of capital. After all, one of the objectives of building an estate is to ensure that a spouse can maintain a certain lifestyle.

The trust-will therefore allows for the fulfillment of two basic objectives: protecting a surviving spouse and also (ultimately) providing capital for one's children.

Income Tax Requirements for Spousal Trusts

For assets to pass into a spousal trust on a tax-deferred basis, the trust must meet two specific conditions:

1. The surviving spouse must get all the income earned by the trust in her (his) lifetime.

And

2. No one other than the surviving spouse may encroach upon the capital of the trust before she (he) dies.

The first rule requires the surviving spouse to receive all *income* earned *irrevocably* and without any strings attached. If you put a clause into a will prohibiting your spouse from deriving income subsequent to a remarriage, or reducing the amount of income that she would then be entitled to receive, this would negate the rollover benefits of the trust for tax purposes. You would still have a valid trust from a legal standpoint, but all assets passing into that trust would be received at fair market value. This would trigger the taxes on death that you are presumably trying to postpone.

The second rule contains another restriction and the difference is rather subtle. You can have a perfectly valid trust for tax purposes even if your spouse is *not* permitted to touch any of the *capital* (provided she receives all the income) as long as no one *else* can encroach on capital *either*.

Capital Encroachment Powers

What is the advantage of a complete prohibition against capital encroachment? If you make up a will prohibiting your spouse from encroaching on capital, you can be quite certain that your children (or other heirs) will inherit at least the same amount of assets as went into the trust in the first place — even if your spouse spends or otherwise disposes of all the income received in her lifetime.

Returning to my $500,000 estate, I think it would be nice to be able to ultimately give $125,000 of assets to each of my children. If I forbid my wife to encroach on capital, this "objective" is easily attainable. On the other hand, is a blanket prohibition against capital encroachment really wise? If I left my wife $500,000 of assets today, it is reasonable to project a conservative annual return of about 12%, or $60,000. While this might be more than adequate for her current needs, what about inflation? Of course, a lot depends on my wife's age, spending requirements, the ages of the children, and so on. To completely prohibit capital encroachment can be somewhat risky in the long run unless an estate is very large. The term "very large" is itself subjective and each person must evaluate the meaning of this independently. Yet to allow my wife an unlimited capital encroachment would negate the value of having a trust in the first place. I would therefore try for a flexible arrangement. The flexibility is achieved by appointing several trustees (generally including my spouse) where each decision on capital encroachment is left to the majority.

"Overprotecting" A Spouse

While providing adequately for a spouse is probably the prime objective of estate planning, I think that there is such a thing as "overprotection". In the classic case, a man dies leaving an estate of $5,000,000 to a trust for his wife, with instructions that on her death, the assets are to pass to the children. At the time of the man's death, his wife is seventy years old. He, of course, has wrongly assumed that she will be dead within two or three years of his own death. He has forgotten that her life expectancy from age seventy is still *another fifteen years* (see Chapter Four). If the wife had her children when she was around the age of twenty-five, the children will then be in their sixties before their mother dies. In novels and movies, the children become disgruntled and help mother along on her way to the pearly gates. In "real life", however, the family relationships often simply disintegrate.

When there are more than enough assets to go around, I think that it might be better social planning to spread these assets either during one's lifetime or at the time the first spouse dies. Even if taxes do become payable, the social benefits could outweigh the tax disadvantages. For instance, in March 1979, a friend of mine asked me to provide some tax and general investment counselling to his widowed mother. My friend's father had just recently died, leaving a will under which all assets were to be held in trust for his wife until her death, at which time there would be a distribution between his two children (average age today, approximately thirty-five). My friend gave me a list of the available assets to work with.

I determined that the value of the estate was approximately $450,000 and that the anticipated income yield was $45,000 a year. When I met with my friend and his mother, the first question I asked was how much she needed for living. She answered, "About $3000." I made some quick calculations and suggested that if her living requirements were $36,000 per annum, and the investment yield was only $45,000, she had best invest rather conservatively. She interrupted, however, and told me that she meant $3000 a year, not each month. When she saw the look on my face, she began to explain. She told me that her house is paid for, she never learned to drive a car, she doesn't have expensive tastes in clothing, never takes vacations, treats herself to a movie only once a week and spends her other leisure time visiting her grandchildren. She assured me that $3000 was more than adequate for her annual needs.

Under these circumstances, if my friend's mother does in fact live to be eighty-five years old, the $450,000 estate should be worth at least three times that amount. This is a good example of "overprotection". With all due respect to the deceased (whom I had never met), an estate of $450,000 is not large by today's standards. I really don't known whether I would have advised him to prepare his will any differently if I were in a position to do so. Perhaps if before his death he had had a frank discussion with his wife on the subject of her living requirements, he himself might have thought differently when making up his will. It might not have been such a bad idea to leave $50,000 directly to each of the two children so that each one could pay off his home mortgage. If this were done, "only" $350,000 would have passed to his wife.

The worst example of bad family-planning that I have ever seen involves the family of another friend. This friend has one brother and one sister and in each case, the family income is approximately forty thousand dollars a year. All three are therefore comfortable but are by no means wealthy. My friend has a father in his early seventies who is a widower. This man is now retired, having made about two million dollars in real estate transactions over the years. In fact, a good deal of his assets today consist of vacant land.

My friend's father has informed his children that under the terms of his will, the assets are to bypass them completely and will vest, on his death, in the grandchildren. His reasoning is that, although he cannot avoid capital gains on his own death, by passing the assets to the grandchildren, there will be no further deemed dispositions for the next sixty years. (After all, if the assets were only to pass to his *children*, the next deemed disposition could conceivably take place thirty years sooner!) Needless to say, my friend, his brother and sister are a little upset with their father's version of estate planning.

One might argue that a father does not owe his children anything once they are out on their own and that, if he wishes to pass his assets to the grandchildren instead, he has every right to do so. However, the motivation here is not that the grandfather does not get along with his own children, but rather a somewhat paranoid desire to reduce taxes otherwise payable. What upsets my friend most is not his own disinheritance, but the fact that his children stand to be considerably wealthier than *he* is within a few short years without having earned anything on their own. This is a clear case of the tax tail wagging the social and economic dog.

Sometimes, it may be necessary to pay more taxes than might otherwise be possible just to maintain good family relationships. Certainly "overprotection" and unnecessary tax avoidance should be considered when estate planning.

Appointment of Executors

One of the most difficult tasks which we all must face is choosing proper executors. It is more than just an honour to be an executor of an estate, it is a responsibility. The executors must be given broad powers and must have good administrative abilities. They must make sure that the deceased's wishes are carried out and that all assets are collected together and allocated properly. There are various "tax elections" which may be made in the year of death in the course of filing final tax returns, and they must be aware of all options. The executors must often deal with matters such as selling property and negotiating the best possible prices. Most of all, there is the responsibility of maintaining a balance between the relative rights of the various beneficiaries. Wherever possible, an attempt must be made to avoid potential conflicts of interest. Often, people appoint their accountants and lawyers as executors because of professional competence but without considering possible difficulties.

One of the most interesting cases that I ever worked on involved such a situation. I received a call one day from an accountant friend of mine who asked me to help him solve a conflict of interest. He had been appointed as an executor of an estate by one of his clients, who then died leaving behind a retarded son as his sole heir. The client also left a thriving business and it was his intention (although not specifically mentioned in the will) that certain key employees be given the opportunity to acquire this enterprise at a "fair price". The employees were more than happy to exercise their option and asked the same accountant to stay on as their auditor and advisor as well. The accountant thus found himself in an awkward position. He could not possibly allow himself to be in a position where, in negotiating a purchase price for the business, he would have to choose between his first client's son and the new prospective clients.

In this case, the conflict was resolved rather nicely. The accountant asked me to act on behalf of the key employees and represent them in formulating a bid. He, in turn, represented the estate. The purchasers of the business understood the necessity of such an arrangement and cooperated fully. An agreement was reached within a short period of time as to the purchase price and method of payment and everybody wound up content. Unfortunately, this does not always happen.

Potential conflicts of interest are not the only problem with which one must contend in appointing executors. In another recent situation, I was asked to help a client reorganize his business holdings and to do some estate planning. The estate was rather complex and the work took several months to complete. By the time of our final meeting in the lawyer's office, the will had already been prepared and had been reviewed several times. All that was left was to fill in a few of the details and sign it. At one point, my client's lawyer asked him to name some executors in addition to his wife. The client thought for a moment and named his brother-in-law — who lived in Lima, Peru. The lawyer and I looked at each other in amazement and then explained to the client that the choice of a brother-in-law in a far-off country as an executor is just not feasible. Fortunately, the client saw the logic behind our arguments and appointed a more suitable substitute.

Special Rules — The Family Farm

So far, this chapter has only dealt with the general rules pertaining to transfers of property on death. However, there are special rules which apply whenever a family farm is transferred from one generation to another. As long as the farm is located in Canada and is transferred to either children, grandchildren or great-grandchildren, a transfer can take place with no capital gain being realized. These rules apply as long as the recipients of the farm are resident in Canada and the property had been used in farming by either the deceased, his spouse or one or more children immediately before death. Vesting in the recipients must take place within fifteen months.

Recently, the Income Tax Act was amended to extend the family farm "rollover" (which originally applied to only unincorporated farms) to interests in family farm partnerships and shares in the capital stock of family farm corporations. In most situations, it would now be advantageous to reorganize the structure of one's farm holdings to take advantage of the corporate tax rules. These have been dealt with in Chapters Nine and Ten and include opportunities to pay dividends and be eligible for the favourable corporate tax rate for small business.

Tax-Free Transfer of Small Business Holdings

The concept of the family farm rollover has also recently been extended to shares of a "qualified small business' which are left to children or grandchildren. A qualified small business is any Canadian-controlled private corporation that earns active business income *except* one which derives fees or commissions from services. Thus, qualified businesses include (among others) companies engaged in wholesaling, retailing, construction, manufacturing, natural resources and transportation.

Under the special tax rules, every owner of shares of a qualified business has a lifetime $200,000 exemption from capital gains. The $200,000 limit applies irrespective of how many businesses the individual owns and/or how many children he has. A taxpayer is free to allocate his $200,000 amount in any way that he desires, and the allocation can take place either in his lifetime or upon his death.

Assume, for example, that a taxpayer has shares in a Canadian private business with a cost of $100,000 and a fair market value of $600,000. If he dies without having previously taken advantage of this special provision and leaves these shares to one or more of his children, his deemed proceeds will only be $400,000 and his capital gain will be $300,000 (instead of $500,000).

Actually, it is not accurate to call the $200,000 difference an "exemption", for it is technically only a deferral. This is because if the child or children ever sell the shares and receive $600,000, they will be faced with a capital gain equal to the difference between their deemed cost of $400,000 and their selling price. This would not, however, result in any hardship for the children since they would be receiving (cash) *proceeds* of disposition.

There are several opportunities for effective planning. First, you need not wait until death to take advantage of this $200,000 limit. If, for example, you wish to admit your children into your business, this special rule will help you greatly in meeting your objective. Using the above numbers, it is possible for a father (or mother) to literally gift 40% of a business "tax free" to one or more children. This would be especially advantageous where the children are already active in the business. The 40% factor just happens to be the percentage that would apply in this particular case:

Portion of business transferred to son/daughter		40%	
Fair market value	$600,000	$240,000	$200,000 gain is "exempt"
Cost for tax purposes	$100,000	$ 40,000	

As long as the difference between the cost of the interest sold and its fair market value is under $200,000, no gain need be recognized. In the above case, however, the child or children would pick up 40% of all future growth.

Effective tax planning also involves taking advantage of the potential to double up on the $200,000 "exemption" by *initially* involving both husband and wife in the ownership of a business. Traditional wills are often obsolete because they fail to incorporate the new small-business rollover provisions. Under the traditional approach, the husband usually leaves all his assets to his wife (either directly or in trust) and it is only on her death that the assets pass to the children. Where there is only one transmission of family business shares to the children, only one $200,000 exemption is obtainable. Where the wife is a shareholder in the business, her will is usually identical to her husband's.

I suggest, instead, that the husband's will be redrafted so that on his death, some shares would pass immediately to the children in amounts sufficient to trigger $200,000 of capital gains (which would be exempt from tax in any event). The balance of his shares could continue to pass to his wife (directly or through a trust), so that she would have control over the business throughout the remainder of her lifetime. On her death, subsequently, the balance of the shares could then pass from her to the children and again the first $200,000 of gains would be exempt. Similarly, the wife's will should incorporate the same provisions, in the event that she dies first.

It is inappropriate to have the Canadian private business capitalized with only a few shares. To take an extreme position, what if a company were owned equally by a husband and wife each of whom had only one share? The problem is that, no matter who dies first, the surviving spouse would not have control of the business if the deceased leaves his or her share to the children. Fortunately, this problem can easily be corrected by simply subdividing the shares (ten for one, or a hundred for one, etc.) as soon as possible. The splitting of shares would *not* attract any income taxes.

What is even more inappropriate, is a case where a company is owned 99% by husband and only 1% by wife. If the wife dies first, all she is capable of transmitting to the children is her 1%. Unless the company is worth somewhere in excess of $20,000,000, there is no possibility that her 1% could have appreciated by $200,000 since its acquisition.

A disproportionate ownership is also not well suited towards income splitting by way of payment of dividends — even where separate classes of shares are held. This has been dealt with in previous chapters. The only time I would suggest that a company be owned completely by a husband (to the complete exclusion of his wife) would be where separate businesses exist, each of which would qualify for the small business tax rate. In these circumstances, if the husband owns 100% of the first company, his wife should own 100% of the second. If the family's intention is to own one business only, the ownership should be spread fairly equally.

If one is faced with a grossly disproportionate ownership among shareholders of a single family business, a reorganization of capital can be accomplished. This is quite technical and requires professional assistance. The reorganization would allow the wife (in the previous example) to participate in *future* growth, which she could pass on to the children as part of her $200,000 exemption if she were to die first. These concepts are all illustrated in the schedule on the next page.

Estate Planning and Life Insurance

The topic of estate planning couldn't possibly be covered without some reference to the role of life insurance as part of the overall picture. As a bare minimum, you should insure your life so that there need be no forced sale of assets at the time of death solely for the purpose of paying income taxes. For that purpose, some kind of permanent insurance is necessary and term insurance will not usually be sufficient. (A term policy will not help if it expires before your death.)

Basically, you should determine the tax consequences resulting from deemed dispositions on death for bequests to beneficiaries other than a spouse. Your accountant can assist you in putting

TO DOUBLE-UP ON
THE TAX-FREE TRANSFER OF SMALL BUSINESS
HOLDINGS REVISE WILLS

TRADITIONAL

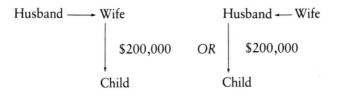

Husband ⟶ Wife   Husband ⟵ Wife

$200,000   OR $200,000

Child   Child

Only one "tax free" transfer is possible no matter who dies first.

ADVISABLE

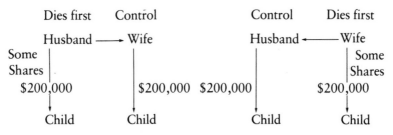

Dies first   Control   Control   Dies first

Husband ⟶ Wife   Husband ⟵ Wife

Some Shares   Some Shares

$200,000 $200,000 $200,000 $200,000

Child   Child   Child   Child

INAPPROPRIATE

1 Share   1 Share   99 Shares   1 Share

Husband   Wife   Husband   Wife

Child   Child   Child

*Survivor has
no control
no matter
who dies first*

*If wife dies first,
what is her
interest worth?*

249

together the figures. You would then apply combined federal and provincial marginal tax rates to the anticipated income. In order to be fairly conservative, you might assume taxes of between 60% and 65%. Of course, the tax implications of death depend largely on the time of year in which you die. If you die early in a given year, the income arising from deemed dispositions might be taxed all by itself at favourable rates. However, if you die late in the year, the income from deemed dispositions is then added to all your other income of that year and the tax burden could be significant.

You should next calculate your available cash, Canada Savings Bonds, and "near cash", such as marketable securities. In addition, liquid assets realizable from the sale of a family business would be relevant if there is a buy-sell agreement between yourself and one or more partners. The minimum insurance you would then require would be that needed to discharge your tax liabilities after applying the liquid assets towards that purpose. Taxes arising from deemed dispositions may be spread over ten years, but each installment presently bears interest at 11%. This installment interest is not tax deductible and the financing therefore becomes expensive.

Of course, life insurance has additional uses beyond just paying taxes. Its role is also to provide a larger income to your heirs, especially for a spouse and dependent children. If your estate is tied up in either vacant land which yields very little income, or growth stocks that do not pay dividends, your spouse may be in a rather embarrassing financial position without proceeds from life insurance with which to generate a future flow of income. If you own a part-interest in a private business, life insurance is almost mandatory to assist the surviving partners in buying out the estates of those who die first.

For taxpayers who maintain liquid estates and who require the bulk of their protection in the early years, perhaps term insurance would be advisable. When it comes to a business situation, however, most advisors would opt in favour of a more permanent type of coverage. This is because most term policies are calculated to expire at age seventy, whereas the average individual will probably not die until one or two years later. Term insurance therefore provides protection for your early needs while your children are young, but it is not adequate for long-range business planning and the preservation of property that is not liquid, such as real estate. When it comes to estate planning, a good insurance agent is just as important a member of the team as your accountant or lawyer.

The Time for Planning is Now

Unfortunately, people tend to postpone estate planning, the preparation of their wills and other similar matters, because the contemplation of death tends to be a bit distasteful. However, ask yourself, what would happen to your family if you died today? If you spend a few minutes thinking about the consequences, tax and estate planning will become much more important. *The time for effective planning is now.*

Taking the "Ax" out of Tax

If you have gotten this far without skipping too many chapters, you should now be quite familiar with just about every legitimate technique for effective tax reduction. Now it is time to apply these suggestions to your own situation. So, start again from the beginning. Open this book to the Table of Contents, and start making notes. Be brief. All you have to do is list some of the areas where you can take the "ax" out of your tax.

Begin with Chapter Two. List the fringe benefit plans that you think are reasonable for you. The next time you are due for a raise, be ready for some serious negotiations. Remember, very often valuable benefits won't cost your employer a penny extra when compared to salary.

Are you ten years or less away from retirement? Is there any chance that you may be leaving the country soon? Are you thinking of selling your business? If the answer to any of these questions is yes, reread Chapter Three and make sure your boss (or accountant) buys a copy of this book and reads it too. If the answer to all these questions is no, go on to Chapter Four.

Do you have a registered retirement savings plan? If you do, continue to contribute. Keep in mind the advantages of spousal plans, as long as you don't have to borrow the funds required. If you still don't believe in RRSPs, reread this chapter — *slowly.*

Do you have $1000 a year of (tax-free) Canadian investment income? If not, start saving your pennies! Do you have more than $8000 to $10,000 of capital and are you in a 50% bracket or higher? Remember, income splitting isn't difficult. One or two loans to family members will do the trick. If you are feeling generous, give your son or daughter $1000 for an RHOSP contribution — as long as he or she is not a minor.

Are you reading this book in the den of your Westmount or Forest Hill home or on a cruise ship bound for warmer weather or on the beach outside your Hawaii condominium? If your answer is yes, consider the benefits of an investment corporation. Dividends to the kids are an excellent way to get them to pay for their *own* vacations, cars, education, and so on.

Do you receive fees or commissions or are you in a position to transform your salary into consulting revenues? Can you *diversify* your activities so that you can be paid by several different customers or clients? If so, make an appointment with an accountant — even if it costs $100 or $150. After about an hour, he will be able to tell you if incorporation is feasible.

If you own your own business, reread Chapters Nine and Ten. I know they have lots of numbers and very few jokes and anecdotes. But they are worth the bother. Then, spend a morning with your accountant and map your strategy. For most of us, guidelines are available which will be effective for at least two or three years — unless the law changes. If that happens, don't worry — I promised my publisher to provide the necessary revisions to this text.

Are you planning to buy (or sell) a business? See your advisors *before* you finalize a deal. Improper tax planning here can be the worst mistake you will ever make. Don't forget — this is the era of the holding company — don't fight progress. It's your money.

Finally, don't ignore the inevitability of death. If you have a spouse, is she (he) adequately protected? Is your spouse "overprotected"? Does your spouse know what you have and where it is? Communicate. Your lifestyles may depend on it.

Writing this book has been fun for me. I trust that reading it has been profitable for you.

Glossary

ACTIVE BUSINESS INCOME: Income from manufacturing, wholesaling, retailing, logging, farming, fishing, natural resource exploration and development, transportation, and in certain instances (as described on pages 166 – 167) services. These incomes qualify for a low rate of corporate tax when earned by *Canadian-controlled private corporations*.

ADJUSTED COST BASE: The cost of property for tax purposes. This may be either the cost to the taxpayer or the value as of December 31, 1971, subject to any adjustments required by the Income Tax Act.

AMORTIZATION: The allocation of an expense or debt over a period of time.

ANNUITY: A series of regular payments (usually equal) consisting of interest and principal.

ARM'S LENGTH: Where the parties to a transaction are unrelated by blood, marriage or adoption.

ASSET: A property which is owned and has value.

ATTRIBUTION RULES: A series of tax provisions whereby income generated from property transferred by a husband to his wife (or vice versa) will be reallocated for tax purposes to the person who made the transfer. Similar provisions also apply for transfers to minors.

BENEFICIARY: A person who receives (or is named to receive) money or property from an insurance policy or *will*. A person for whose benefit a *trust* exists.

BUY-SELL AGREEMENT: An undertaking among owners of a business whereby those that remain agree to acquire the interest in the business of an owner who dies, retires or becomes disabled.

CANADIAN-CONTROLLED PRIVATE CORPORATION (CCPC): A company incorporated in Canada where the majority of the shares are not held by non-residents or public companies or by any combination of non-residents and public companies.

CAPITAL COST ALLOWANCE: A provision for depreciation as permitted under the Income Tax Act to recognize wear, tear and obsolescence and to allocate the cost of an asset over the period for which it is useful to generate revenue.

CAPITAL GAINS: The profit realized when certain assets such as real estate and shares of a public or private company are sold for proceeds in excess of cost. A taxpayer's capital gain is measured as the difference between the selling price of property and its *adjusted cost base*. One-half of a capital gain is taken into income when proceeds are received. This is called a taxable capital gain.

CLASSES OF ASSETS: For tax depreciation *(capital cost allowance)* purposes, assets are divided into pools or groups. Each pool has its own depreciation rate, which is usually related to the useful life of the assets which it contains.

COLLATERAL: Stocks, bonds, or other property pledged as security for a loan. A lender has the right to sell collateral in the event of a borrower's default.

COMBINED INDIVIDUAL TAX RATES: Rates (usually expressed in percentages) which take into account the effect of both federal and provincial taxes.

CONTROLLING SHAREHOLDER: Usually, a shareholder who owns more than 50% of the voting shares of a corporation.

CURRENT SERVICE CONTRIBUTION: A contribution made to an employer-sponsored pension plan by either the employee and/or the employer in respect of the present year.

DEEMED DISPOSITION: An event such as death, departure from Canada or the making of a gift, where an individual is considered for tax purposes to have sold his property for consideration (generally) equal to its *fair market value*.

DEFERRED ANNUITY: An *annuity* under which payments of principal and interest will only begin some time after the annuity is acquired.

DEFERRED COMPENSATION: An arrangement under which income is postponed until some future time, usually until retirement from employment.

DEFERRED PROFIT-SHARING PLAN (DPSP): An employer-sponsored fringe-benefit program under which up to $3500 per participating employee may be set aside out of profits in order to provide a *deferred annuity* subsequent to the employee's retirement.

DIVIDEND: A distribution out of after-tax earnings or profits which a corporation pays to its shareholders.

DIVIDEND TAX CREDIT: A reduction from taxes otherwise payable by an individual who receives a dividend from a Canadian corporation. The tax credit takes into account the fact that a dividend is a distribution by a corporation out of previously taxed profits.

256

EARNED INCOME: The sum of incomes from employment, self-employment, rentals, pensions and alimony minus losses from self-employment and/or rentals. Up to 20% of earned income qualifies for an annual investment into an individual's *registered retirement savings plan* (maximum $5500).

EFFECTIVE TAXES: Combined federal and provincial taxes as a percentage of total income. (Compare *marginal rate of tax*.)

EQUITY CAPITAL: The funds in a business which have been invested by the owners and not loaned by others.

ESTATE FREEZING: An exchange of assets whereby properties with growth potential are exchanged for properties whose value remains constant from time to time.

ESTATE PLANNING: The orderly arrangement of one's financial affairs so that assets may be transferred on death to persons designated by the deceased with a minimum loss of value due to taxes and forced liquidations.

EXECUTOR: A person named in a *will* to carry out the provisions of that will.

FAIR MARKET VALUE: The price for property that a willing buyer would pay to a willing seller on the open market in circumstances where both parties deal at *arm's length* and neither is compelled to transact.

FRONT-END LOAD: An administration charge for handling investment capital which is levied against the initial contribution(s) to a savings plan, such as an RRSP.

GIFT TAX: A tax imposed on the donor of property where the value of a gift exceeds certain maximum allowable deductions. In Canada, at the present time, only the province of Quebec levies a gift tax.

GROSSED-UP DIVIDEND: When an individual resident in Canada receives a dividend from a Canadian corporation, the amount which is taxable is one and one-half times the actual payment received. The individual is then allowed a *dividend tax credit* approximately equal to the 50% gross-up.

GUARANTEED TERM: A minimum term under which annuity payments are guaranteed. In the case of a life annuity with a guaranteed term, the payments will continue through the guarantee period even if the recipient of the annuity dies before the end of that period.

INCOME-AVERAGING ANNUITY: A special type of annuity designed to spread the impact of Canadian taxation on certain (generally non-recurring) types of lump sum receipts. See page 52 for the nineteen categories of income which qualify for a purchase of this kind of annuity.

INVESTMENT DEDUCTION: A provision under which the first $1000 of *arm's length* interest, grossed-up dividends and taxable capital gains received by an individual from Canadian sources is deductible annually in arriving at taxable income.

MANAGEMENT COMPANY: A corporation set up by professionals such as doctors, dentists, lawyers and accountants to provide administrative services to the professional business of the practitioner(s).

MARGINAL RATE OF TAX: The combined federal and provincial tax rate that would apply to the next dollar of taxable income earned by a taxpayer in a given year. Compare *effective taxes*.

MANUFACTURING AND PROCESSING PROFITS DEDUCTION: A special reduction from corporate income taxes otherwise payable, computed as either 5% or 6% of taxable income from manufacturing and processing activities.

NET INCOME: Gross income from all sources less expenses to earn this income, but before personal exemptions and taxes.

NON-RESIDENT WITHHOLDING TAX: A flat rate of tax imposed on investment income such as interest, rents, dividends and annuities paid to a non-resident recipient. In Canada, the rate of withholding tax is 25% unless reduced by a tax treaty with the country in which the non-resident lives.

PARTICIPATING SHARES: Shares in a corporation which participate in the growth of a business and its assets and on which (theoretically) unlimited dividends may be paid.

PAST SERVICE CONTRIBUTION: A contribution made to an employer-sponsored pension plan by either the employee and/or the employer in respect of prior years of employment.

PENSION INCOME DEDUCTION: A provision under which the first $1000 of annual pension income (other than the Canada/Quebec Pension or the Old Age Pension) is deductible from an individual's income for tax purposes. The pension deduction applies to a pension received at any age, while amounts received from an RRSP qualify if the recipient is at least sixty-five.

PERSONAL EXEMPTIONS: An automatic deduction permitted to any individual in arriving at taxable income. For 1980, the basic personal exemption is $2890. There are additional personal exemptions available to individuals who support other dependants, such as a spouse or children.

PERSONAL SERVICE CORPORATION: A corporation formed to earn fees for services or commissions where the income can be attributed to the personal efforts of one or a few individuals.

PRINCIPAL RESIDENCE: A housing unit ordinarily occupied by an individual during a given year and designated as being his (or her) principal residence. Only one such residence may be designated for each year. Where an accommodation which was a principal residence throughout the period of its ownership is subsequently sold, the *capital gain* thereon is exempt from tax.

REGISTERED HOME OWNERSHIP SAVINGS PLAN (RHOSP): A savings program whereby qualified individuals may contribute up to $1000 a year on a tax-deductible basis towards the purchase of a home.

REGISTERED RETIREMENT INCOME FUND (RRIF): One of the settlement options available to taxpayers over age sixty who wish to draw an annuity from their registered retirement savings plans. Under this option, payments received increase annually until the recipient is ninety.

REGISTERED RETIREMENT SAVINGS PLAN (RRSP): A government-approved program whereby individuals may make annual, tax deductible contributions of up to 20% of their *earned income* to a maximum of $5500 as a savings towards retirement.

RECAPTURED DEPRECIATION: *Capital cost allowances* previously claimed which are determined (in the year that depreciable property is sold) to be in excess of the actual amount by which the property in question has depreciated.

REFUNDABLE TAX: A portion of corporate taxes previously paid by a private corporation on its investment income. Initially, the investment income is subject to a 50% tax rate although an amount equal to $16\frac{2}{3}\%$ of the investment income is refundable back to the corporation upon payment of dividends to shareholders. The net corporate tax on investment income is thus reduced to $33\frac{1}{3}\%$.

REPLACEMENT PROPERTY: In certain circumstances, gains on the disposition of property may be deferred for tax purposes if other property (i.e., replacement property) is acquired. The tax cost of the replacement property is reduced by an amount equal to the deferred gain.

RETIREMENT ALLOWANCE: A payment made by a former employer to an employee in recognition of long service or for loss of employment. Retirement allowances may be transferred to *income-averaging annuity* programs or *registered retirement savings plans*.

ROLLOVER: A transfer of property from one person to another where the tax rules permit a deferral of gains at the time the transfer is made.

SMALL BUSINESS TAX RATES: A special incentive available to *Canadian-controlled private corporations* earning *active business income*. The first $150,000 of annual profits is taxed at approximately 25% (the rate varies from province to province), until $750,000 is earned cumulatively.

SOFT COSTS: Various specific components of a construction project which may be deducted for tax purposes during a construction period instead of being subject to a long-term write-off through depreciation *(capital cost allowance)*. Soft costs include landscaping, interest on money borrowed during the construction period and certain administrative expenditures.

SPOUSAL RRSP: An option available under a *registered retirement savings plan* whereby a taxpayer may earmark all or a portion of his annual contributions into a program for his (or her) spouse. This option is designed to ensure future *annuity* benefits for that spouse.

T-4 SLIP: A form prescribed by the Canadian government for employers to use in reporting salaries, wages, and benefits paid to employees.

TAX CREDITS: A direct deduction against taxes otherwise payable. Among others, tax credits are available to individuals with respect to Canadian dividends received and to all taxpayers with respect to foreign taxes previously paid on foreign source income.

TAX DEDUCTIBLE: Amounts which may be subtracted in arriving at one's income for tax purposes.

TAX DEPRECIATION: See *capital cost allowance*.

TAX DEFERRED: This refers to opportunities whereby taxes on income or benefits may be postponed until some future date.

TAX LOSS VS. TAX SHELTER: A tax loss is a loss from business or property which is deductible in arriving at income for tax purposes. A tax loss becomes a tax *shelter* in circumstances where it is created by claiming *capital cost allowances* and does *not* involve an actual outflow of cash or a reduction in the value of one's investment.

TAX SHELTERED: Income which is not taxable currently but will be taxed at some future time.

TAXABLE BENEFIT: A benefit provided by an employer to an employee where the value is taxed in the hands of the employee as additional remuneration received.

TAXABLE INCOME: Net income from all sources minus personal exemptions, the investment and pension deductions, a provision for medical expenses and donations, and miscellaneous other deductions. For Canadian corporations, taxable income is computed after deducting dividends received from other Canadian corporations. Taxable income is the base on which income taxes are levied.

TERM INSURANCE: Life insurance which only pays if death occurs within a specific time period. There is usually no cash value under such a policy. Compare *whole life*.

TESTATOR: A person who makes a *will*.

TRACKING: Earmarking the flow of borrowed funds to clearly indicate the purpose for which these funds have been used. In Canada, this is important since it is only interest on funds borrowed for investment purposes which is tax deductible.

TRANSFEREE: A person to whom a transfer of title, rights or property is made.

TRANSFEROR: A person who makes a transfer of title, rights or property.

TREASURY SHARES: Shares which a corporation has the authority to issue but which are still unissued.

TRUST: An arrangement made in a person's lifetime or effective upon death whereby legal title and control of property is placed in the hands of a custodian *(trustee)* for the benefit of another person or group of persons who are known as *beneficiaries* of the trust.

TRUSTEE: A person who acts as custodian and administrator of property held in *trust* for someone else.

UNDEPRECIATED CAPITAL COST: The cost of depreciable assets minus accumulated *capital cost allowances* previously claimed.

VESTING: The process whereby a right to property passes unconditionally to a particular person, such as where an employee becomes entitled to the full benefits from contributions previously made by an employer to a pension or *deferred profit-sharing plan*.

WILL: A legal statement of a person's wishes about what shall be done with his property after he is dead.

WHOLE LIFE: Life insurance which remains in force until the insured dies, irrespective of when this occurs. Whole life insurance policies usually have cash values which increase over time and which may be borrowed against, or for which the policy may be surrendered.

YEAR END: The end of the business cycle each year. For tax purposes, a business must file an annual report disclosing its profits. Initially, the year end may be selected to fall on any date. However, no change in the year end may be made subsequently except with the permission of the Revenue authorities.

YIELD: Return on investment, usually computed as the percentage of the anticipated (or realized) annual income relative to the capital invested.

Acknowledgements

This book is dedicated to the many executives, professionals and business owners who have attended my tax seminars and have asked me to put it all down in writing.

I wish to thank my good friend Dr. Norman Schachar, who was kind enough to read the text and whose valuable criticism helped me to keep sophisticated and technical material simple.

Above all, however, I would like to thank my wife, Shana, for typing this manuscript (all three drafts), and our children for their patience in putting up with us during all those late nights and weekends.

H.B.Z.